The failure of

world monetary reform, 1971–74

The failure of
world monetary reform,
1971–74

John Williamson

New York, New York University Press, 1977

Published in the USA by New York University Press
First published in Great Britain by
Thomas Nelson and Sons Ltd, 1977

332.45
W731f

Library of Congress Catalog Card Number: 77-71278

ISBN 0 8147-9173-5 cloth
0 8147-9174-3 paper

Typeset by Computacomp (UK) Ltd,
Fort William, Scotland
Printed in Great Britain by
The Camelot Press Ltd, Southampton

194172

Preface

This book concerns the birth, life, death and possible after-life of the worthwhile, though unsuccessful, attempt to design an international monetary system to replace the one that collapsed in 1971. For the 2 years that the Committee of Twenty met in pursuit of this aim, I was privileged to watch its deliberations from the vantage point of the most junior IMF official whose duties involved regular participation in the work of the Committee. The issues that arose in those negotiations seem to me of sufficient importance to justify my drawing on the insights thus gained to present a reasonably comprehensive analytical account to the wider public that takes an interest in these questions but have, up to now, had to piece the story together from newspaper stories and official pronouncements. While I have used the experience gained from my temporary official position, I have endeavoured to avoid revealing what is not in the public domain: revelations, in so far as there is anything left to be revealed, come more appropriately from elder statesmen. Most of the facts in the book could, with sufficient diligence, be unearthed from published sources. I conceive my role as being that of exposing and clarifying analysis and where, for example, I describe national attitudes, this is motivated by the fact that one cannot hope to analyse international negotiations without probing into the positions adopted by governments and the national interests that motivate these postures.

I make no attempt to conceal the fact that I hold strong views on many of the subjects discussed in this book. I hope that this has not prevented my portraying contrary views as clearly and generously as I can, and explaining why they are held, as well as why I believe them to be mistaken, for there is nothing that I hold in greater intellectual contempt than the erection of straw men. But I do not pretend to be impartial, any more than I did before entering the Fund (as some of my writings make transparently clear) or, for that matter, during the time I was employed by the Fund. I hold the view, which is reflected in Chapter 7, that it is no part of the duty of an international civil servant

v

to free himself of preferences between the alternative proposals under discussion; he needs a sympathy with the interests and hopes of the many countries he is charged with indirectly serving, but his usefulness depends on his willingness to work for particular proposals that have the potential of reconciling those interests, and not on a preparedness to give equal credence to all views, irrespective of their merit.

Chapter 7, which attempts to analyse why the reform negotiations failed, is the most speculative chapter in the book, although it is by no means the only chapter in which inherently speculative comments about motivations occur — generally with a word such as 'perhaps' to serve as a warning. The chapter was also the most difficult to write, for I am conscious that my professional expertise does not extend to some of the subjects that it is necessary to consider in this context. The viewpoint from which this chapter is written is less that of the expert academic observer than of the bemused participant who felt that mistakes were being made and has tried to analyse their nature, but who remains acutely aware that this analysis is offered without any background of study in the relevant discipline.

The remainder of the book is concerned with subjects that I have studied, with increasing concentration, for the past 10 or 15 years. It draws on a number of my previously-published papers, in particular: *The Choice of a Pivot for Parities*, Princeton Essays in International Finance No.90, Princeton, 1971; 'International Liquidity — A Survey', *Economic Journal*, September 1973; 'Payments Adjustment and Economic Welfare', IMF *Staff Papers*, November 1973; and 'The Future Exchange Rate Regime', Banca Nazionale del Lavoro *Quarterly Review*, June 1975. I am grateful to the editors of these journals for their consent to my free adaptation of the arguments first developed there. To a lesser extent I have also drawn on a number of my other papers, references to which are somewhat liberally scattered through the book.

This book has benefited, directly and indirectly, from help received from individuals ranging from my former teacher, Fritz Machlup, to those who offered valuable comments on part or all of the first draft of the manuscript: Benjamin J. Cohen, J. J. Polak, William Wallace, Denise Williamson, Geoffrey Wood and, most particularly, Fred Hirsch and Wolfgang Rieke. The responsibility for any remaining errors and for the opinions expressed remains, of course, exclusively mine. I also owe an immense debt to my former colleagues in the Fund, and in particular to J. J. Polak and the late J. Marcus Fleming, whose death was, sadly, announced shortly after the manuscript was completed. International monetary economics has suffered a profound loss in being deprived of the always stimulating and often provocative views of one of its leading thinkers just before his retirement. It goes without saying that the views of my former colleagues cannot necessarily be inferred from the opinions that I express in this book, just as my former employer, the IMF, can in no way be implicated in my views. Mrs J. Gardner has earned my permanent gratitude for her typing of the manuscript. Finally, I wish to record my appreciation of the forbearance shown by my wife and family while the book was being written; but at least my wife, as an economist and former Fund employee, appreciated the cause more than most.

To Denise

Contents

Introduction

The Bretton Woods system is generally regarded as having come to an end when President Nixon announced his 'New Economic Policy' on 15 August 1971 and included in it a suspension of the right of foreign monetary authorities to convert their official dollar holdings into gold. Although this action terminated only one of a number of features that collectively constituted the Bretton Woods system, it was sufficient to render it emotionally impossible for the rest of the world to maintain its previous acquiescence in the slide towards a dollar standard. And since the United States' action was precipitated by a loss of patience with the passive or 'nth-currency' role assigned her by a dollar standard, there emerged a general desire to attempt the ambitious task of consciously redesigning the international monetary system on a new and more symmetrical basis. There followed a series of tortuous international negotiations, which culminated in the work of the Committee of Twenty (hereafter referred to as the C-20) from the autumn of 1972 to June 1974. During that period the international monetary system changed dramatically, but the changes owed little to the process of negotiation. The aims of this book are to provide an analytically-oriented history of these negotiations, to examine the economic issues with which the C-20 grappled, to offer an explanation of why the negotiations achieved so little and to extract such lessons as these events offer for the future.

By way of background, Chapter 1 is devoted to a short history of the Bretton Woods system. The chapter outlines the major issues that arose in designing the Bretton Woods system, the provisions that were incorporated in that system, its functioning and evolution over time, and the academic and official debate that developed on the problems of the Bretton Woods system and the means by which it might be reformed. In principle, this exposition is self-contained and assumes no prior knowledge of international monetary economics; in practice, however, the treatment is somewhat condensed and may in places prove obscure to those who lack a familiarity with international monetary economics equivalent to that normally reached in the later stages of a specialist undergraduate course in international economics.

Chapter 2 analyses the reasons for the breakdown of the Bretton Woods system. It considers separately the factors that led to the suspension of dollar convertibility in August 1971 and those that led to the abandonment of the Bretton Woods exchange rate regime, the adjustable peg, in March 1973. So far as the suspension of convertibility is concerned, it is argued that, while the timing of the crisis was a product of particular historical circumstances, notably the Vietnam War, the ambiguities of the Bretton Woods system as to the responsibility for initiating adjustment, and the absence of a viable is-proof method of effecting adjustment, would in any event have led to a similar dénouement at some time or other. The breakdown of the adjustable peg is interpreted as the inevitable consequence of the increase in capital mobility.

Chapter 3 describes the course of the negotiations that took place from August 1971 to the winding up of the C-20 in June 1974. It covers the negotiations on exchange rate realignment that culminated in the Smithsonian Agreement, the preparations for the C-20, and the work of the C-20 itself, including its failure to secure agreement on a comprehensive blueprint for a reformed system along the lines that were initially envisaged. The following chapter contains a survey of the attitudes and interests of the major groups of countries involved in the negotiations.

The heart of the book is the economic analysis of the issues that arose in the course of the C-20 negotiations. These are grouped under the headings of adjustment (Chapter 5) and reserve assets (Chapter 6). The chapter on adjustment deals with the questions of defining appropriate balance-of-payments objectives, of creating inducements for countries to pursue these appropriate objectives, and of selecting the techniques to be used to secure payments adjustment. An appendix deals with the related topic of the intervention system. The chapter on reserve assets covers the proposals for reform of the special drawing right (SDR) regarding its valuation, yield and use; for adoption of the link; for the future of gold; for reducing the role of reserve currencies through consolidation; and then discusses the problems of establishing, and exercising, control over the volume of global liquidity.

Chapter 7 considers five competing hypotheses about why the reform negotiations failed. It is argued that this failure was not the inevitable result of the disturbed state of the world economy or of the existence of irreconcilable national interests, but that it resulted from a combination of weak political will and technical inadequacy, reflected particularly in the decision to rename rather than to reform the exchange rate regime.

The final chapter turns to the future. It outlines the way in which a reformed system, satisfying the general aspirations that emerged in the C-20 as well as respecting the particular interests of individual countries, would fall into place once an appropriate proposal for the exchange rate regime were envisaged. It is argued that such a system would have significant advantages over the *ad hoc* non-system that emerged from the rubble of the C-20. Whether a reformed system is in fact likely to emerge in the future is another matter altogether.

1

The Bretton Woods system

The Bretton Woods system was easily the nearest thing to a consciously designed international monetary system that the world has yet experienced. Without this example before them, the negotiators of the early 1970s might never have conceived the aim of 'writing a new monetary constitution for the world' (as Marina Whitman aptly described the task attempted by the C-20).

The Bretton Woods system was in large measure the product of ambitious Anglo-American planning during the Second World War. John Maynard Keynes in Britain and Harry Dexter White in the United States were the brains behind the attempt to design a new and liberal international economic order that would abolish the economic evils of the 1930s, which were generally held to have contributed to the outbreak of the war — depression, commercial warfare, bilateralism and competitive depreciation. The results of their deliberations in the monetary field were incorporated in the draft Articles of Agreement of the International Monetary Fund (IMF), which were, in due course, submitted to the historic conference convened at Bretton Woods, New Hampshire, in July 1944. The IMF Articles that were agreed at that conference did not merely create the legal framework for a new international institution, but also shaped the international monetary system that was aspired to for the next quarter of a century and that was, in substantial measure, actually achieved between 1959 and the mid-1960s.

An international monetary system can be characterized by the arrangements made in five areas: market convertibility, the exchange rate regime, balance-of-payments adjustment, the supply of reserve assets and the management of the system. The present chapter outlines the provisions and history of the Bretton Woods system and the main strands of academic and official discussion, grouped under these five headings. The Bretton Woods system contained explicit provisions on four of these subjects: the exception was the adjustment mechanism. The system broke down in two areas in the early 1970s: the adjustable peg exchange rate regime and the gold exchange standard, which governed the supply of reserves. It was the breakdown of the latter feature that precipitated the C-20. But two of its other key features — market convertibility and the arrangements for cooperative international management of the system — have endured. Perhaps the ultimate tribute to the architects of the Bretton Woods system is that these arrangements are now so taken for granted that people no longer associate them with Bretton Woods.

Market convertibility

The question of 'market convertibility'[1] concerns the circumstances under which the holder of one currency can sell it in order to acquire another. A multilateral system, which the architects of Bretton Woods aspired to create, requires that someone who is paid in one currency be able to convert that currency into any other currency that they need to make payments, since in the absence of such a right they are under pressure to spend their earnings on goods from the country in which the currency is acquired. The IMF Articles therefore contained an obligation on member countries to make their currencies convertible (Article VIII, Sections 2-4). This obligation was, however, qualified in two important ways. First, countries were entitled (under Article XIV) to avail themselves of a transitional period of undefined length before accepting the obligation. Second, it was only currency balances acquired in the course of, or needed to make, current-account transactions that the issuing country was obligated to convert on request: in fact it was assumed that most countries would control capital transactions.

All members of the IMF, except for the United States, Mexico, and three of the Central American republics, initially availed themselves of the loophole provided by the transitional period allowed under Article XIV. The era of post-war reconstruction and recovery proved far longer than had been contemplated at the end of the war, and, although exchange controls were gradually liberalized during the 1950s, it was not until late 1958 that the principal European countries felt strong enough to accept non-resident convertibility. The assumption of Article

1. Gottfried Haberler invented the term 'market convertibility' to emphasize the distinction between the convertibility of one currency into another by private parties, as opposed to the right of a monetary authority to convert a reserve currency into other reserve assets ('official convertibility' or 'asset convertibility'). See G. Haberler, 'Prospects for the Dollar Standard', *Lloyd's Bank Review*, July 1972.

VIII status — i.e., the formal and irreversible convertibility obligations specified in the IMF Articles — was further delayed: until 1961 on the part of the Europeans and 1964 on the part of Japan. Most developing countries, except for some of the oil producers and some Latin American countries that had hard currencies in the early post-war period, still have inconvertible currencies. They show no signs of wishing to relinquish their Article XIV status, and the IMF exerts no pressure on them to do so.

Most countries maintained a system of exchange control after the adoption of convertibility. There was a general, though frequently interrupted, trend toward liberalization until the mid-1960s, which culminated in most other industrialized countries joining the United States in extending current account convertibility to residents, except for periods of acute payments deficits when some tended to restrict tourist expenditure abroad. Capital transactions, in contrast, remained restricted to some extent by most countries for most of the time: even the United States adopted a programme of controls over capital outflows in the mid- and late-1960s that amounted to *de facto* exchange control over large corporations and banks. Country after country found that these exchange controls were of limited effectiveness, especially as regards short-term capital flows: the opportunities for disguising capital movements through leading and lagging current payments and other devices are too great to make exchange control an effective weapon in an international economy with the degree of interdependence achieved by the 1960s. The United States abolished her capital controls in January 1974 in the wake of the oil crisis, and German controls (over capital inflows) have again been relaxed since the move to floating, but most other countries still maintain significant controls over capital movements.

The exchange rate regime

The exchange rate regime incorporated in the Bretton Woods system has become generally known as the 'adjustable peg'. The essential characteristics of this system are that at any time a country undertakes to maintain the value of its currency within a narrow margin of a par value, while the par value can be changed under certain circumstances. This arrangement was intended to provide a compromise between the desire to stabilize exchange rates in order to avoid the disorderly markets and competitive depreciations of the 1930s, and the desire to avoid forcing countries to revert to the gold standard 'rules of the game', under which defence of the exchange rate override the pursuit of domestic full employment policies.

The adjustable peg is one form of the par value system.[2] As the name implies, a par value system requires each currency to have a par value — i.e., a central value in terms of some numeraire. The numeraire of the Bretton Woods system was gold. This was to some extent obscured by the fact that many countries chose to express their par values in terms of the US dollar; but since the relevant IMF Article spoke of 'the United States dollar of the weight and fineness in effect on July 1, 1944' (Article IV. 1(a)), a dollar devaluation (a) was legally possible; (b) did *not* automatically change the par value of any other currency in terms of gold; and (c) *did* change the parities of other currencies in terms of the dollar. (The ratio of two par values is known as a parity; it describes the central value of one currency in terms of another.) All these points were suppressed — whether from ignorance or attempted wish-fulfilment — in much discussion by both academic economists and officials before the dollar devaluation of 1971.

There are two aspects of the operation of a par value system: the provisions for the defence of a par value and those for selecting and changing par values. The Bretton Woods system contained two methods by which a country might defend its par value. One method, which was written for and used by the United States, was to buy and sell gold in exchange for its currency at rates close to par. The other technique, which was adopted by all other countries, was to prevent the market exchange rate deviating from its parity against an intervention currency by more than 1 per cent. This was accomplished by buying (or selling) unlimited quantities of the intervention currency at a rate no more than 1 per cent above (below) parity. Most countries chose to intervene in terms of the US dollar: thus the dollar was pegged to gold and other currencies were pegged to the dollar, so that all were pegged with narrow margins of ± 1 per cent to the numeraire.[3] The dollar was therefore the dominant intervention currency in the Bretton Woods system. A consequence of this was that the intra-margin flexibility of the dollar was only half that of any other

2. The par value system is sometimes treated as synonymous with the adjustable peg. In my view this is wrong: the crawling peg is also a par value system, but it is sufficiently distinct to merit classification as a separate exchange rate regime. The essential difference is that a crawling peg includes a limitation on the size of permitted par value changes, so that a necessary change is effected gradually in a number of small steps.
3. The sterling area and franc zone countries pegged respectively to the pound sterling and French franc, which meant that the values of their currencies could deviate by up to 2 per cent from par. The cross rate between two currencies which both pegged to the dollar could, of course, deviate from parity by ± 2 per cent, which was contrary to the requirement of Article IV.3(i) that spot rates should be kept within 1 per cent of parity. The Fund exercised its considerable legal ingenuity to find a way of condoning these practices.

currency in the sense that the maximum possible exchange rate change between the dollar and any other currency was 2 per cent, while between any other pair of currencies it was 4 per cent (which occurred if one currency appreciated 2 per cent in terms of the dollar while the other depreciated 2 per cent in terms of the dollar).

There was considerable controversy between Britain and the United States regarding the provisions for selecting and changing par values in the discussions leading up to Bretton Woods. The White Plan had originally envisaged par values being determined by the IMF. This was vigorously resisted by the British and was eventually replaced by a provision that countries should propose their initial par values and any changes therein, and that the IMF should have no right to take an initiative with regard to par value changes, but that IMF consent to the country's proposals would be required. Countries were forbidden to propose a change in par value except to correct — famous phrase — a 'fundamental disequilibrium" (Article IV.5(a)), and the Fund was required to concur in the proposal provided that it was satisfied that the change was indeed necessary for that purpose. It was specifically precluded from objecting because of 'the domestic social or political policies of the member proposing the change'. (Article IV.5(f)). This provision was occasioned by the British (and very Keynesian) preoccupation that countries should not be forced into the abandonment of full employment policies by an obligation to defend an over-valued exchange rate. It is ironical that in the 1960s Britain did voluntarily what she had gone to such lengths to avoid being forced to do. In fact the Fund has not objected to a proposed par value change since 1948,[4] although it is possible that the knowledge that its approval was required has deterred countries from seeking changes that would otherwise have been made.

The adjustable peg operated until March 1973. In the initial post-war period most currencies were overvalued relative to those of the dollar bloc, but this was corrected — indeed, with the aid of hindsight, overcorrected — by the substantial devaluation of most non-dollar currencies in 1949. The par values of all major currencies except the French franc, which was devalued twice, remained stable throughout the 1950s, despite periodic intense speculation — particularly on a revaluation of the Deutschmark (DM) and a devaluation of the pound sterling. Canada, however, adopted a floating exchange rate in 1950 because of her concern over the inflationary consequences of a large

4. In 1948 the Fund objected to a proposed par value change by France largely on the ground that it considered some proposed associated multiple-currency practices unacceptable. See J. K. Horsefield, *The International Monetary Fund 1945-65*, IMF, Washington, DC, 1969, Vol.I, p.202.

capital inflow stemming from the market's disbelief in the viability of the previous parity. She reverted to a pegged rate in 1962 following a particularly inept piece of economic management, which was widely, though erroneously, attributed to floating.

There then followed a period when exchange rate changes were relegated to the status of confessions that the adjustment process had failed, and an attempt was made to operate a fixed rate system. This was the joint result of several factors: (a) the intense speculation that accompanied the long-anticipated revaluation of the DM (in the event joined by the Dutch guilder), which had finally occurred in 1961; (b) the personal hostility to exchange rate changes of the then Managing Director of the IMF, Per Jacobsson; and (c) the anxiety of the reserve-currency countries, the United States and Britain, to avoid anything that might disturb confidence in their currencies and thus undermine the international roles of the dollar and the pound. And, for over 5 years, from 1962 to 1967, there was no par value change by a major currency. In 1963 a major run on the lira was defeated with the aid of the central bank swap network and at the cost of a severe deflaticnary programme. Between 1964 and 1967 the pound was defended from a series of speculative runs, occasioned by the growing evidence of its overvaluation, once again by large short-term borrowing and at the cost of a series of disruptive internal measures. Such flexibility as survived was confined to the periphery of the system: many developing countries devalued periodically, the Lebanon continued to float and several Latin American countries with high inflation rates - led by Chile in 1962 and encouraged by the IMF - adopted a fast crawling peg.

In November 1967 Britain finally faced the facts of life and devalued the pound by 14 per cent. Six months later the French students rioted, in one of the manifestations of the widespread student unrest of the late 1960s, and on this occasion, unlike others, they persuaded the workers to join them. The 12 per cent general wage increases that ended 'les Evénements' transformed the French franc from one of the prides of Gaullist grandeur to an obvious devaluation candidate. Meanwhile the chronic German surplus had re-emerged and the DM once more became a candidate for revaluation. The resulting speculative pressures led to a 3-day closing of many foreign exchange markets in November 1968 (market closures occurred at irregular intervals during the following 5 years), and the convening of a conference of the Finance Ministers of the Group of Ten (G-10) at Bonn. This was the first time that an international conference discussed possible exchange rate realignment, but it ended by issuing a communiqué that declared that no par values would be changed. President de Gaulle, who vetoed the devaluation that his technicians had conditionally promised, declared that a devaluation of the franc would be 'the worst absurdity'. In 1969 the German press could still oppose revaluation with the argument that one should cure the sick man and not the healthy man, and a senior spokesman for the German government could still declare the DM parity to be valid 'for eternity'. But these proved to be the last gasps of the supporters of a doomed system.

Academic support for greater exchange rate flexibility had been building up ever since the famous advocatory writing of James Meade and Milton Friedman in the early 1950s.[5] During the 1960s the literature on fixed versus floating exchange rates was supplemented by much discussion of limited flexibility, in the specific form of a wider band for exchange rates to fluctuate around parity (the 'band proposal'), or for a series of very small parity changes to replace the occasional jumps of the adjustable peg (the 'crawling peg', alias 'sliding parity', 'gliding parity', etc.).[6] In 1969 the force of events gave significance to these intellectual developments. In January Paul Volcker, who was sympathetic to flexibility, got the key job of Under Secretary for Monetary Affairs in the US Treasury; in April de Gaulle resigned following his defeat in a referendum; in September the SPD won enough votes in the German elections to form a coalition with the FDP and displace the CDU/CSU from the Government. The monetary consequences were not long in following. In August the French franc was devalued; in September the DM embarked on a transitional float and the IMF Executive Board was instructed, under American pressure, to study the issue of the exchange rate regime; in October the DM was repegged at a new higher par value. In May 1970 Canada again floated, thus dissociating herself, even before it was published, from the ultra-cautious IMF report *The Role of Exchange Rates in the Adjustment of International Payments* (whose main virtue was its title, which at least implied that exchange rate changes were a legitimate instrument of adjustment). A year later the DM and Dutch guilder were floated ('they'll have to build a bigger dog house now', one Canadian official is reported

5. J. E. Meade, *The Balance of Payments* (The Theory of International Economic Policy, Vol.I), Oxford University Press, London, 1951; M. Friedman, 'The Case for Flexible Exchange Rates', in his *Essays in Positive Economics*, University of Chicago Press, Chicago, 1953.
6. G. N. Halm, *The 'Band' Proposal: The Limits of Permissible Exchange Rate Variations*, Princeton Special Papers in International Economics No.6, Princeton, 1965; J. E. Meade, 'The International Monetary Mechanism', *Three Banks Review*, September 1964; J. Williamson, *The Crawling Peg*, Princeton Essays in International Finance No.50, Princeton, 1965; C. F. Bergsten, G. N. Halm, F. Machlup, R. V. Roosa, eds., *Approaches to Greater Flexibility of Exchange Rates: The Bürgenstock Papers*, Princeton University Press, Princeton, 1970.

to have quipped), to be joined by all the other principal currencies (except the French franc) after the United States closed the gold window on 15 August. The adjustable peg, with wider margins of 2.25 per cent instead of the previous 1 per cent, was patched together again at the Smithsonian Conference in December. The realignment was greeted in Nixonian hyperbole as 'the most significant monetary agreement in the history of the world'. The pound was floated within 7 months. After a further 7 months, Italy introduced a 2-tier market, Switzerland floated, the United States devalued, Japan floated, Italy floated. Within 3 weeks of the US devaluation there was a new run from the dollar into the DM. At that point the rate between the European snake and the US dollar was allowed to float. The adjustable peg was dead.

Balance-of-payments adjustment

There are two aspects to the subject of payments adjustment:[7] first, the question of which country has the responsibility to initiate adjustment action and when; and second, the question of the techniques that should be used to effect adjustment when adjustment is desired. In the end, the Bretton Woods system was not particularly explicit on either of these questions. This was not because they were forgotten by Keynes and White. On the contrary, the original Keynes Plan provided for interest to be paid on both excessive accumulation of bancor balances — i.e., excessive reserve accumulation — and excessive bancor indebtedness — i.e., an excessive cumulative deficit — reflecting the view that the system should contain explicit obligations on both surplus and deficit countries to maintain reasonable balance in their external accounts in the medium term. And the original versions of both the Keynes Plan and the White Plan contained specific provisions on the measures that countries could be required to take to effect adjustment: the unpublished first draft of the White Plan went as far as vesting control of exchange rates with the Fund and allowing the Fund to veto members' monetary and banking

7. Payments adjustment was defined as 'the process by which deficits and surpluses are eliminated' in the influential taxonomy of international monetary problems compiled by the Bellagio conferees in 1964. See F. Machlup and B. G. Malkiel, eds., *International Monetary Arrangements: The Problem of Choice*, International Finance Section, Princeton University, Princeton, 1964, pp.32-3. This definition can be criticized on the ground that there are times — as, for example, when a country has an excessive or deficient reserve level — when it is appropriate to create, or not to eliminate, a deficit or surplus; but the definition is easily amended to refer to 'the process by which payments balances are adjusted to conform to objectives'.

policies.[8] There was, however, a direct conflict between the interests of creditor countries and of debtor countries on such points: creditor countries had a strong national interest in ensuring that they did not end up carrying the major share of the burden of adjustment, and debtor countries had a strong interest in ensuring that they were not forced to adjust by measures unnecessarily harmful to their well-being. Since the United States took it for granted that she would be a permanent surplus country and Britain expected to be a debtor country for a lengthy period (which turned out to be a far more permanent state of affairs than the US creditor position), this conflict of national interests was direct and acute. The result was that the substance of both plans was whittled away in the course of negotiation.

The principle that both surplus and deficit countries had a responsibility to seek payments adjustment was, however, implicitly incorporated in the Bretton Woods system. Deficit countries have only finite reserves, and are, therefore, faced with the threat of reserve depletion if they allow a deficit to persist too long. There is no similar natural limit to the reserves that a surplus country can accumulate but the 'scarce currency clause' provided a potential sanction on chronic surplus countries. This clause permitted the IMF to declare a currency 'scarce' if its holdings of that currency were depleted to an extent that threatened its ability to continue lending that currency to other countries, whereupon the Fund would be authorized to ration the currency and members would be authorized to discriminate against the exports of the country whose currency was scarce (Article VIII.3). This proposal was apparently advanced by the United States because of a concern for the technical viability of an institution that would otherwise have promised rights to borrow a particular currency that might collectively have exceeded its resources of the currency.[9] At Harrod's instigation,[10] the proposal was seized on by the British and elevated into a major assurance that creditors would play a part in the adjustment process and so be constrained from inflicting deflation on the rest of the world.

The Bretton Woods system was equally ambiguous about the techniques that were supposed to be employed to effect adjustment. Current account restrictions were frowned on. Capital account restrictions were permitted, but, quite apart from their limited

8. R. N. Gardner, *Sterling-Dollar Diplomacy*, McGraw Hill, London, new edition, 1969, pp.74, 90-1.

9. *Ibid., p.91, n.6*

10. *See R. F. Harrod, The Life of John Maynard Keynes*, Macmillan, London, 1951, p.545, for Harrod's account of his excitement when he first read of the US proposal on a midnight train to Oxford in the middle of the war.

effectiveness, they cannot by their nature contribute to current account adjustment. Exchange rate changes could be proposed by a country in 'fundamental disequilibrium', subject to the Fund's concurrence, but the Fund had no power to propose a par value change, and in practice countries proved extremely reluctant to exercise their rights in this matter. Fiscal and monetary policies were principally devoted to the pursuit of internal stabilization objectives in the post-war world, although on occasion they were modified by external needs. Hence there was no agreed strategy as to the mechanisms that should be used to secure adjustment.

The early post-war years were marked by a longer and more acute dollar shortage than had been foreseen during the negotiations to plan the brave new post-war world. After an initial lag the United States responded as a model creditor country, generously dispensing aid, encouraging foreign spending and not objecting to foreign devaluations or discrimination against her exports. Variations in aid flows and direct controls served as the principal adjustment mechanisms during the era of dollar shortage, which lasted until about 1953. From then on European recovery, coupled with the delayed effects of the 1949 currency realignment, led to a progressive strengthening in the European payments position. European surpluses were kept in check by progressive import liberalization, which tended to be undertaken as and when the payments position permitted. This process exhausted itself by the early 1960s, by which time countries were largely fulfilling their international commitments on trade liberalization.

It was therefore in the 1960s that the great ambiguity of Bretton Woods became apparent. Since the climate of the time was strongly hostile to exchange rate flexibility, an attempt had to be made to reinstate financial policies — i.e., monetary and/or fiscal policy — as sufficient instruments for payments adjustment. Perhaps the most firmly established theorem in international monetary economics states that if a country wishes to maintain a fixed exchange rate it had better follow the gold standard rules of the game by inflating the money supply when it has a payments surplus and deflating it when it has a deficit, irrespective of the state of the domestic economy. The IMF began to preach the association between domestic credit expansion (DCE) and deficits, in a suitably guarded way, as early as 1958.[11] Subsequently the international monetarists[12] came along with the cheering message that the achievement of external balance through monetary

11. J. J. Polak, 'Monetary Analysis of Income Formation', IMF *Staff Papers*, November 1958.
12. The international monetarists have their intellectual home in Chicago. The two leading members of the school are Harry Johnson and Robert Mundell.

policy would be essentially painless, contrary to the entrenched Keynesian orthodoxy, as amplified and interpreted by James Meade,[13] which was full of dilemma situations caused by differential cost-push inflation. The first theory advanced to support this fantasy was the Mundellian fiscal/monetary mix: internal and external balance could supposedly be reconciled at fixed exchange rates by choosing the appropriate *combination* of policy — e.g., a country tending to deficit was supposed to tighten its monetary policy so as to attract a capital inflow, while offsetting the contractionary effect of this on internal demand (and therefore also on the current account) by fiscal expansion.[14] It was always unrealistic to regard this as a method of payments adjustment, rather than as a method of temporarily financing a deficit by attracting short-term capital inflows instead of using reserves, because, although it is perfectly rational to contract loans to finance investment, it can be little more than a temporary palliative when there is no presumption that investment will be expanded and no mechanism to secure the current account adjustment needed to service and ultimately to repay the loans contracted.[15] Those countries, such as Britain, that adopted this expedient in the 1960s and relied on the attraction of capital inflows rather than ensuring current account adjustment, found that their position became progressively more difficult and ultimately untenable. However, by the time that this refutation of the Mundellian mix had won wide acceptance, the international monetarists had developed the monetary theory of the balance of payments, according to which payments imbalances were simply the result of allowing the domestic creation of money (DCE) to get out of line with the increase in the demand for money.[16] The theory in its original form asserted that a change in DCE would produce a corresponding change in the level of reserves without exerting a significant effect on the domestic economy. An exchange rate change

13. J. E. Meade, *The Balance of Payments*, op. cit.
14. R. A. Mundell, 'The Appropriate Use of Monetary and Fiscal Policy for Internal and External Stability', IMF *Staff Papers*, March 1962.
15. The first criticism along these lines appears to have been by H. G. Johnson, 'Theoretical Problems of the International Monetary System', *Pakistan Development Review*, spring 1967. See also J. Williamson, 'On the Normative Theory of Balance-of-Payments Adjustment'', in G. Clayton, J. C. Gilbert and R. Sedgwick, eds., *Monetary Theory and Monetary Policy in the 1970s*, Oxford University Press, Oxford, 1971, and F. Modigliani and H. Askari, 'The International Transfer of Capital and the Propagation of Domestic Disturbances Under Alternative Payments Systems', Banca Nazionale del Lavoro *Quarterly Review*, December 1973.
16. H. G. Johnson, *Further Essays in Monetary Economics*, Allen and Unwin, London, 1972, chap.9; R. A. Mundell, *Monetary Theory*, Goodyear Publishing Co., Pacific Palisades, Calif., 1971, Part II; H. G. Johnson and J. A. Frenkel, eds., *The Monetary Approach to the Balance of Payments*, Allen and Unwin, London, 1976.

was viewed as producing its effect by inducing a change in the real value of the money supply, as domestic costs and prices are adjusted to match the world level at the new exchange rate, thus implying that monetary policy provides a more or less perfect substitute for exchange rate changes. These properties hold *asymptotically* in virtually every coherent model of the balance of payments; what led to the striking policy conclusions of the first-generation monetarist models was the assertion that they held even in the short run. Despite the appeal that this theory achieved among academic economists, these first-generation models[17] never achieved much influence in official circles, primarily because they did not seem consistent with the events through which the officials were living and the problems with which they were confronted. To take an extreme example, when, in May 1968, Daniel Cohn-Bendit momentarily forged the worker − student alliance that paralysed France during 'les Evénements', the whole sequence of consequences was inconsistent with monetarist theory. The money supply increased by 8 per cent immediately after the 'Events';[18] the increase in domestic credit did not all immediately leak out abroad; prices did increase relative to those in the rest of the world; it did take a devaluation of the French franc to restore French competitiveness; French prices did not rise in line with the devaluation. It was experiences such as these that forced the official world, much against its will, to accept exchange rate flexibility.

Nevertheless, it was not until the early 1970s that there was any acceptance of the idea that exchange rates should play a central role as instruments of payments adjustment.[19] One little-noticed but crucial result of inflexibility is to increase the importance of the issue of which country bears the responsibility for initiating adjustment. If adjustment is effected with the aid of an exchange rate change, which country initiates the rate change has little effect on the location of the

17. The second-generation models inspired by the monetary approach to the balance of payments, as represented by the work of the International Monetary Research Programme at LSE and Geneva or the papers presented to the Stockholm Conference in August 1975 and published in the *Scandinavian Journal of Economics*, 1976(2), are another matter altogether. These models differ from the mainstream tradition stemming from Meade essentially in postulating that the balance on the capital account depends on the excess demand for money. They do not suggest the same strong policy implications as the first-generation models did.

18. *International Financial Statistics*, December 1968. This provides the most striking example of endogeneity in DCE of which I am aware.

19. The extent to which exchange rates were disregarded in the mid 1960s can be gauged by the fact that the official report on the subject of adjustment contained only two grudging references. See OECD, *The Balance of Payments Adjustment Process*, Paris, 1966.

burden of adjustment. There may be some political loss of face to the country that takes the initiative. The relative valuation of reserve assets will be affected if the question is, for example, whether to devalue the dollar or revalue a number of other currencies; and it is convenient, in an *n*-country world, if the country whose costs are out of line with the generality is the one that makes the move;[20] but which country takes the initiative does not affect the level of activity or rate of inflation in either country. It is quite different if adjustment is to be effected by financial policy at a fixed exchange rate: whether country A deflates or country B inflates is a question that affects the vital national interests of both. This perhaps explains why the early 1960s witnessed a major attempt to develop international consultation over the adjustment process.

Since at that time this was a problem of primary concern to a limited group of the major developed countries, it was natural that a more limited forum than the IMF should be chosen for the development of 'multilateral surveillance'. The obvious organ was the Organization for Economic Cooperation and Development (OECD), which also had the advantage of allowing a more senior level of representation than was possible in the Fund Executive Board. (OECD had just been expanded from the former Organization for European Economic Cooperation by the addition of the United States, Canada and the new honorary member of the North Atlantic Community, Japan.) OECD created a ministerial-level Economic Policy Committee to discuss members' economic policies and problems, especially as they impinged on other members. The Committee set up four working parties, of which the most important rapidly became Working Party No.3 (WP3), which was charged with surveillance of members' payments policies. WP3 has since met frequently (every 6 weeks or so) at senior civil servant level, and is the principal forum in which the key national officials seek to coordinate their payments policies (which inevitably involves some discussion of anti-cyclical policies), to establish consistency between their objectives, to criticize the adequacy of one another's policies, and to defend their own policies before their international peers. Despite the fact that the lack of an effective adjustment mechanism has at times turned the consultations on payments objectives into something of an academic exercise and the discussions on policy into slanging matches about the failure of other countries to take actions that solve one's own problems, the meetings have widely been judged valuable in developing

20. J. Williamson, *The Choice of a Pivot for Parities*, Princeton Essays in International Finance No.90, Princeton, 1971, p.14.

understanding and even at times making a modest contribution to the achievement of consistency.

The continuing discussions on payments adjustment never resulted in an attempt to invoke the scarce currency clause to discipline a surplus country. It was not used in the years of dollar shortage because US aid largely supplanted borrowing from the IMF so that the Fund never ran short of dollars. It would therefore have been technically impossible to invoke the clause, even if any other country would have cared at that time to challenge US power by seeking to have the dollar declared scarce. No attempt was made to revive the clause when Germany replaced the United States as the world's chronic surplus country in the late 1950s. The clause's status as a dead letter was ratified by the conclusion of the General Arrangements to Borrow (GAB) in 1961, since the GAB had the incidental effect of enabling a chronic surplus country to lend additional quantities of its currency to the IMF and thereby avoid its currency becoming technically scarce. The disappearance of any international sanction on chronic surplus countries led to the accusations that the system suffered from a deflationary bias (or a devaluation bias, if exchange rates rather than demand-management policy were regarded as the main adjustment weapon). It seems doubtful, however, whether the absence of an institutional sanction can in itself be considered decisive. An excessive volume of reserves is costly to hold, since it involves foregoing real resources or incurring foreign debt in exchange for assets with a low yield, and reserve inflows may prove difficult to sterilize, with a consequent disruption of internal stabilization policy. Surplus countries, therefore, have an incentive to seek adjustment beyond some point, and the critical question is whether that point is so great in relation to the volume of global liquidity as to throw an excessive part of the adjustment burden on to deficit countries.[21] After the liquidity explosion of 1971 and the spread of worldwide inflation, it seemed far more plausible to accuse the system of an inflationary bias, as Dr Otmar Emminger, the Deputy Governor of the Bundesbank, did.[22] Even before then, the fact that one country — the United States — did not have a reserve constraint, but could finance her deficits by having other countries accept her liabilities, tended to impart an inflationary bias that was overlooked by those economists who claimed to diagnose a deflationary bias in the system.

The honour for first recognizing the importance of the disappearance

21. D. E. Roper, 'On the Theory of the Devaluation Bias'', *Kyklos*, 1972.
22. O. Emminger, *Inflation and the International Monetary System*, Per Jacobsson Foundation, Washington DC, 1973.

of the US payments constraint belongs to Jacques Rueff.[23] He contended that her ability to run a 'deficit without tears' robbed the United States of any incentive to seek adjustment and that this, coupled with the institutional fact that a payments deficit did not produce a monetary contraction in the United States, explained the maintenance of the US deficit during the 1960s. A radically different interpretation of the persistence of the US deficit was offered by the 'dollar standard' school.[24] It agreed with Rueff that the US payments constraint had been abolished, so that the world was effectively on a dollar standard, but argued that the US deficit was to be welcomed as providing the rest of the world with the liquidity that it desired, rather than that the deficit represented an involuntary appropriation of the rest of the world's real resources or business investments by the United States. In this view the dollar standard provided a convenient resolution of the '(N-1) problem' — i.e., that if all countries had their own balance-of-payments objectives, there was a strong probability that they would prove inconsistent and that this would lead to self-defeating policies such as competitive devaluation, interest rate wars or competitive deflation. The solution was for the reserve centre to treat its balance of payments with 'benign neglect', which would enable other countries to adjust to secure the payments objectives they desired, and would make the US payments balance demand determined. In the early years of the Nixon Administration, the United States showed signs of following this advice, to the considerable annoyance of most Europeans who proved to be unappreciative of the opportunity of determining the size of the US deficit. Then, in 1971, the US deficit exploded and the cause was obviously the relaxation of US monetary policy rather than a sudden increase in the appetite for dollars of monetary authorities in the rest of the world. In August the United States, by accompanying the closing of the gold window with demands that other countries should take action to remedy her deficit, effectively rejected the policy of benign neglect. How the responsibility for initiating adjustment should be distributed emerged as a major issue that had been fudged at Bretton Woods but that could no longer be papered over.

23. J. Rueff, 'The West is Risking a Credit Collapse', *Fortune*, July 1961.
24. The principal members of this school have been Emile Despres, Gottfried Haberler, Charles Kindleberger, Ronald McKinnon, Walter Salant, Thomas Willett and, at one time, Lawrence Krause. The most impressive exposition of the school's views is in R. I. McKinnon, *Private and Official International Money: The Case for the Dollar*, Princeton Essays in International Finance No.74, Princeton, 1969.

Reserve assets

A central feature of the Keynes Plan was its ambitious proposal for the creation of an international fiduciary reserve asset, bancor, in very large quantities, and the virtually unlimited obligation of surplus countries to accept payments in bancor. In contrast, the White Plan was modest in its objectives for supplementing international liquidity: it merely envisaged the creation of a pool of currencies and gold from which deficit countries could borrow in limited quantities. The war-end realities of power being what they were, the IMF was modelled on the White Plan; and the Bretton Woods system therefore accepted in its essentials the existing situation regarding the supply of reserve assets.

The status quo was the gold exchange standard. Gold was the major reserve asset and it was assumed that it would remain so. Sterling was the major reserve currency, mainly as a result of British success in financing much of her foreign war expenditure through the creation of reserve liabilities. The dollar was also a reserve currency on a small scale by 1945. Its reserve currency role expanded rapidly after 1950 as the rest of the world moved into collective surplus and found dollars as good as gold in terms of safety and somewhat superior on the grounds of their convenience in transactions and their interest yield.

The IMF did play a minor role in supplementing international liquidity. Each member subscribed a sum equal to its quota — one quarter in gold and the remainder in its national currency. This provided a pool of currencies (and gold) from which members in need could borrow up to 125 per cent of their quota.[25] After a protracted Anglo-American dispute on the automaticity of drawing rights, the IMF resolved in 1952 that it would give the 'overwhelming benefit of the doubt' to members wishing to borrow within the gold tranche — i.e., up to the 25 per cent of their quota that they had paid for with gold — but that beyond that point borrowing would be subject to conditions that became increasingly stringent as the member utilized more of its 'credit tranches'. Countries could, therefore, count their gold tranche and 'super-gold tranche' positions — i.e., any net creditor position they established in the Fund as a result of other countries borrowing their currency — as part of their reserves, since they were unconditionally available, while the rest of their drawing possibilities constituted conditional liquidity. Conditional liquidity expanded when quotas were increased, as happened in 1959, 1965 and 1970. Unconditional liquidity

25. Technically members do not 'borrow' from the Fund, but 'purchase' a designated strong currency (which the central bank of that country then converts into a reserve currency usable in intervention) with their own currency. It is, however, more revealing of the economic content of the transaction to refer to this as 'borrowing' or 'drawing'.

expanded as a by-product of the use of conditional liquidity: when, for example, Britain drew DM from the Fund, Germany obtained a super-gold tranche position which counted as a part of her reserves.[26]

IMF lending was on a minor scale at first, with the United States effectively assuming the role of lender of last resort during the period of dollar shortage. The IMF emerged into its own right in 1956 with the appointment of a more forceful Managing Director in the person of Per Jacobsson, and the need to bail out Britain and France from the financial consequences of their Suez escapade. Britain established a reputation at that time, which was reinforced during the 1960s, of being the Fund's principal debtor.

During the 1950s the countries in surplus chose to convert part of the dollars that they were earning into gold and to retain the remainder. This was an unconstrained portfolio choice. Matters changed shortly after the phrase 'dollar problem' ceased meaning dollar shortage and came instead to mean dollar glut — an event that may be dated around 1957, when the extensive and imaginative literature inventing reasons for expecting a permanent dollar shortage ceased to expand.[27] In the autumn of 1960 there was a brief flurry in the gold market as the realization that the dollar might not remain permanently as good as gold first dawned. The United States responded by informally requesting her partners to use restraint in exercising their right to convert dollars into gold so as to give her time to effect adjustment, and there is evidence that they responded.[28]

1960 was also important as the year in which Robert Triffin published his short but influential book *Gold and the Dollar Crisis,*[29] which launched the debate on reform of the international monetary system.

26. The analogy between the way in which utilization of an overdraft expands a country's money supply and the way in which a Fund drawing expands the world reserve stock appears to have been overlooked before publication of the paper by H. Ezekiel, 'The Present System of Reserve Creation in the Fund', IMF *Staff Papers*, November 1966.
27. Major contributions to the literature on the dollar shortage included T. Balogh, *The Dollar Crisis: Causes and Cure*, Blackwell, Oxford, 1950; J. R. Hicks, 'An Inaugural Lecture'', *Oxford Economic Papers*, June 1953; and D. MacDougall, *The World Dollar Problem*, Macmillan, London, 1957.
28. P. B. Kenen, *Reserve-Asset Preferences of Central Banks and Stability of the Gold Exchange Standard*, Princeton Studies in International Finance No.10, 1963; P. Høst Madsen, 'Gold Outflows from the US 1956-63', IMF *Staff Papers*, July 1964; M. L. Greene, 'Reserve-Asset Preferences Revisited', in in P. B. Kenen and R. Lawrence, eds., *The Open Economy*, Columbia University Press, London, 1968; L. H. Officer, 'Reserve Asset Preferences in the Crisis Zone, 1958-67', *Journal of Money, Credit and Banking*, May 1974.
29. R. Triffin, *Gold and the Dollar Crisis*, Yale University Press, New Haven, 1960.

Triffin's central thesis was that the gold exchange standard contained an inherent dilemma that was ultimately bound to undermine the satisfactory functioning of an international monetary system based on the use of national currencies as international reserves. He argued, convincingly, that the demand for reserves was growing faster than the supply of gold, so that a liquidity shortage would emerge unless the United States continued to run a balance-of-payments deficit to supply additional reserves in the form of dollars. But, if the United States did continue to run a deficit, this would progressively undermine confidence in the dollar, and when other countries responded by seeking to convert dollars into gold the result would be to precipitate a crisis. The gold exchange standard had, after all, collapsed before, in 1931, and the effect was to prolong and intensify the most disastrous slump the world has ever experienced. Triffin's conclusion was that the world was faced with a dilemma, in which either a growing liquidity shortage would stifle the growth of trade and real income, or the system would collapse.

This simple but powerful argument was initially resisted by the official world. A defensive IMF report published in 1958[30] had explicitly argued that reserves were at that time adequate and that prospective reserve growth gave no cause for concern. This complacency was vigorously attacked by Triffin, and although many were unconvinced that international liquidity was already inadequate, his thesis that it was bound to become so — unless a confidence-eroding US deficit were maintained — was rapidly accepted by most academic economists. The academics, led by Triffin, began searching for a remedy, which most of them inferred could be found by inventing a reserve asset whose supply could be expanded without the need for a US deficit. Many and varied plans to this end were proposed.[31]

These academic calls for a revolution in the international monetary system provoked a series of assurances from official quarters that revolution was unnecessary because a satisfactory process of evolution was already in train. The principal exhibits pointed to were (a) the 1959 increase in IMF quotas; (b) the creation of the 'Gold Pool', a cartel of the eight principal central banks on whose behalf the Bank of England intervened in the London gold market to stabilize the market price of gold within narrow margins around its official price to prevent a

30. IMF, *International Reserves and Liquidity*, Washington DC, 1958.
31. A detailed account and comparison of many of the early schemes can be found in F. Machlup, *Plans for the Reform of the International Monetary System*, Princeton Special Papers in International Economics No.3, Princeton, revised edition, 1964. Many of the original papers were reprinted in H. G. Grubel, ed., *World Monetary Reform*, Stanford University Press, Stanford, 1963.

repetition of the confidence-eroding flare-up in the gold price in October 1960; (c) the development of multilateral surveillance; (d) the invention of 'Roosa bonds', which had a maturity of just over 1 year (and were, therefore, for US balance-of-payments purposes statistically 'long-term'), and carried an exchange guarantee so that they could be sold to monetary authorities that might otherwise have been tempted to convert their dollars into gold; (e) the creation of a network of 'swap' agreements among the major central banks, whereby each central bank made available a reciprocal line of credit to its partners up to an agreed maximum sum for a limited period; and (f) the conclusion of the GAB in late 1961, under which the 11 major financial powers[32] concluded a stand-by agreement with the IMF to enable it to borrow additional sums of their currencies if the Fund's own resources threatened to be insufficient. All these changes, except the quota increase, were of almost exclusive interest to the developed countries, but the developing countries achieved a significant innovation in their interests in 1963 when the IMF introduced a facility for the compensatory financing of export fluctuations, which permitted a country experiencing a shortfall in export receipts below the level indicated by a formula based on previous experience to borrow from the Fund without the usual conditions and beyond the normal limits.

Academic critics labelled this combination of *ad hoc* financing and arm-twisting 'ad hoccery', and it was not long before official opinion also started to question whether the system was so resilient that natural evolution would suffice. Bolder steps were first called for at the 1962 Annual Meetings of the IMF, when Reginald Maudling, the British Chancellor, and other Governors advanced proposals for new measures to increase international liquidity. By the following year there was general acceptance that the subject needed exploration, whereupon both the G-10 and the IMF initiated studies, but with the G-10 making it clear that their deliberations were the important ones (to the considerable resentment of the countries excluded). After a year's deliberations the G-10, while reaffirming its 'conviction that a structure based ... on fixed (*sic*) exchange rates and the established price of gold, has proved its value ... '', got to the point of conceding that the 'continuing growth of world trade and payments ... in the longer run, may possibly call for some new form of reserve asset',[33] and set up a study group chaired by Rinaldo Ossalo of the Banca d'Italia to study

32. The 11 were the Group of Ten (G-10) — the United States, Germany, the United Kingdom, France, Italy, Japan, Canada, the Netherlands, Belgium and Sweden — and one non-member of the IMF, Switzerland.
33. Ministerial Statement of the Group of Ten, 1 August 1964, reprinted in R. V. Roosa, *Monetary Reform for the World Economy*, Harper and Row, New York, 1965.

alternative ways in which a new reserve asset could be created.[34] At that stage the main discussion centred around alternative forms of composite reserve unit (CRU), an idea first developed by Edward Bernstein (the former Economic Counsellor to the IMF), under which each member of the G-10 would subscribe a sum of its own currency to a pool and receive in return a corresponding number of CRUs, which could then be used as equivalent to gold. A French version of the CRU had been proposed by Giscard d'Estaing in 1963-64, according to which, countries would be eligible to subscribe to the CRU account in proportion to their gold holdings, and gold and CRUs would then circulate together in fixed proportions. The United States initially opposed such ideas on the ground that they would undermine the role of the dollar, preferring instead a system in which other strong currencies became reserve currencies (the 'multiple currency system'). But in July 1965 the new Secretary of the Treasury, Henry Fowler, announced an about-turn in US policy that made the United States the foremost advocate of the creation of a new reserve asset.

France had, however, anticipated the American volte-face by one of her own. On 4 February 1965, President de Gaulle gave one of his famous press conferences. In terms calculated to bring despair to the heart of every serious technocrat, he declared:*

Quelle base? En vérité, on ne voit pas qu'à cet égard il puisse y avoir de critère, d'étalon, autres que l'or. Eh! oui, l'or qui ne change pas de nature, qui se met, indifféremment, en barres, en lingots ou en pièces, qui n'a pas de nationalité, qui est tenu, éternellement et universellement, comme la valeur inaltérable et fiduciaire par excellence. D'ailleurs, en dépit de tout ce qui a pu s'imaginer, se dire, s'écrire, se faire, à mesure d'immenses événements, c'est un fait qu'encore aujourd'hui aucune monnaie ne compte, sinon par relation directe ou indirecte, réelle ou supposée, avec l'or.

France was thereafter committed to espousing a return to the gold standard, with the implicit corollary of an increase in the price of gold. As part of a systematic policy of making the gold exchange standard

---

34. Its taxonomy was presented in Group of Ten, *Report of the Study Group on the Creation of Reserve Assets*, 1965, generally known as the Ossola Report.

* 'What basis? Actually, it is difficult to envisage in this regard any other standard than gold. Yes, gold, which does not change in nature, which can be made into bars, ingots or coins, which has no nationality, which is considered, in all places and at all times, the immutable and fiduciary value par excellence. Furthermore, despite all that it was possible to imagine, say, write or do in the midst of major events, it is a fact that even today no currency has any value except by direct or indirect relation to gold, real or supposed.' (Quoted in F. Hirsch, *Money International*, Penguin, London, 1967, p. 277.)

unworkable, she initiated regular and substantial conversions of dollars into gold. The reason for this policy was a straightforward antagonism to the power of the United States, as manifested specifically in the 'inordinate privilege' of financing a deficit by issuing additional dollar liabilities instead of transferring reserve assets. The same motivation had underlain Giscard's proposed CRU, which was also intended to replace the use of reserve currencies. But, whereas Giscard's proposal had been a serious attempt to find a viable technical solution to what was widely recognized as the real problem posed by the asymmetrical position conferred on the United States by the reserve currency role of the dollar, de Gaulle's solution was widely felt to be archaic and justly felt to be non-viable.[35] French intellectual prestige in international monetary affairs suffered a blow from which it took years to recover, and France soon found herself isolated and therefore with little more than nuisance value at the conference table. De Gaulle's action represented a renunciation of the responsibility of power in favour of the emotional warmth of instant opposition of the type more usually associated with the far left.

So far as the reform negotiations — as they had now become — were concerned, the joint result of Fowler's initiative and de Gaulle's assumption of the direction of French policy was to place leadership firmly in American hands. A protracted series of negotiations took place in the G-10, the IMF Executive Board and joint meetings of these two bodies, between 1965 and 1967.[36] What emerged from these meetings, to be formally ratified by the IMF 1967 Annual Meeting in Rio de Janeiro, was an agreement to create a new reserve asset called the 'special drawing right' (SDR).

As Fritz Machlup has said,[37] the nature of the SDR is best revealed by its Spanish name, 'derechos especiales de giro'. 'The word *giro* ... suggests transfer from one account to another, a gyration or circulation of the amounts that, once created, remain in existence. A giro-right exercised by its holder merely passes on to another holder.' This system would operate by the IMF creating a Special Drawing Account

35. The fundamental reason for the non-viability of a pure gold standard is that the costliness of commodity money creates a strong economic incentive for individual countries on both sides of the market for reserves to substitute credit money, which ensures that a gold standard will rapidly be transformed into a gold exchange standard. See M. Friedman, 'Commodity Reserve Currency', *Journal of Political Economy*, June 1951, reprinted in his *Essays in Positive Economics*, University of Chicago Press, Chicago, 1953.

36. A detailed account of these negotiations can be found in S. D. Cohen, *International Monetary Reform 1964-69*, Praeger, London, 1970.

37. F. Machlup, *Remaking the International Monetary System: The Rio Agreement and Beyond*, Johns Hopkins, Baltimore, 1968, p.13.

which all members, and not just a select inner group,[38] would be entitled to join. Participants would be credited a number of SDRs proportional to their share in Fund quotas when an SDR allocation was made, and would be obliged to accept SDRs when designated to do so by the IMF, provided that their holdings were less than three times their cumulative allocation. SDRs were to rely for their acceptability on the fact that other countries were in turn obliged to accept them, which is the essential basis for the acceptability of all money, rather than on 'backing' provided by a pool of currencies or gold. In this sense, indeed, the SDR had no backing, and the recognition that a monetary asset did not need any backing was hailed as a minor breakthrough in monetary practice.[39] However the SDR carried a (low) rate of interest that was paid to net creditors and debited to net debtors in the SDR Account, so that in a real economic sense the backing was provided by all participants in proportion to the SDRs they were allocated. Use of SDRs was restricted to occasions when a country had a payments deficit, thus preventing the SDR from being an instrument for changing the composition of reserves, and each participant was obliged to maintain an average balance over a 5-year period of at least 30 per cent of its allocation. (This 'reconstitution provision' was the concession extracted by the conservatives who wanted to create only a 'credit instrument' and not a 'reserve unit'.) Apart from these two provisos, countries were free to use SDRs unconditionally, so that they were true reserve assets, although the semantics were designed to veil this fact out of deference to French feelings. A country wishing to use SDRs would notify the Fund, which would in turn designate a surplus country to receive the SDRs and provide an equal value of some convertible currency for use in intervention, and the IMF would then adjust the computer entries for both parties' SDR holdings. The SDR was defined in terms of gold (hence the nickname 'paper gold', though this is mildly libellous in suggesting that SDRs were old-fashioned paper money rather than computer entries), and 1 SDR was set equal to US$1 at the then-current par value of the dollar.

Even France eventually subscribed to the SDR agreement, after winning a number of concessions both semantic and substantive — the latter involving (a) an undertaking that SDRs would not be activated until there was evidence of a 'better working of the adjustment process', which was generally interpreted to mean that the US deficit

38. The proposal to confine the newly-created reserves to an inner group of supposedly responsible countries died during 1965-66, with Pierre-Paul Schweitzer, the Managing Director of the IMF, playing a possibly important role in arguing that 'international liquidity is the business of the Fund'.
39. Machlup,lop. cit., p.34.

had been eliminated, and (*b*) removal of the proposal to permit substitution of SDRs for reserve currencies. The agreement was a historic step. It was the first time that a fiduciary reserve asset had been deliberately created by international agreement, and the design of the asset was superior to most of the initial proposals in technical terms. There are three basic issues that monetary theory indicates to be of importance in a monetary asset.[40] The first concerns the question of confidence: if asset holders are liable to lose confidence in an asset and are free to switch their portfolios among assets, the result will be to exaggerate the normal effects of payments variations as holders switch from weak to strong assets, and to produce capricious variations in total liquidity; for example, because a reserve centre is forced to surrender primary reserve assets without a corresponding gain in liquidity elsewhere in the system. The SDR agreement did not solve the confidence problem so far as the reserve currencies were concerned, but the restriction on the use of SDRs to occasions when a country had a payments deficit, prevented the introduction of this new asset intensifying the confidence problem by providing an additional possibility for portfolio switches. The second issue concerns stabilization: all schools of thought are agreed that the prime criterion of an efficient monetary system is its performance in contributing to stabilization of the level of activity and either the level or trend of prices.[41] The SDR agreement provided the international community with the ability to create reserves deliberately so as to avoid a reserve shortage arising from the accidents of geology or capricious variations in the payments imbalances of reserve centres. Its failing, which became glaringly apparent after 1971, was in not providing a constraint on reserve growth through the deficits of reserve centres or the operation of the Euro-currency markets. The third basic question is commonly referred to as the 'seigniorage' issue. It concerns the question of whether the real resource cost of providing money should be minimized, and who reaps the social saving thus achieved. The SDR agreement involved the creation of an international fiat money and thus

40. See the more extensive discussion of this subject in my survey article 'International Liquidity - A Survey', *Economic Journal*, September 1973, Section III.2.
41. The classical expression of what this implies in the international sphere was that of Keynes: 'We need a *quantum* of international currency, which is neither determined in an unpredictable and irrelevant manner as, for example, by the technical progress of the gold industry, nor subject to large variations depending on the gold reserve policies of individual countries; but is governed by the actual current requirements of world commerce, and is also capable of deliberate expansion and contraction to offset deflationary and inflationary tendencies in world demand.' (Cmd 6436 (1943), the Keynes Plan for an International Clearing Union.)

reaped the social saving from avoiding the reinstatement of an international commodity money such as gold. It distributed the bulk of the social saving as seigiorage rather than as interest.[42] Since SDRs are allocated in proportion to countries' quotas, the SDR scheme is distributionally neutral to the extent that IMF quotas provide a measure of countries' long-run demands for reserves, since, to that extent, countries are on average neither long-run net users nor net holders of SDRs in excess of their cumulative allocations. Since developing countries were permitted to participate in the SDR scheme, they reaped a part of the social saving; but they did not secure a disproportionate part, as the proponents of an aid link — who naturally came to include virtually all the developing countries — desired.

Discussions on activation of SDRs commenced in 1969, as the SDR agreement was grinding its way to ratification in the world's parliaments. These negotiations resulted in activation on a considerably larger scale (SDR 9·5 billion over 3 years) than had been envisaged during the negotiations to create the SDR facility. It would seem that this was the joint result of three factors.[43] First, there was a feeling that the degree of reserve ease prevailing up to the mid-1960s was about right, and all the methods used by the IMF to extrapolate this degree of reserve ease into the early 1970s suggested there would be a substantial shortfall in liquidity in the absence of SDRs. This largely reflected the facts that reserves had scarcely grown between 1965 and 1968 and that no subsequent major growth in any other form of reserves was anticipated. (In particular, the explosion in dollar holdings that actually occurred from 1970 on was unanticipated.) Second, it seems that there was a growing conviction in official circles that —

42. The term 'seigniorage' originally meant the mint charge for turning metal into money, but in the modern context it refers to the net value of the resources accruing to the issuer of money. The term, and most of the analysis, was introduced into international monetary economics by the international monetarists at a conference held in Chicago in 1966, the proceedings of which were published in R. A. Mundell and A. K. Swoboda, eds, *Monetary Problems of the International Economy*, University of Chicago Press, Chicago, 1969. (See the papers by H. G. Grubel, H. G. Johnson, R. A. Mundell and W. E. Schmidt.) A basic conclusion of the analysis is that the social saving resulting from technical progress in the money supply industry may be distributed either through the payment of interest on money (as would happen in a competitive system) or through seigniorage. Since the SDR interest rate was only 1·5 per cent per annum until 1974, the bulk of the social saving was originally distributed as seigniorage. A natural benchmark of distributional neutrality (implicity employed in the text) is the distribution that would result if the social saving were all distributed through interest payments.
43. Most of the papers on which the decision regarding SDR allocation was based are reproduced as appendices to IMF, *International Reserves: Needs and Availability*, IMF, Washington DC, 1970.

contrary to the views of the international monetarists — the main response to reserve stringency was to be found in restrictions and controls rather than demand-management policy, so that the conflicting signals for reserve policy provided by the simultaneous intensification of restrictions and inflation were resolved in favour of the former. Third, the temporary US official settlements surplus resulting from acute monetary stringency produced the prospect of a liquidity famine in Europe that provided both a perceived need for additional reserves and an occasion for contending that the condition for SDR activation regarding the prior elimination of the US deficit had been satisfied.

The first SDRs were therefore allocated to IMF members on 1 January 1970. In the event, the supplement to liquidity that they provided was rapidly overshadowed by the outflow of dollars from the United States that initially reflected the relaxation of US monetary policy and that fed on itself as confidence in the dollar waned. In the decade since the dollar glut first emerged as a serious problem, countries had become accustomed to holding most of their reserve accruals in the form of dollars rather than demanding conversion into gold. Initially this had been a short-term act of help to the United States to give her time to effect adjustment. As time progressed, but the deficit persisted, countries found themselves increasingly locked in to holding dollars: conversion of dollars into gold became an act of political hostility to the United States, especially after de Gaulle launched his gold war in 1965. In 1968, following the sterling devaluation, there had been a run into gold by private speculators, which was terminated by the Washington Agreement of March 1968. The Washington Conference dissolved the Gold Pool (from which France had already withdrawn in June 1967), and its former members undertook not to sell monetary gold on, or buy gold from, the private market. This creation of a 2-tier market did not formally interfere with the right of foreign monetary authorities to convert their dollars into gold, but it became increasingly recognized that in fact any major moves to exercise this right would result in the United States 'closing the gold window'. Reserve increases were therefore taken in the form of dollars, though with increasing reluctance. At the beginning of August 1971 a number of countries apparently decided that it would be wise to try to get some gold while the going was good, even if this did threaten formally to end the Bretton Woods arrangements regarding dollar convertibility; after all, these were already no more than a formality. They ceased to be even that when the United States responded as anticipated on 15 August.

International management

The IMF's Article I(i) states the first of the Fund's purposes as that of '[promoting] international monetary cooperation through a permanent institution which provides the machinery for consultation and collaboration on international monetary problems'. The ideal of cooperative international management of the system has been largely realized for most of the post-war period, even though the cooperation was at times reserved and the management was not of a sufficiently forward-looking character to avert the ultimate breakdown of the system. The IMF, with its wide membership (excluding only Switzerland and the bulk of the socialist bloc), has been the central organization involved, but its work has been supplemented by a number of organizations of more limited scope — OECD, the Bank for International Settlements (BIS), the United Nations Conference on Trade and Development (UNCTAD), the General Agreement on Tariffs and Trade (GATT), the G-10, and so on.

The work of the IMF may be divided into that involving relations with individual member countries, and that concerning the general operation of the international monetary system. Before the introduction of SDRs, the main formal powers of the Fund — the approval of par value changes and of loans by the Fund — both fell in the first category, as did the vast body of regular consultations with member countries, which give the international community an opportunity to express views on the policies of individual countries. The work in the second category, which has tended to become increasingly important in recent years, concerns matters such as revision of the policies governing Fund lending, the drafting of occasional reports on proposed reforms of the international monetary system and — latterly — the operation of the SDR system. Quite apart from the specific items of business that arise, the very fact that business needs to be done ensures frequent contact between the officials who constitute the elite of the international financial community. The members of this elite, many of whom either are serving or have previously served in the IMF, either on the Executive Board or on the staff, tend to develop a certain internationalist perspective from which they influence the governments to which they are responsible, at the same time that they are seeking to promote the interests of their governments in the international arena.

The official governing body of the Fund is the Board of Governors, an unwieldy body representing all Fund members,[44] at Minister of Finance/Central Bank Governor level. This is the body that meets at the

44. Fund membership has grown from 39 in 1946 to 126 in September 1975.

Annual Meetings, which are an important occasion for numerous informal contacts. The formal sessions are significant mainly as a talking shop; the resolutions passed do no more than ratify formally what is decided elsewhere. The other decision-making organ of the Fund is the Executive Board, which meets one to three times a week and is drawn from the intermediate levels of the civil service or central banking fraternity. The Board currently has 20 members, five of whom are appointed by the members with the largest quotas (the United States, the United Kingdom, Germany, France and Japan), with the other 15 representing the remaining members grouped into constituencies that are formed biennially by a complex voting procedure and that in practice tend to consist of groups of countries with common interests. The Executive Board is chaired by the Fund's Managing Director and serviced by its multinational staff, which consists predominantly of professionally trained economists. In general the Executive Board resolves matters of only secondary importance: the strategic principles tend to emerge from higher level meetings of smaller groups of countries, although the Board often does important preliminary work which forms a basis for the strategic decisions.

In the early years of the Fund the real power lay with its two largest members, who had been essentially responsible for its creation, the United States and the United Kingdom, and major decisions — in so far as there were any — tended to be determined in bilateral talks between the two. By the early 1960s this no longer reflected the realities of power. One of the causes of the creation of the GAB in 1961 was the determination of the new creditors of continental Europe to create an inner directorate, the G-10, who were the Fund members that established lines of credit with the Fund under the GAB. The Group's meetings rapidly became the forum where the key negotiations on such issues as the establishment of a new reserve asset were conducted. Many of the same officials from essentially the same group of key countries also started meeting regularly in other contexts as well, notably the meetings of the OECD Economic Policy Committee and its Working Party No.3 and the monthly meetings of the central bankers at the BIS at Basle.[45] The latter became of major importance because of their role in supervising the operation of the swap network, which was called on time after time in the 1960s to provide swift help to countries struggling to defend a pegged parity against the vast speculative flows that inevitably occurred in a system in which international capital

---

45. The overlap between the participation in these various forums was studied by R. W. Russell, 'Transgovernmental Interaction in the International Monetary System, 1960-72', *International Organization*, Autumn 1973.

mobility had become one of the dominant facts of international economic life.

The developing countries were naturally affronted by their exclusion from effective decision making. They responded by organizing themselves into a coherent pressure group, which was first reflected in the creation of UNCTAD in 1964. They played a small part in the SDR negotiations when these were broadened from the G-10 to joint meetings of the G-10 Deputies and the IMF Executive Directors in 1966, and succeeded in gaining the right to participate in the SDR scheme — although they found little sympathy among the developed countries for their desire to go further than this and establish a link between the allocation of SDRs and the provision of aid.

As the 1970s opened there was some tendency for countries to coalesce into three groups: the United States and a handful of sympathizers, which had no objection to the prospect of a dollar standard; most of the remaining developed countries, virtually all of whom (momentarily even including Britain) were major surplus countries, and who increasingly regarded Germany as *primus inter pares*; and the developing countries, many of whom were at last beginning to enjoy a significant measure of economic progress and whose success whetted their appetite for greater power. The story of the C-20 was in large measure the story of how these three groups tussled with each other in the attempt to refashion the international monetary system so as to further what they conceived to be their interests.

2

Why Bretton Woods collapsed

The account of the history of the Bretton Woods system in the previous chapter described both the events that led up to its breakdown in the early 1970s and the academic prognostications of its collapse. It did not, however, attempt to explain why the system ultimately broke down. Since the C-20 negotiations were strongly influenced by the participants' interpretation of the causes of this breakdown and because any reformed system needed to learn from these experiences, it is important to analyse the causes of the breakdown of the Bretton Woods system as a prelude to an examination of the C-20 negotiations.

It was argued in the previous chapter that it is wrong to think of the whole structure erected at Bretton Woods as having disintegrated. The arrangements made in two important respects, market convertibility — i.e., the ability of the private sector to convert one currency into another — and international management, survived. In another area, that of adjustment responsibilities and incentives, the Bretton Woods system was always highly ambiguous. These ambiguities gave rise to increasing tensions as the 1960s progressed, and an important part of the work of the C-20 was devoted to the attempt to legislate a framework of rules in this area. Such an endeavour was in any event overdue, but the immediate cause of the creation of the C-20 was not a sudden realization of the inadequacies of the existing system in this respect, important as I shall argue these inadequacies to have been in contributing to the suspension of official convertibility. It was quite clearly the suspension of official convertibility* — the right of foreign monetary authorities to convert official holdings of dollars into primary reserve assets (gold or SDRs) — in August 1971 that provoked the

---

* Unqualified use of the term 'convertibility' in the remainder of this book should be interpreted as referring to 'official convertibility'.

reform negotiations. Another aspect of the Bretton Woods system, the adjustable peg, also collapsed, but the final breakdown here did not come until the C-20 was in full operation.

Since two distinct aspects of the Bretton Woods system failed, it is proper to inquire separately into the causes of the failure of each. It should not be taken for granted that there was a common cause of these two distinct developments, or that the breakdown of one feature caused the breakdown of the other, although it would perhaps be surprising if there were no interconnections between the two sets of events. Accordingly, this chapter will first seek to explain the breakdown of the gold exchange standard, and will subsequently examine the causes of the abandonment of the adjustable peg.

The gold exchange standard

The gold exchange standard is a system under which reserves consist of both a primary reserve asset, gold, and foreign exchange, which the reserve centre stands ready to convert into the primary reserve asset on request. When the peripheral countries are confident that the reserve currency is not going to be devalued relative to gold, it is attractive to them to hold reserves in the form of a reserve currency rather than gold, since foreign exchange yields interest and is directly usable in intervention. A strong currency that is widely used in international payments and that has an active money market is, therefore, likely to emerge as a reserve currency, unless the issuing country takes steps to discourage other countries holding its currency in their reserves. As long as the reserve centre is concerned to maintain convertibility, the fact that its currency is serving as a reserve currency does not avoid the need to maintain a satisfactory payments position: failure to do so results in a loss of confidence which is liable to provoke requests for conversion of its currency into gold. The economic function of convertibility is, therefore, that of providing a discipline on the policies of the reserve centre, analogous to the discipline exerted by the threat of reserve depletion on other countries.

In academic circles it had been more or less taken for granted, ever since the publication of Triffin's *Gold and the Dollar Crisis* in 1960, that the gold exchange standard was inherently unstable. It will be recalled that Triffin's analysis had suggested that, failing a basic reform that would place the creation of liquidity on a more rational basis, the world would either experience a progressive strangulation of trade and activity as liquidity became increasingly inadequate as a result of the correction of the US deficit, or else there would, at some time, come a crisis of confidence in the dollar that would provoke massive

conversions of dollars into gold and thus drastically reduce
international liquidity, provoke the suspension of convertibility, and
cause a disintegration of the world economy on the lines experienced in
1931. Triffin's forecast went wrong in assuming that the United States
would respond to a confidence crisis, as Britain had in 1931, by trying
to maintain the gold exchange standard. In fact, however, by the time
that confidence broke, the system had evolved into something much
closer to a dollar standard, and the United States was therefore able to
suspend convertibility without curtailing international liquidity. The
period was, in fact, marked by an explosive growth in dollar reserves
that fuelled worldwide inflation rather than deflation. The basic
instability diagnosed by Triffin nonetheless existed, even though the
form of the ultimate breakdown took a different form from the one he
had predicted.

Once the Triffin dilemma had been recognized in official circles, plans
were set in motion to try to sidestep it. The strategy that evolved under
US leadership was to shore up the existing system by encouraging
countries to hold dollars rather than convert them into gold while the
US balance of payments deficit was being corrected, and to create a
new reserve asset to supply the needed increase in international
liquidity once the US deficit had been eliminated (an event that was
anticipated with some confidence). For a considerable time this
strategy did not seem unrealistic. Other countries responded to US
appeals to exercise restraint in converting dollars into gold (as they also
responded to British appeals for credits between 1964 and 1969). Up to
the mid-1960s, it was reasonable to hope that the US deficit was in the
process of being corrected: inflation was lower than in Europe, the
current-account surplus climbed to a peak of $6 billion in 1964,
earnings on foreign investments were growing rapidly, and a part of the
statistical deficit could be explained away as the result of financial
intermediation.[1] Meanwhile plans to create a new reserve asset went
ahead slowly, culminating in the Rio Agreement to create the SDR in
1967. In happier circumstances this might have paved the way to an
orderly evolution to a gold/SDR exchange standard. In the event,

---

1. The deficit as measured on the 'liquidity basis' counted increases in short-term
liabilities to private foreigners below the line, even though it was reasonable to assume
that foreigners were building up their holdings of liquid dollar assets voluntarily (and were
prepared to borrow long term in the United States to accomplish this; hence the view of
the United States as a banker country engaged in financial intermediation). To the extent
that foreign monetary authorities wanted to build up their dollar holdings much the same
thing could be argued of the deficit as measured on the 'official settlements basis'. See
C. P. Kindleberger, *Balance-of-Payments Deficits and the International Market for
Liquidity*, Princeton Essays in International Finance No. 46, Princeton, 1965.

however, US involvement in the Vietnam War, which was to a significant extent financed more by monetary expansion than by the belt-tightening that was called for by the fully employed state of the domestic economy, reversed the earlier progress made in correcting the US payments deficit.

The above strategy for seeking orderly evolution to a gold/SDR exchange standard was not universally endorsed. The dissentients who initially attracted most of the limelight were those who wished to rely on the traditional primary reserve asset, gold, rather than to introduce a new one, the SDR. Peter Oppenheimer has subsequently gone as far as to argue that the breakdown of the Bretton Woods system had nothing to do with any inadequacies of the system itself, but was entirely attributable to the refusal to revalue gold, the solution provided by the founding fathers.[2] It is probably true that, had the United States been prepared to reverse her previous stand and urge a decisive increase in the price of gold,[3] it would have been possible to re-establish a functioning gold exchange standard, at least for a short time. (It is not obvious, however, what economic function convertibility is supposed to serve if the reserve centre is empowered to write up its assets whenever its reserve constraint starts to bite.) What most economists doubted was not the feasibility of such a strategy, but its desirability, as opposed to the alternative of developing a fiduciary reserve asset.

The advocates of gold revaluation were always reluctant to concede that development of the SDR *was* an alternative. But they were never very specific as to what it was that gold revaluation was supposed to be able to accomplish that could not also be achieved by development of the SDR. Perhaps the most obvious answer is that gold revaluation would have achieved an immediate strengthening in the external liquidity position of the United States that would have enabled her to repay the dollar balances in gold, thus permitting the restoration of a full gold standard, as persistently advocated by Jacques Rueff. It is true that the SDR agreement did not provide the potential for securing a similar quick strengthening in the liquidity position of the United States: to accomplish that it would have been necessary to amend the rules to allow a substitution operation on the lines contemplated by the C-20.

2. P. M. Oppenheimer, 'World Monetary Developments and the Committee of Twenty', *Aussenwirtschaft*, September 1974.
3. There would, however, have been a major difficulty facing any attempt by the Administration to reverse policy in this area: the fact that Congressional consent to a gold price increase was required. Representative Henry Reuss, the Chairman of the Joint Economic Committee's Sub-committee on International Trade and Payments, could have been relied on to oppose any such proposal, and he carried great influence with Congress on questions of international finance.

However, as Robert Mundell has emphasized,[4] this case for gold revaluation made sense only as a part of a package that included abolition of the reserve currency system and the abandonment of monetary sovereignty in favour of the price-specie-flow mechanism of the gold standard, and there is no reason whatsoever for believing that the peripheral countries would have been prepared to trade in their dollars for gold once the economic incentive to do so had been destroyed by gold revaluation, or that any countries — least of all the United States — would have been prepared to abandon their monetary sovereignty. The other principal advocates of gold revaluation[5] did not emphasize the stock effects of a gold price increase, but rather its effect in recreating a net inflow of new gold reserves into the system, thus enabling some countries to have surpluses without others having deficits — in particular, enabling the rest of the world to build up its reserves without the United States having a deficit. For this purpose SDRs are not merely a perfect substitute for gold but a superior substitute, in so far as the volume of the inflow is not dependent on a host of unpredictable and capricious factors concerned with mining technology, geology, the use of gold in building spaceships and the elasticity of demand for jewellery. Even if one assumes that countries are irrational enough to be seeking current account surpluses *per se* rather than reserve increases, a modified SDR could meet the need better than gold revaluation: all that would be necessary would be to adopt the aid link. It remains possible that the advantage of gold revaluation perceived by its advocates lay in the belief that, whatever they may say to the contrary, deep in their hearts central bankers regard the SDR as funny money and gold as real money. There is no published research on the psychology of central bankers that would enable one to test this conjecture, but its relevance may be questioned on the ground that the worst possible way to try to engender confidence is to pander to irrational prejudices rather than to seek to construct a system with the objective conditions necessary for efficient operation. The latter view leads one straight back to the need to compare the merits of gold and the SDR as the basic reserve asset.

Seven considerations are generally thought to be relevant to such a comparison. First, in an inflationary age there is no question of a once-for-all gold revaluation leading to a permanent solution of the need for steadily growing liquidity (such as can be provided through regular SDR

4. R. A. Mundell, 'The Economic Consequences of Jacques Rueff', *Journal of Business*, July 1973, p.390.
5. Milton Gilbert, whose analysis was published in *The Gold-Dollar System: Conditions of Equilibrium and the Price of Gold*, Princeton Essays in International Finance No. 70, Princeton, 1968, and Peter Oppenheimer.

allocations at a controlled rate). In due course gold accruals would have dried up again and the liquidity position of the United States would again have started to deteriorate, leading to a renewed desire of reserve holders to switch out of the dollar and a repetition of the whole unhappy cycle of the 1960s, no doubt at a much accelerated pace. Second, some advocates of the reinstatement of gold see this as a way of restoring financial discipline on governments. However, the willingness of governments to be disciplined was dependent on their belief that there was no alternative. One cannot recreate a myth. Once governments have learned to change the gold price whenever the discipline of gold threatens to become irksome, gold is merely another form of funny money with the capacity for provoking particularly disruptive speculative shifts in anticipation of changes in its price, and with the added complication that it has alternative uses as a commodity. Third, SDRs are cheaper to produce — not only because the mining of gold absorbs real resources, but also because the substitution of SDRs would permit existing stocks of gold to be released for useful purposes such as filling teeth or creating ornaments. This is not only an economic gain in itself, but also means that the SDR is potentially capable of paying a rate of return competitive with that on currencies, which would eliminate the economic incentive for a reserve currency system with its tendency for destabilizing portfolio switches between reserve assets. Fourth, even while the primary reserve asset co-exists with reserve currencies, the restrictions embodied in the SDR agreement on the use of the SDR in portfolio switching operations reduce the confidence problem as compared to that inherent in a resurrected gold exchange standard. Fifth, the supply of SDRs can be managed with a view to contributing to stable growth of the world economy, whereas the supply of gold is subject to a mass of capricious influences. Sixth, the sudden massive increases in international liquidity that would have occurred whenever gold was revalued would have had highly inflationary effects. Finally, the distribution of the seigniorage benefits of SDR creation is at least roughly neutral, and could, with sufficiently general agreement, be varied to reflect any consensus that might be established on a desirable international redistribution of income. The distribution of the seigniorage benefits of gold revaluation would have been at best capricious and at worst perverse, with the major gold producers (South Africa and the Soviet Union) and the gold hoarders (those countries that had rocked the boat when it still appeared that an orderly reform was possible) benefiting substantially, and most of the developing countries gaining virtually nothing.

To most economists, if not to all newspaper editors, these considerations seemed to add up to an overwhelming case against trying to resurrect the gold exchange standard by a revaluation of gold. The bulk of the case was endorsed by most officials as much as by the academics. Indeed, the pride that the officials took in their role in pioneering the introduction of a new reserve asset created a willingness to entertain solutions involving the development of the SDR that was prone to be underestimated by some academics. There was also another factor, though it is difficult to say to what extent its importance was consciously appreciated by those involved. This arises from the fundamental irrelevance of restoring convertibility unless this act symbolized a commitment by the United States that in future she would accept the discipline of a reserve constraint similar to that under which other countries operated. In the absence of such a commitment, which there is no reason whatsoever to suppose the United States would have been prepared to give, gold revaluation would merely have papered over the ambiguities of the Bretton Woods system regarding the distribution of the responsibility for initiating adjustment.

Although gold revaluation did not offer a solution that met the needs of the situation or that had very wide appeal, its advocacy by the French was not without effect. In addition to stimulating private demand for gold and thus ending the modest growth in gold reserves that had prevailed till then, President de Gaulle's declaration of the gold war tended both to stiffen US resolve not to reward the gold hoarders, and to make substantial gold conversions into acts of political hostility to the United States. The net result was almost certainly counterproductive from a Gaullist standpoint: countries became more willing to refrain from requesting conversion of dollars into gold. This was highly significant because it was at this time that the deterioration in the US balance of payments resulting from the Vietnam War was beginning to undermine the hope of orderly evolution to a gold/SDR exchange standard, and to raise the prospect that instead the gold exchange standard would evolve into a dollar standard.

A dollar standard may be defined as a pegged exchange rate system in which the dollar is the ultimate reserve asset — i.e., in which there is no obligation on its issuer, the United States, to convert dollars into anything else. This implies that the United States need have no concern about financing her payments deficits, since other countries can be relied on either to accumulate dollars or, if they do not so wish, to undertake adjustment. The United States can therefore pursue a passive payments policy. Indeed, it was argued by the proponents of the dollar standard not only that she could adopt a policy of 'benign neglect' but that she should: this would permit other countries to adjust their payments positions so as to achieve their desired reserve accumulation objectives. However, the most ardent advocates of a dollar standard always added the important proviso that the centre country had a crucial obligation to maintain internal stability, so that the rest of the world could adjust around a stable fulcrum rather than be obliged to import inflation or deflation.

There is no denying that there would be considerable technical virtues in a dollar standard. It would provide an instantaneous solution of the confidence problem (except in so far as secondary reserve currencies were concerned). It would resolve the '(N-1) problem', by allowing the reserve centre's payments position to adjust to whatever was required for consistency with the policies chosen by other countries. And, in view of the interest paid on dollar reserves, the degree of seigniorage that would accrue to the United States is minimal, provided at least that interest rates in the United States are not artificially depressed. (In fact, the main source of seigniorage arises from the fact that the United States is relieved of the necessity to tie up resources in low-yielding reserves in order to provide the necessary insurance against possible future deficits.) There are also some technical disadvantages. First, one component of a passive payments policy involves the complete sterilization of the effects of reserve movements on the domestic money supply (a policy that has long been pursued by the United States). Complete sterilization in a fixed exchange rate regime means that the whole burden of adjustment is avoided by the sterilizing country and thrown on its partners; if they too try to sterilize, the system tends to become unstable.[6] This might be immaterial if the centre country could really be relied on to pursue an optimal stabilization policy, but economic management cannot aspire to that degree of perfection, and, in any event, cyclical needs will sometimes differ between the centre country and its partners. It seems reasonable to suppose that global adjustment costs would be minimized by a more equal distribution of the responsibility for initiating adjustment. Second, there will be times — especially if the centre country is atypical in its determination to resist inflation — when its costs get out of line with those in the generality of other countries. In view of the difficulties of engineering exchange rate changes except under a floating regime, it is easier in such circumstances to introduce the necessary realignment if the centre country is able to change its par value than if this has to be done by a series of changes by other

6. This point was developed during the first Wingspread Conference on the international monetary system, the proceedings of which were published in R. Z. Aliber, ed., *National Monetary Policies and the International Financial System*, University of Chicago Press, London, 1974. See especially the papers by R. N. Cooper, R. I. McKinnon, and V. Argy and P. J. K. Kouri.

countries.[7] Third, there may be a cost to the reserve centre in losing control of its current account balance. Desite these disadvantages, however, it is difficult to argue that — so long as the centre country provided a stable fulcrum — the dollar standard did not offer strong attractions on technical grounds.

But technical issues were never really the heart of the matter. The central political fact is that a dollar standard places the direction of world monetary policy in the hands of a single country, which thereby acquires great influence over the economic destiny of others. It is one thing to sacrifice sovereignty in the interests of interdependence; it is quite another when the relationship is one way. The difference is that between the EEC and a colonial empire. Charles Kindleberger demonstrated his appreciation of this when he proposed that the Federal Open Market Committee be expanded into an Atlantic Open Market Committee containing European and Japanese representatives.[8] But the proposal never aroused much interest in policy-making circles on either side of the Atlantic, and it is difficult to see how it could have been made acceptable to both parties. An effective foreign representation would have subjected US domestic monetary policy to foreign pressures of a type with no parallel elsewhere, while an ineffective presence would hardly have met the problem. The fact is that acceptance of a dollar standard necessarily implies a degree of asymmetry in power which, although it actually existed in the early post-war years, had vanished by the time that the world found itself sliding to a reluctant dollar standard.

Despite the distaste for a dollar standard on the part of the developed countries, there were strong pressures pushing the system in that direction. Even when policy makers came to realize the extent to which the US balance of payments was likely to deteriorate in the wake of the Vietnam War, it was not obvious to them what they could do about it. They had no illusions that requests for conversion of their dollars into gold would serve to discipline the United States into adjustment measures: such requests might have undermined the fight against exchange rate changes, which was at its most intense in the mid-1960s; they might have driven the United States into closing the gold window, and thus faced the rest of the world with a choice between formalization of the dollar standard and a break up of the pegged exchange rate system that was still the ark of the covenant; or

7. J. Williamson, *The Choice of a Pivot for Parities*, Princeton Essays in International Finance No. 90, Princeton, 1971, p.8.
8. C. P. Kindleberger, *The Politics of International Money and World Language*, Princeton Essays in International Finance No. 61, Princeton, 1967, p.7.

they might have caused a crisis that was ultimately resolved by gold revaluation. But the United States was simply not prepared to contemplate adopting adjustment measures beyond the occasional tightening up of restrictions on capital exports. The reluctance to subordinate demand management policy to external needs was particularly well-founded in the case of a country with an economy as closed as that of the United States, which implied that any effective adjustment measures had to include a change in the exchange rate. But the adjustable peg was singularly ill-suited to the task of engineering a devaluation of the dollar. A dollar devaluation that was not large enough to convince dollar holders that no further devaluation was conceivable would have jeopardized the willingness to continue restraint in converting dollars into gold, but the devaluation necessary for that purpose would have been larger than other countries would have dared accept for fear of undermining their competitive positions. The Europeans* were therefore confronted by the fact that the series of steps in which they had acquiesced to prevent the immediate disintegration of the system had led them to a position where they were effectively locked in to a dollar standard.

In retrospect it may appear strange that the prospect of exchange rate flexibility should have loomed as a threat to be avoided at all costs. It is a fact, however, that it was so regarded. In the minds of most policy makers, floating carried overtones of a return to the economic conditions of the 1930s. Even some of those who were convinced of the need to make exchange rate changes a major instrument of payments adjustment could not see how a system of floating exchange rates could be absorbed within the framework of the cooperative arrangements established at Bretton Woods. One of the principal sources of support for limited flexibility of exchange rates, as opposed to floating, lay in the belief that they could be introduced into the Bretton Woods system without threatening what was valuable in it, such as market convertibility, international cooperation and the recognition that exchange rates were inherently a matter of international rather than purely national concern. In contrast, a system of widespread floating seemed too much of a gamble. The attempt to preserve a system of fixed exchange rates started to crumble in 1967, when the pound sterling was finally forced into devaluation. The pound had long been regarded as the dollar's first line of defence, in the sense that the dollar was safe from speculative pressure as long as there was another important currency that was unambiguously weaker and would

---

* The Japanese should be counted as honorary Europeans for the purposes of the remainder of this chapter.

therefore be almost certain to be devalued first. The sterling devaluation had the expected effect of undermining confidence in the dollar and provoking a run into gold by the private sector, which was stemmed only by the Washington Agreement of 1968. In principle this did not interfere with the right of official convertibility. In practice, however, it was another acknowledgement that free portfolio choice between gold and dollars — the basic tenet of a gold exchange standard — was no longer possible, and it became ever clearer that any major exercise of the notional convertibility right would provoke the United States into closing the gold window.

Meanwhile the view was growing in the United States that, however much they might protest to the contrary, a dollar standard was pretty much what the rest of the world really wanted. The particular experience cited to support this belief was the failure of the substantial improvement of the US current account in the mid-1960s to bring with it a corresponding improvement in the official settlements deficit.[9] This suggested that the US deficit was essentially determined by the reserve accumulation policies of other countries. If the United States took some action to improve her payments position — whether by restraining demand, so as to improve its current account, or by introducing controls on capital exports — there was no presumption that the overall payments deficit would be reduced, because the action could be counteracted by the policies of other countries. If every other country had a payments objective that it pursued successfully (a hypothesis that always struck a Briton as somewhat implausible), then the US deficit would be the mirror image of the surplus collectively desired by the rest of the world, and it would be largely unresponsive (except perhaps in the short run) to US payments policies. This theory implied that, so long as the rest of the world desired a trend growth in reserves, the only way to remedy the US deficit was to provide an alternative source of reserve growth.

It had been envisaged that the injection of SDRs into the system would provide this alternative source of reserve growth. A potential difficulty with this approach was that the price of obtaining French consent to the SDR agreement had included a provision that SDRs should only be activated when there was evidence of a 'better working of the adjustment process', meaning that the US deficit had already been eliminated, whereas the demand determined theory suggested that the US deficit would not be eliminated until the SDRs were flowing into world reserves. However, the tight monetary policy pursued in the

9. The most explicit development of this case is by R. Z. Aliber, *Choices for the Dollar*, National Planning Association, Washington DC, 1969.

United States in 1969 produced a temporary official settlements surplus that provided the occasion for reaching agreement on activation. Had the demand determined theory been correct, the early 1970s should have then witnessed elimination of the US deficit, since it was no longer necessary to provide the desired reserve growth. The fact that the deficit exploded rather than disappeared would seem to constitute rather decisive evidence that the demand determined theory was incorrect, and that the deficit in fact depended on a complex of such factors as demand, costs and monetary policy in the United States *vis-à-vis* those in the rest of the world — much as the deficit of any other country depends on its relative position in these respects.

This was not, however, as evident at the time as it is in retrospect. The belief that the US deficit was demand determined continued to grow in the United States in the early 1970s in parallel with the increasing support for exchange rate flexibility. The two together nurtured the conviction that, if the surplus countries truly disliked their surpluses, they could eliminate them by revaluing; and if they chose not to revalue, that was evidence of their insincerity in claiming to want an end to the US deficit. This logic seemed quite uncompelling viewed from the other side of the Atlantic. With the exception of Germany (who did revalue) — and, from 1969 or 1970, Japan — no countries had payments positions that were strong enough to make it possible for them to consider an individual revaluation, since this would have reduced the competitiveness of their exports against the whole range of their competitors rather than just against the United States. The counterpart of the US deficit was a widely diffused surplus; and the change necessary to remedy it was essentially a change in the rate between the dollar and the currencies of all the other industrialized countries. Given the political loss-of-face involved in initiating an exchange rate change at that time, it seemed to most Europeans to be impertinent for the United States to demand that such a change be effected by a series of decisions on their part rather than by a single decision on her part, especially in view of the organizational problem of coordinating the series of changes that would be needed.

Not that such opinions were voiced explicitly by the Europeans, most of whom were too scared of provoking speculative capital flows even to acknowledge that a realignment between the dollar and their currencies was needed. Moreover, the Europeans were paralysed by their disagreement on almost everything except their dislike of the subordinate political status assigned them by a dollar standard. Some were politically antagonistic to the United States, others regarded trans-Atlantic partnership as the central principle of their foreign policy; some wanted to restore gold, others to demonetize it; some

favoured liberal capital movements, others capital controls; some
wanted to discipline the United States into deflating, others were ultra-
Keynesians who never thought any country should deflate; some
wanted more flexible exchange rates, and thought the United States
should not stand aloof from this movement, while others were
opposed to greater flexibility in principle; some wanted to press ahead
quickly with the development of a European Monetary Union, others
deplored the very idea. These disagreements destroyed any capacity
for constructive action and left them willing to drift along, praying that
adjustment by faith would score a final triumph, so long as the United
States refrained from flaunting the reality of the dollar standard.

The gradual transmutation of the gold exchange standard into a
reluctant dollar standard had enabled the gold convertibility of the
dollar to be maintained, at least in principle, for far longer, and in the
face of more adverse circumstances, than most of Triffin's readers
might have thought possible in 1960. But as the US deficit exploded in
1970-71, it became ever clearer that the only hope of maintaining the
system lay in the adoption of firm adjustment policies. There were two
basic difficulties preventing this: the disagreement about whose
responsibility it was to initiate adjustment and the lack of any effective
crisis-proof adjustment mechanism. To Europeans it seemed obvious
that the principal cause of the US deficit was the inflationary financing
of the Vietnam War and that there were no major maladjustments
between the European currencies* so that an American initiative was
called for. But the United States continued to regard herself as the
victim of the rest of the world's struggle for ever-increasing exports
and reserves (with Japan cast in the role of principal offender).
Moreover, given the inadequacy of the existing set of adjustment
techniques, the United States had every incentive to avoid accepting
any share of the responsibility for initiating adjustment: a dollar
devaluation engineered under the adjustable peg could not have hoped
both to restore confidence and to win acceptance by the rest of the
world. That is why it seemed to me that the key to preventing the
breakdown of the gold exchange standard lay in a reform of the
exchange rate regime.[10] Given the unthinkability at that time of a step
as revolutionary as widespread floating, the only possible reform lay in
adoption of the crawling peg (coupled with a widening of the band). In
the light of subsequent history — regarding both the magnitude of
capital outflows from the United States and the time taken for the
dollar devaluation to make an impact on the US payments position — it

* Japan is not to be treated as a part of Europe so far as this statement is concerned.
10. Publication of this argument was somewhat belated: see Williamson, *op.cit.*

must be judged highly doubtful whether a downward crawl of the dollar initiated as late as 1970 or 1971 would in fact have averted the crisis of August 1971. But, had it been accompanied by a renunciation of 'benign neglect' and the dollar standard, which would have implied a more cautious monetary policy than that actually adopted by the United States and perhaps an earlier initiative on the incomes policy front, it might have induced the Europeans to continue holding the fort a good bit longer, and this might have enabled a sufficiently forceful initiative to succeed in securing the orderly evolution to the gold/SDR exchange standard that was once hoped for.

The United States was not, however, in any mood to undertake sacrifices to defend a system, the gold exchange standard, in which she had ceased to believe. And as 1971 developed the Europeans found it increasingly difficult to maintain their acquiescence in a system that was ever more clearly a dollar standard. The press talked more and more of 'benign neglect', and an over-expansionary US monetary policy was maintained despite vast capital outflows. It became increasingly difficult to sustain the belief that the basic prerequisite for the economic efficiency of a dollar standard, that the reserve centre provide a stable fulcrum, was being satisfied in view of the after-effects of the inflationary financing of the Vietnam War — the large US deficit and the resulting generalization of world inflation. The first country to find the inflationary consequences of the dollar standard intolerable was, predictably, Germany, which floated the DM in May (and was joined by the Netherlands). By August other countries had lost the willingness to prop up a system that had become offensive to their conception of what partnership was about. They therefore started converting dollars into gold while the possibility remained open.

The US authorities were in no doubt that the conversion demands would rapidly snowball unless they acted. They had two choices: to propose a dollar devaluation and try to maintain convertibility at the new par value, or to close the gold window and confront the world with the reality of the dollar standard. Given the depth of the US commitment to avoiding a major revaluation of gold (including the Administration's doubt as to what Congress could be persuaded to agree to), her belief that other countries would resist a revaluation of their currencies against the dollar, her loss of faith in the value of fixed exchange rates and the gold exchange standard, and the taste of the Nixon Administration for power politics (which was at that time reinforced by an uncharacteristically chauvinist Secretary of the Treasury in the person of John Connally), it was inevitable that the first option would be rejected. But the Administration had also lost patience, in so far as it ever had any, with the passive 'nth currency' role of the dollar that was the logical corollary of a dollar standard, but that was blamed for the deterioration of the US current account and resulting loss of US jobs. Hence, instead of the apologetic announcement that convertibility was temporarily suspended, hedged around by assurances that this really changed nothing material, that observers had long expected would ultimately come, the closing of the gold window was accompanied by bellicose demands that other countries should revalue their currencies so as to eliminate 'unfair exchange rates', backed up by the imposition of a 10 per cent import surcharge until such time as they complied. This schizophrenic rejection of benign neglect, which coupled an active concern about the payments outcome with a dogmatic assertion that it was the duty of other countries to take the measures necessary to change the outcome, made it impossible for the rest of the world to acquiesce in the final step to a formal dollar standard, as might conceivably have occurred had the step been accompanied by the customary bromides. Since the gold exchange standard had finally succumbed to its long-predicted fate, while the system to which it had seemed to be evolving had been rejected by both the United States and the Europeans, the need for a reconstruction of the international monetary system was evident and universally accepted.

The adjustable peg

When the United States closed the gold window and announced that she believed the currencies of other industrial countries should be revalued relative to the dollar, the countries involved had little choice but to float. The Japanese held out for a couple of weeks and the French invoked strong exchange controls and sat tight, but the other industrial countries joined Canada, Germany and the Netherlands in floating. The immediate cause of the first adoption of widespread floating was therefore the breakdown of the gold exchange standard, coupled with the US decision to press for the revaluation of other currencies, which created a massive incentive to shift funds out of the dollar into the revaluation candidates that only the most dedicated and dirigiste countries could contemplate facing. Just over 4 months later a new structure of pegged exchange rates was agreed at the Smithsonian Conference in Washington. The effective devaluation of the dollar was not as great as the United States had wished, but it was sufficient to induce the US Administration to endorse the new rate structure. However, there was a new run on the dollar some 14 months later, which provoked a rapid formal devaluation of the dollar by another 10 per cent. The new rate lasted less than 3 weeks before there was a renewed run from the dollar to the DM that provoked the European decision to let the European snake out of its tunnel and ushered in the era of generalized floating.

The ultimate demise of the adjustable peg in March 1973 cannot be explained away as the consequence of a crisis in some other aspect of the international monetary system. One can perhaps argue that the immunity of the United States from the financial penalties of successful speculation blunted her incentive to defend the agreed structure of exchange rates, and there was some suggestion in Europe that the particular crisis of March 1973 might have been averted but for the detachment she showed in the defence of her new parity.[11] But there is no reason to think that this would have done more than delay the final débâcle, and in any event it can hardly explain why Canada, Britain, Italy, Japan and Switzerland had already decided to float or why France, Iceland, Malaysia, Portugal, Singapore, South Africa and Spain floated subsequently. One obviously has to seek a more general explanation for the abandonment of the adjustable peg than the suspension of convertibility.

It is sometimes said that it was the outbreak of worldwide inflation in the early 1970s that caused the resort to floating. It is certainly true that in an inflationary environment there is a far greater need for exchange rate changes than in a period of price stability — not just because in practice inflation rates are less uniform when the general rate of inflation is higher, so that some countries (such as Britain) have a greater need to neutralize a domestically generated inflation, but also because some countries with a greater determination to prevent inflation (such as Germany) have a greater need to repel an imported inflation. But Bretton Woods did not provide for a fixed rate system (despite the attempt to construe it that way during the 1960s): it provided for the indefinite — as opposed to permanent — pegging of parities. The regime was supposed to allow for pegs to change when necessary. The critical question is why it proved inadequate to the task of accommodating changes.

One explanation attributes the breakdown of the adjustable peg to deficiencies in the decision-making process. This explanation points, in particular, to the repeated failures to adjust par values until a major disequilibrium had already developed. Delayed adjustment led to prolonged misallocation of resources and distortion of domestic policies. The large parity changes imposed major shifts on international trading and investment patterns when they eventually occurred, although trade was sometimes sluggish to adapt itself to the new price

11. See, for example, *Frankfurter Allgemeine Zeitung*, 24 February 1973, p.1.

signals because of the decay of the necessary productive facilities during the lengthy preceding period of malvaluation. The delay in making parity changes made their need plainly evident to the market, which was thus presented with the possibility of speculation on a one-way option.[12] The key to avoiding these ills, it was argued, most notably in the 1970 IMF report *The Role of Exchange Rates in the Adjustment of International Payments*, lay in abandoning the attempt to run a fixed rate system and returning to the spirit of Bretton Woods, by changing par values promptly when the need arose.

This explanation always struck me as superficial. One cannot, of course, deny that the system did suffer from delayed adjustment, or that this entailed the disadvantages described above. What can be questioned is whether the adjustable peg really offers any hope of doing significantly better. It can, for example, be argued that national authorities are inevitably going to be subject to bureaucratic delays while the evidence that change is needed builds up to a decisive case, and that even then political pressures will frequently favour procrastination in a system where a positive decision to change the rate is required.[13] More fundamental, to my mind, is the claim that, in a world of capital mobility such as developed during the 1960s, success in achieving prompter adjustment would do little or nothing to pre-empt the speculative flows that plagued the adjustable peg (unless, at least, par values were changed so freely as to make a mockery of the idea of having a par value at all). The theory of portfolio equilibrium tells us that people who are free to do so will shift between assets on a massive scale when presented with the opportunity of a riskless gain from so doing, and this is precisely what the adjustable peg presents them with whenever the need for a significant exchange rate change arises. Neither the interest rate nor the exchange rate can in general adjust immediately so as to neutralize the incentive to shift funds that is created by the expectation of a parity change. The interest rate cannot adjust sufficiently (under the adjustable peg, as opposed to the

12. Some writers make a great point of arguing that the capital flows that precede anticipated parity changes are 'precautionary' rather than 'speculative'. I do not usually find such semantic distinctions of great interest, but I have to confess that shifting money from one currency to another in pursuit of a capital gain (measured in currency A) or to avoid a capital loss (measured in currency B) strikes me as corresponding rather closely with the everyday use of the term 'speculation' — whether the speculator's home currency is A or B.

13. See, for example, S. N. Marris, 'Decision Making on Exchange Rates', in C. F. Bergsten, G. N. Halm, F. Machlup, R. V. Roosa, eds., *Approaches to Greater Flexibility of Exchange Rates*, Princeton University Press, Princeton, 1970, and C. J. Oort, *Steps to International Monetary Order*, Per Jacobsson Foundation, Washington DC, 1974, pp. 18-19.

crawling peg) because anticipated discrete changes in the market exchange rate cannot be neutralized by acceptable interest rate differentials. And the exchange rate cannot always be permitted to adjust immediately, no matter how prompt the government is in making changes recognized to be necessary, unless it resorts to routine and uncritical acceptance of the market's judgement, which means floating in all but name.

Contemporary — i.e., 1975 — work on the theory of floating exchange rates demonstrates the fundamental deficiencies of the adjustable peg more clearly than ever before. The new theories argue that, in a world of capital mobility, the short-run level of the exchange rate is determined by the conditions of asset market equilibrium* — i.e., by the condition that the existing stocks of the several currencies be willingly held. This requires that the risk-adjusted expected yields, which consist of the own interest rate plus the expected rate of appreciation, be equated.[14] One cannot hope to satisfy the conditions of asset market equilibrium both before and after administratively determined discrete changes in market exchange rates unless expectations are formed by some arbitrary, irrational and improbably convenient process. Hence the adjustable peg is bound to generate a series of crises.

At the time of Bretton Woods the working assumption was that the post-war world would be one of very limited capital mobility. The international capital market had collapsed in the 1930s; it was indeed to provide a substitute for it that the International Bank for Reconstruction and Development (IBRD or the World Bank) was created as a sister institution to the IMF at Bretton Woods. There had of course been troubling flows of 'hot money' in the 1930s. Because these had no rationale in terms of the classic resource allocative functions of capital movements, it was, however, assumed at Bretton Woods that it would be desirable to suppress such movements in the post-war world. That is why the (market) convertibility obligation placed on the IMF members specifically excluded capital transactions. The adjustable peg was not,

---

* Throughout the book I discuss the conditions of asset market equilibrium without introducing the forward market, as though all speculation took place through the spot market. This simplifies reasoning and in no way detracts from the generality of the conclusions.

14. See in particular the papers of R. Dornbusch, P. J. K. Kouri and M. Mussa presented to the Stockholm conference on 'Flexible Exchange Rates and Stabilization Policy' in August, 1975, printed in the *Scandinavian Journal of Economics*, 1976(2). (My own paper obscured the conclusion by utilizing a flow rather than a stock model of exchange rate determination, but the spirit of the model was similar in that it assigned a key role to the equilibrium stock of foreign lending and this was assumed to be determined by similar factors.)

therefore, an irrational choice of exchange rate regime for the world
that it was expected it would be used in. The post-war world did not,
however, materialize as anticipated in these respects. International
trade, with its opportunities for shifting funds between currencies by
leading and lagging payments, grew at an unprecedented pace: its
value multiplied more than 5-fold between 1950 and 1971, and import
penetration rose substantially in most countries. An international
capital market re-emerged in the 1950s and expanded dramatically with
the emergence of the Euro-currency market after 1958: one of the
attractions of the offshore currency markets was, indeed, their greater
immunity from exchange controls. Multinational corporations, which
have ample opportunities for avoiding exchange control through
variations in the timing of payments between subsidiaries, became a
major economic force. (For example, the earnings on US direct foreign
investment expanded from $1·8 billion in 1950 to $10·3 billion in
1971.[15]) As a result, the world of the late 1960s had become one of
intense capital mobility.

Some idea of the increasing force of currency speculation as a result
of the growth of capital mobility can be gleaned from the increase in
the magnitude of central bank intervention. I have assembled some
figures for reserve changes in the two countries that suffered the
greatest speculative flows, Germany and the United Kingdom. Table
2.1 shows weekly changes in the foreign exchange holdings of the
Bundesbank for selected years from 1949 to 1973. Figures for every
third year, plus all the years in the periods of intense speculation on a
revaluation of the DM in the late 1950s and late 1960s, have been
calculated. Foreign exchange holdings are not an inclusive measure of
reserves, and there are occasions when they give a misleading picture
of reserve changes — e.g., because of a conversion of dollars into gold.
However, most of the other items are relatively stable; some are of
dubious relevance — e.g., World Bank bonds; and the classifications
have changed over time; so that foreign exchange holdings probably
give as good a measure as can be constructed from published sources.
The one important error in the use of foreign exchange holdings
involves the valuation adjustments which are made on the occasion of
a par value change; these lead to a writing down in the DM value of
foreign exchange reserves, which would, for example, cause a major
underestimation of the reserve inflow in the crisis week in which the
dollar was devalued in February 1973 if no correction were made. The
Bundesbank has kindly supplied figures to enable an appropriate

15. Marina v. N. Whitman, 'The Current and Future Role of the Dollar: How Much
Symmetry?', *Brookings Papers on Economic Activity*, 1974(3), p.555.

correction to be made in the two relevant weeks in October 1969 and February 1973.

The second column of Table 2.1 shows the average absolute weekly change in reserves, and the third column the maximum increase

Table 2.1

Weekly changes in Bundesbank holdings of foreign exchange 1949-73 (Million DM)

year	average absolute weekly change	maximum weekly increase
1949	35	104
1952	73	184
1955	56	146
1958	129	774
1959	146*	424
1960	204	514
1963	127	369
1966	150	1089
1967	147	570
1968	477	3036
1969	1310	11482
1970	567	3270
1971 (pre-floating)	1230	8040
1972	581	6261
1973 (pre-floating)	3735	16064

* Excluding the week ending 31 March 1959, in which unique factors operated.

SOURCE: Deutsche Bundesbank, *Annual Reports*, Appendix 4, Weekly Returns of the Deutsche Bundesbank.

recorded in any week during each year. It will be observed that both columns show striking increases — even in comparison with the 23-fold growth in German trade between 1949 and 1972. And the increases would have been larger still if measured in dollars rather than DM. What is particularly significant is the 20-fold increase in the size of the maximum weekly inflow between the late 1950s and the end of the adjustable peg era (over which period German trade increased less than 5-fold). Since both were periods of intense speculation on a DM revaluation, the increase must be a reflection of the increase in capital mobility, coupled with the commitment to prompt adjustment of par values in the later period, which provided an obvious incentive for the market to react faster than was previously necessary.

Comparable British experience is summarized in Table 2.2. This shows monthly changes in net reserves, defined as official reserves

Table 2.2
Monthly Changes in British Net Reserves* 1948-72
(Million pounds)

year	average absolute monthly change	maximum monthly decrease
1949	21	82
1951	63	133
1952	31	107
1955	20	58
1956	33	103
1957	36	104
1958	33	52
1961	79	258
1963	22	66
1964	67	320
1965	86	190
1966**	81	355
1967**	155	341
1968	139	505
1969	113	133
1970	153	198
1971 (pre-floating)	256	—
1972 (pre-floating)	219	1072

Intervention in the forward market is not reflected in the figures.

* Net reserves are defined as official reserves minus official borrowing from the IMF and other central banks.
** Figures for February 1966 and November 1967 were adjusted to eliminate the effect of the adsorption of the dollar portfolio in the reserves.

SOURCE: Bank of England. The assistance of the Bank of England in compiling and releasing these data is gratefully acknowledged.

minus official borrowing from the IMF and on the swap network, for selected years from 1949 to 1972. Figures for every third year plus all the periods of intense speculation are shown, together with one abnormally 'normal' year, 1963. Appropriate allowance has again been made for valuation adjustments on the occasion of par value changes, so that the figures represent an estimate of net intervention. The second column of Table 2.2 shows the average absolute monthly change in net reserves, and the third column the maximum decrease recorded in any month during the year. One again observes striking increases in the size of the figures in both columns, especially if it is recognized that the figures of 1951-52 reflected a severe underlying deficit. The rises are not as dramatic as the increases in the German figures, but one has to remember that British trade only multiplied some three times between 1949 and 1972. In the British case one finds roughly a 10-fold increase in the size of the maximum monthly outflow between the late 1950s and the end of the adjustable peg, demonstrating that at least one feature of the British economy recorded substantial growth. (Trade grew some 150 per cent over the same period.)

By the time that the adjustable peg was abandoned, capital mobility had developed to the point where the Bundesbank could take in well over $1 billion in an hour when the market had come to expect that another parity change was impending. This is the fact that has to be faced by those who argue that the only thing wrong with the adjustable peg was the reluctance of governments to change the peg promptly. It is irrelevant to point out that in 1964 Britain had ample time to devalue the pound after it had become evident to all informed observers that this step was necessary but before any speculative outflow had commenced. In 1964 the market took it for granted that a par value would be defended as long as possible, and the outbreak of speculation was therefore delayed until long after doubts about the long-term tenability of the parity had become widespread. This forbearance could hardly be expected to survive official declarations that in future par values would be adjusted promptly. The consequence of this change in attitude was entirely predictable: the market came to react far more rapidly to incipient signs of disequilibrium than it had done previously, and hence one began observing the billion-dollar-per-hour flow.

To maintain that prompt adjustment can make the adjustable peg work in this environment, one either has to believe that the authorities can always anticipate the market — or at least not lag behind it by more than 10 or 15 minutes — or else that they can be persuaded to be indifferent to the exchange losses involved in rewarding successful speculation. One does not need to have great faith in the percipience of the market or great cynicism about the forecasting abilities of the authorities to believe that the former is out of the question, particularly if one regards exchange rates as legitimate subjects for public debate and international consultation. So far as exchange losses are concerned, it was at one time regarded as sophisticated to dismiss them (in the abstract, though never in any concrete case). Some officials liked to regard them as a cross they had to bear. And some US economists, whose wealth did not suffer in view of US abstinence from market intervention, were prepared to dismiss them as mere transfer payments. Transfer payments they indeed are, but they nonetheless involve a real call on the wealth of the country whose central bank finds itself selling a currency at a lower price than it bought it for. Governments have never been indifferent to such wealth transfers in the past, and they will not be in the future until such time as they abandon a concern for their national interests.

The formal abandonment of dollar convertibility in August 1971 was the end of a long road. Although it might have been delayed had the United States not become ensnared in the Vietnam War, the system that it symbolized contained basic inadequacies which, in the absence of reforms, would have been bound to precipitate its collapse on some subsequent occasion. Even the conclusion of the SDR agreement, which would have enabled the system to survive a move of the US balance of payments into surplus, was irrelevant to the strains produced by a large deficit. *What the system lacked was both a clear assignment of responsibility for initiating adjustment and a crisis-proof method of effecting adjustment.* The rest of the world was not prepared to accept sole responsibility for securing adjustment, as called for by a dollar standard, and the American authorities had convinced themselves that they were powerless to initiate adjustment. (There was in fact an important element of truth in this, given the inability to contemplate using exchange rate changes without provoking massive portfolio shifts.)

The adjustable peg broke down because it did not provide a viable crisis-free method of changing exchange rates in an era of capital mobility.[16]   While the inadequacies of the adjustable peg were an important factor contributing to the demise of the gold exchange

16. The fragility of the adjustable peg had been a part of the conventional wisdom of academic international monetary economists at least since Meade (*The Balance of Payments*, especially p.228). It was a major theme of L. B. Yeager, *International Monetary Relations*, Harper and Row, New York, 1966. My own view is on record: '... the adjustable peg is unlikely to be viable indefinitely. Ever increasing destabilizing speculation will result if pegs are apt to jump ... ' J. Williamson, *The Crawling Peg*, Princeton Essays in International Finance No. 50, Princeton, 1965, p.8.

standard, the breakdown of the adjustable peg would have occurred even if by some series of miracles the US balance of payments had evolved in a manner that permitted the maintenance of the gold exchange standard. This breakdown was foreseeable and foreseen, inevitable and irreversible.

3

Negotiations

The abandonment of convertibility in August 1971 set in train a series of negotiations aimed at international monetary reconstruction that lasted almost 3 years. These negotiations fell into three distinct phases. The first came to a climax with the Smithsonian Conference in December 1971, when an agreed realignment of exchange rates was achieved. The second, which occupied the first 9 months of 1972, was concerned with establishing the forum in which it was hoped that a basic reform of the international monetary system would be negotiated. This period also witnessed a preliminary study of the options for reform in the Executive Board of the IMF. The final phase covered the negotiations within the C-20, which met periodically between September 1972 and June 1974. It is the purpose of this chapter to provide an account of these negotiations, although discussion of the substantive issues that involved the C-20 is postponed until Chapters 5 and 6.

Exchange rate realignment: August-December 1971

The rest of the world reacted to the US decision to suspend convertibility of the dollar with a mixture of anger and consternation. It was not the suspension of convertibility in itself that aroused anger, for it had long been foreseeable that the United States would be obliged to take this step as and when demands for conversion began to escalate, but rather the aggressive manner in which the step was announced. The reason for the consternation was that the aggressiveness of the approach removed the possibility of the rest of the world acquiescing in the final step to a full dollar standard, which most Europeans were convinced was a system that was in the national interest of the United States.

Most foreign exchange markets were closed in the week following

15 August, as governments that had failed to make contingency plans sought how to react to the US measures. In fact, however, their choice was very limited, in view of the attitude of the United States in urging revaluation and the costliness of acquiring dollars prior to a revaluation. Either they had to invoke draconian exchange controls to limit the influx of capital, or they had to allow their currencies to float. France chose the first course, accompanied by a dual exchange market. The other industrial countries all floated, after an initial delay on the part of the Japanese.

When the foreign exchange markets reopened, all the floating currencies moved up to some extent against the dollar. However, virtually every country endeavoured to limit its appreciation by a combination of intervention to buy dollars and exchange controls designed to repel capital inflows. This was not surprising in view of the recession that the world was then experiencing, which resulted in each country fearing that its demand management problems would be intensified by any loss of external markets. The Germans, who were less fearful of the trade implications of appreciation and more concerned about the inflationary impact of intervention on the money supply than any other country, coined the emotive phrase 'dirty floating' to describe the system that had emerged. It is perhaps unfortunate that this phrase has since been applied to any version of floating with intervention, irrespective of whether or not the intervention is well intentioned and well conceived. The other industrial countries (except Canada) remained reluctant floaters. In large part this was no doubt a hangover from the long years when advocacy of floating had been akin to sedition, but in part it was more rationally based. In particular, many thoughtful European officials felt that, at least in certain circumstances (such as during the recession then being experienced), the interests of countries in regard to their exchange rates were antagonistic, so that, if there were no international framework for reaching agreement on what exchange rates ought to be, the resulting competitive policies could be highly destructive. Their interpretation of contemporary experience, with the United States pumping out an excessive quantity of dollars secure in the knowledge that this would depreciate the dollar while the rest of the world countered by a proliferation of exchange controls designed to repel the unwanted influx, was hardly more reassuring than their recollections of the 1930s.

A primary requirement for the restoration of international monetary order was therefore regarded as the re-establishment of a par value system. A ministerial meeting of the G-10 was convened in late August, in a first attempt to examine the possibilities. The United States did not share the feeling of urgency about the need to end floating, but her primary aim had become that of securing a large enough effective devaluation of the dollar to promise rectification of her payments deficit — an objective that came to take the concrete form of a desired turnaround on current account of $13 billion per annum. She therefore came to welcome the prospect of a realignment that would imply that other countries were willing to allow her the improvement she aspired to. But there were two difficulties preventing a prompt realignment. One lay in finding a mutually acceptable pattern of exchange rates, which was complicated by trans-Atlantic differences of view over whether there should be a formal devaluation of the dollar. The second was that simply re-establishing a new set of par values would lead straight to a dollar standard unless it were accompanied by other reforms such as a restoration of the convertibility of the dollar — which was quite obviously infeasible in view of the dollar overhang and the loss of confidence in the dollar occasioned by the events of mid-1971.

In the weeks following the suspension of convertibility, about the only proposition that commanded universal assent was that there was a need for a thorough reform of the international monetary system. President Nixon had accompanied the announcement of his 'New Economic Policy' by a call for such a fundamental reform, and the recognition in other countries that restoration of convertibility was impracticable in the absence of such reform meant that at least this part of US thinking was welcomed in the rest of the world. There was a certain amount of discussion during the IMF Annual Meetings at the end of September about the desirable nature of long term reform. Anthony Barber, the British Chancellor of the Exchequer, made a powerful impact with a speech that in effect called for an SDR standard. He proposed that the SDR should be the numeraire in terms of which par values were expressed, thus restoring the possibility of an active exchange rate policy to the United States; and that the SDR should be the principal reserve asset, with holdings of reserve currencies largely confined to working balances and the excess converted into SDRs through substitution. The almost rapturous reception given to these proposals might be judged paradoxical, in view of the facts that the second proposal was merely a revamped version of what Triffin had been saying for 11 years, while the first proposal differed only presentationally from the existing legal situation in which gold was the numeraire and the value of the SDR was rigidly linked to the monetary price of gold. The political importance of a speech cannot necessarily be judged by the intellectual novelty — or cohesion — of its contents, however, and there is no question but that Anthony Barber's speech was important, both because it specified the nature of the steps needed to realize the widely acclaimed but ill-defined objective of 'making the SDR the centre of the reformed system', and because it crystallized the growing recognition that it was desirable for the United States to be able to exercise the initiative with respect to the exchange rate of the dollar.

Discussion of the possible nature of fundamental reform made it evident that the necessary measures could not be introduced overnight. The re-establishment of exchange rate stability was, however, regarded as too urgent a task to postpone until a comprehensive reform had been agreed. There therefore emerged a consensus that international monetary reconstruction should be sought in two stages. The first stage would involve securing agreement on a new structure of par values, while the second and more protracted phase would involve fundamental reform of the system. Even though convertibility would not exist, at least until this reformed system were in place, the implicit promise of its ultimate restoration made the prospect of an interim dollar standard no more intolerable than the *de facto* dollar standard existing before 15 August had been.

The IMF Annual Meetings instructed the Executive Board to undertake studies of the desirable nature of long-term reform. The immediate task, however, was conceived as being that of negotiating a new exchange rate structure. The IMF staff, on the basis of its multilateral exchange rate model (known affectionately as MERM), [1] and the OECD Secretariat had already calculated the changes in parities needed to induce what they regarded as appropriate sets of current account changes. It became evident, however, that just about all the countries involved found that their implied effective exchange rate was higher than they cared to accept. There followed a series of rancorous meetings (whose tone was not helped by the knowledge that someone had leaked the results of the IMF calculations to the press and that this had influenced the market) in the G-10, WP3 and the Executive Board of the IMF, in which the industrial countries wrangled with one another about the shape that the realignment should take. There were three separate sources of disagreement: the size of the changes in current account positions that it was desirable to secure; the size of the parity changes needed to secure a given set of current account adjustments; and the way in which a given set of parity changes should be implemented in terms of par value changes.

So far as the question of current account targets was concerned, the United States wanted a bigger improvement than most other countries

---

1. The MERM is described in J. R. Artus and R. R. Rhomberg, 'A Multilateral Exchange Rate Model', IMF *Staff Papers*, November 1973.

deemed necessary or desirable — a turnround of some $13 billion per annum. The OECD's WP3 undertook one of its exercises on reconciling current account targets, and came to the conclusion that the collective surplus implied by the individual aspirations of its members exceeded the deficit that the less developed countries would be able to finance by an enormous $8 billion or $10 billion per annum. (In those days, when exploitation of the international capital market by the developing countries was in its infancy, the collective current account deficit of these countries was treated as almost a natural constant.) However, OECD also came to the conclusion that a good part of the apparent inconsistency could be explained by the incomplete account that most countries were taking of the impact of the recession then in process. Countries typically made a full allowance for the effect of their own recession in reducing their imports below the level that could be expected when they were operating at full employment, but made an inadequate allowance for the impact of other countries' recessions in reducing their exports below a normal ('cyclically adjusted') level. Hence the typical country felt itself unable to concede as large a reduction in its current surplus as it could have if it had made appropriate allowance for the departure from full employment abroad as well as at home. The calculation of a consistent set of cyclical adjustments by the OECD went a considerable way towards reducing the apparent inconsistency in payments objectives; this provides a good illustration of the way in which, by adopting a cosmopolitan standpoint, an international organization can hope to play a role in reducing national differences. Even with consistent cyclical adjustment, however, there remained an important inconsistency in national objectives. There are two views as to why this was so. One is that it was explained by a widespread neo-mercantilist obsession with the achievement of current surpluses as a means to the promotion of export-led growth. The other is that the fact that the world was currently in a recession gave all countries an interest in maintaining an undervalued exchange rate in the short term in order to maintain employment.

The issue that generated the least polemical interchanges involved the size of the parity changes needed to secure a given redistribution of current account balances. The models used to calculate the necessary changes by the IMF and OECD embodied comparatively high figures for the relevant long-run trade elasticities, based on the findings of most econometric research in this field in the last 20 years or so, and also assumed — more controversially — that the bulk of any exchange rate changes would be reflected in enduring changes in competitive positions. Hence the models suggested that the necessary parity changes were relatively modest, provided that one were prepared to sit out the initial — but perhaps quite lengthy — period during which payments flows might even respond perversely to the exchange rate changes (the 'J-curve'). Some national authorities gave signs of scepticism about this intellectual framework; in particular, the US Treasury seems to have suffered from a degree of elasticity pessimism that is uncharacteristic among advocates of flexible exchange rates.

The final and most sensitive source of disagreement was about how a given realignment of parities should be translated into a new set of par values. By calling for exchange rate changes by other countries to correct the overvaluation of the dollar, President Nixon had claimed that the dollar's par value should be left unchanged and that the entire realignment should be effected by other countries revaluing their currencies. This position was publicly and quickly disputed by the Managing Director of the IMF, Pierre-Paul Schweitzer, who called for a formal devaluation of the dollar as a part of the realignment, thereby incurring such enmity from the US Administration as to ensure that the United States would in due course veto his reappointment for a third term of office (especially in combination with the IMF's calculations of desirable exchange rate changes, which failed to produce the answer the United States wanted). During the autumn of 1971 the call for a US 'contribution' to the realignment gathered force; by November it was clearly endorsed by all the other members of the G-10. There were some who delighted in dismissing the question of 'the price at which the United States did not sell gold' as a childish argument that affected political prestige alone and was devoid of economic substance. This was not so: in fact two important economic questions were involved.

The first question concerned the relative valuation of different reserve assets. A formal dollar devaluation resulted in an appreciation of the monetary price of gold, which was admittedly of little significance in view of the virtual cessation of gold transactions at the official price, but hence — and far more importantly — to an appreciation of the SDR in terms of the dollar. To many Europeans, one of the main attractions of creating the SDR had been that it would provide a chance to invest a part of their dollar earnings in an asset that would not depreciate if and when the dollar was devalued. It was the assumption that appreciation in terms of the dollar was possible that provided the SDR with some appeal as an investment medium despite its low nominal interest rate. Had the SDR proved to be merely a dollar with a 1·5 per cent interest coupon, it would have lost all such appeal.

The second question was whether it was desirable for the United States to pursue an active payments policy, and therefore have the right to an independent initiative with regard to her exchange rate. In the period before August 1971 a widely held belief had developed, in the United States at least, that the existing system precluded any such initiative, either because other countries defined their par values in terms of the dollar, or because the dollar's role as the dominant intervention currency meant that, whether or not there was a dollar devaluation, other countries were faced with essentially the same decision of whether to adjust their rates in terms of the dollar. The first contention was unambiguously wrong, as a matter of legal fact, because the relevant Fund Article (IV. I(a)) referred to a dollar *with a given gold content* as an alternative measure in terms of which par values might be expressed to gold itself. A dollar devaluation would therefore have caused a change in the parity of currency A, in terms of the dollar, unless currency A were also devalued to the same extent as the dollar. The second contention, however, involved an element of judgement. It would have been convincing enough if the rest of the world were a single currency area, so that the only exchange rate was the rate in terms of the dollar. In fact, however, the rest of the world consists of a number of relatively small countries, any one of which may hesitate to propose a revaluation of its own currency even when it is perfectly prepared to adjust its own intervention margins to give effect to a dollar devaluation, because, in contemplating a revaluation of its own currency, it is considering not merely revaluation against the dollar but also revaluation against a large number of other (and in most cases collectively far more important) trading competitors. [2] Hence a US initiative with respect to the dollar exchange rate was neither precluded by the legal situation nor condemned to futility by the economics of the situation. One route to establishing the legitimacy of a US initiative might have been to adopt the presentational changes in the numeraire envisaged in the Barber Plan. Another and more immediate route was to persuade the United States to exercise the rights she already possessed.

Since the United States was so anxious to achieve an effective devaluation of the dollar, her long resistance to conceding a formal devaluation seemed odd. It was never clear, however, whether this was genuine resistance rather than the retention of a bargaining counter in order to extract as big an effective devaluation as possible. In the event, the principle of a US 'contribution' was conceded in the course of a summit meeting between Presidents Nixon and Pompidou in the Azores in mid-December. Together with the lengthy preliminary work on the more technical questions, the way was then open to reach an agreement. This was achieved at a ministerial conference of the G-10 at

2. I developed this argument in J. Williamson, *The Choice of a Pivot for Parities*, Princeton Essays in International Finance No.90, Princeton, 1971, p.8.

the Smithsonian Institution in Washington on 18 and 19 December. The outcome was not that different from that urged all along by the staffs of the IMF and OECD. Political jockeying resulted in adjustments of 1 per cent or 2 per cent here and there, but the proposals of the international civil servants provided a focus with some sort of analytical basis from which it was impossible to deviate far without producing an intolerable feeling on the part of some countries that misery was being shared unequally. The Smithsonian realignment, therefore, provided for a devaluation of the dollar of 7.9 per cent; no changes in the par values of the pound sterling or French franc; revaluation of the yen, DM, Swiss franc, Belgian franc and Dutch guilder; and a mini-devaluation of 1 per cent for the lira and Swedish krone. Effective exchange rates [3] generally changed significantly less than par values, because most countries tended to move in the same direction as their principal trading partners. The Canadian dollar continued to float. The margins around parity within which fluctuations were permitted were widened from 1 per cent to 2.25 per cent. Most currencies of non-members of the G-10 were subsequently devalued part or all of the way with the dollar (and a few by even more). In return for these exchange rate adjustments, the United States abolished the import surcharge and put its demands for trade concessions and burden sharing into abeyance. Amid sighs of relief that the dangers of floating and economic warfare had been averted, the first stage of the restoration of international monetary order had been accomplished.

Preparations for the C-20: January-September 1972

Once the Smithsonian realignment had been achieved, attention was turned to the organization of a forum in which the long-term reform of the international monetary system could be negotiated. The G-10 had filled the role of discussing such issues for the previous decade and it had been active in the preceding months as the natural body in which to negotiate the exchange rate realignment — the currencies that were sufficiently important to require simultaneous determination were, after all, pretty much those of the members of the G-10. There were, however, two decisive objections to basing the reform negotiations in

3. The concept of the effective exchange rate came into its own at this time, precisely because of the realization that, in the context of a major realignment, changes in par values or in parities against a single other currency bear no systematic relationship to the changes in competitiveness that result from the package of exchange rate changes. A change in the effective exchange rate is defined as the trade-weighted average change in the exchange rate against all other currencies. See F. Hirsch and I. Higgins, 'An Indicator of Effective Exchange Rates', IMF *Staff Papers*, October 1970.

the G-10. The first was that the G-10 entirely excluded the developing countries, whose consent to the shape of any fundamental reform was indispensable, most concretely because any agreed reform would require amendment of the IMF Articles and the developing countries collectively had more than enough votes to prevent ratification of any amendments that they did not endorse. The second was that, since August 1971, the United States had found herself completely isolated in the G-10. She was, therefore, anxious to see the negotiations transferred to some other forum where her influence might be wielded to greater effect. After wavering between a smaller group — which has subsequently been realized in occasional meetings of the Big Five (the United States, Germany, Britain, France and Japan, to which Italy has been added on occasion) — and a larger group, the United States eventually plumped for the latter, harbouring the hope that bringing in the new (southern) world might redress the imbalance that had developed in the old (northern) one. Hence it was decided to base the negotiations within the near-universal framework provided by the IMF. The difficulty with this was that the Fund did not have any organ suitable for conducting such an important negotiation. The Board of Governors was far too unwieldy, and in any event it had no provision for meetings at the level of Deputies — i.e., senior civil servants. The Executive Board was unsuitable, both because of the relatively junior level of most Executive Directors and also the absence of any provision for ministerial-level meetings. The solution adopted was to create a purpose-made *ad hoc* committee within the framework of the Fund, as had been considered from time to time over the preceding 3 years.

This was the Committee of Twenty. It derived its name from the fact that representation was based on the 20 constituencies that appointed or elected Executive Directors to the Fund. The official title of the Committee was the 'Committee of the Board of Governors on Reform of the International Monetary System and Related Issues': the final phrase was in response to US insistence that a range of issues concerned with trade should be considered in conjunction with monetary reform. It was formally created as a result of a postal ballot of the Board of Governors held in July 1972.

During the spring of 1972 the Executive Board of the Fund took up the mandate given it at the previous Annual Meetings to study all aspects of the international monetary system with a view to reporting on possible measures of reform. After the usual marathon series of sessions, a report entitled *Reform of the International Monetary System*, popularly known as the *Reform Report*, was issued in August. The *Reform Report* aimed to lay out the options available in constructing a reformed system, rather than to draw conclusions about the desirable shape of reform. After a preliminary chapter on the need for reform, the report devoted a chapter to each of what were at that stage regarded as the five main areas in which reform was needed. It is worth summarizing the contents of these chapters, since they indicate the state of the discussion on the eve of the reform negotiations proper.

Chapter II, on the exchange rate mechanism, reiterated quite a bit of the analysis and options contained in the Fund report on *The Role of Exchange Rates in the Adjustment of International Payments* published 2 years previously. There was still a touching faith that prompter adjustment was in itself capable of mitigating the problem of disequilibrating capital movements. Slightly wider margins (wider than 1 per cent, not wider than 2.25 per cent) and temporary floating were again viewed sympathetically. There were, however, three interesting developments. First, and least surprising, was the explicit attention paid to the problem of enabling the United States to take the initiative in adjusting the exchange rate of the dollar. Second, there was a more sympathetic treatment of the proposal to allow the IMF to take the initiative in suggesting par value changes, so as to ensure that the international interest was taken into account in preventing the maintenance of inappropriate par values as well as in preventing inappropriate changes in par values. Finally, and most significantly, the suggestion that automatic indicators should be used to determine small par value changes was no longer rejected out of hand, but was discussed, under the heading of 'objective indicators for par value changes', in a way that suggested the existence of strong differences of opinion. What lay behind this became clear when the new US Secretary of the Treasury, George Shultz, unveiled US thinking on reform at the IMF Annual Meetings in September; apparently US planning crystallized too late to be fully reflected in the *Reform Report.*

The major contribution of the *Reform Report* came in Chapter III, 'Convertibility and the Settlement of Imbalances'. One interesting innovation was the discussion of the possibility of adoption of a system of multicurrency intervention (MCI) in the interests of greater symmetry. The principal novelty, however, was the emphasis placed on securing 'asset settlement' in the future system, rather than on restoring on-demand convertibility of the traditional type. Asset settlement, which was a new term to describe a concept whose significance had previously only rarely been appreciated, [4] was used to

---

4. The importance of the concept of asset settlement appears to have first been explicitly recognized by M. Stamp, 'The Reform of the International Monetary System', *Moorgate and Wall Street*, Summer, 1965.

describe a system under which the deficits or surpluses (on an official settlements basis) of all countries are reflected in a loss or gain of reserve assets (or by a change in negotiated credits — e.g., by borrowing from the IMF or on the central bank swap network), rather than sometimes being financed by a change in reserve liabilities. Countries other than reserve centres are, in any event, subject to asset settlement, so that the implication of adopting a system of asset settlement would have been to extend the normal disciplines exerted by reserve changes to the reserve centres. This would have (*a*) prevented future demands for net conversion of outstanding dollar (or, for that matter, sterling) balances into primary reserve assets by the United States (United Kingdom), requiring the US (UK) to draw on her reserves, and (*b*) prevented future financing of US (UK) deficits by official foreign accumulation of dollars (sterling). Two reasons were given as to why asset settlement might be considered desirable: first, that it was a necessary condition for collective international control of the volume of reserves to be exercised through variations in SDR creation; and, second, that asset settlement would ensure that a reserve centre in deficit would be exposed to the same pressure to take adjustment action as any other country. The *Reform Report* also indicated that some doubt had been expressed as to the feasibility of introducing a system of asset settlement, on the ground that such a system might preclude an adequate degree of flexibility in meeting sudden strains and might therefore require either very large reserves or a great deal of exchange rate flexibility.

The *Reform Report* sketched three possible mechanisms for achieving asset settlement. One technique, called the 'second approach', followed the lines that had long been proposed by those who were fearful of the inherent instability of the gold exchange standard — its tendency to amplify the payments swings of reserve centres, who found countries anxious to accumulate their currencies so long as they remained strong but all trying to switch out simultaneously when a deficit developed, thus depriving the reserve centre of liquidity at the very time it was needed. This approach would have involved each country declaring a specific level for its reserve currency holdings (perhaps equal to working balances), and regularly presenting any acquisition in excess of this level for conversion into primary reserve assets, as well as regularly selling primary reserve assets to the reserve centre to replenish its currency holdings whenever these ran down as a result of a deficit. Had every country acted in this way, the total of all reserve currency balances outstanding would have remained approximately constant over time, thus achieving asset settlement. The drawback with this approach, from the standpoint of non-reserve centres, was that it would have deprived them of any substantial measure of freedom in managing the composition of their reserve portfolios; and this was a freedom that many countries, particularly many developing countries, had come to value.

However, the *Reform Report* also pointed out that there were two other ways in which asset settlement could be achieved, neither of which would involve as much sacrifice of freedom of portfolio composition (or, for that matter, as rapid a rundown in the proportion of reserves held in reserve currencies). It was pointed out that the real need, from the standpoint of achieving asset settlement, was that the global total of reserve currency holdings should remain constant, rather than that the holdings of each individual country should remain constant. One alternative technique (the 'first approach') would have allowed countries in the first instance to choose freely how they wished to hold their reserves, but would then have had the Fund at regular intervals calculate the net increase or decrease in total currency balances outstanding, and then reverse whatever change had occurred through a designation procedure akin to that involved in operating the SDR account. If, for example, there had been an increase in outstanding dollar holdings as a result of a US deficit, the United States would have been required to sell primary reserve assets equal to her deficit, and certain countries would have been designated by the Fund to purchase these primary reserve assets in exchange for dollars, which the United States would have received in return for the primary reserve assets she was surrendering. Conversely, a US surplus would have led to certain countries being designated to surrender primary reserve assets to the United States, which would thus have been certain of being able to build up her reserves when she ran a surplus.

The final scheme for achieving asset settlement (known as the 'third approach') would have extended the freedom of portfolio composition even further. It would have accomplished this by using the dollar holdings of a Fund Substitution Account as a buffer stock with which to secure asset settlement with the United States, without requiring other countries to engage in transactions they would have preferred to avoid (or preventing them from engaging in transactions they would have liked to make). It was envisaged that some countries would initially choose to swap — technically, to 'substitute' — some of their dollar holdings for SDRs with a special account at the Fund (the Substitution Account). In the event of a US deficit, the Substitution Account would have sold some of these dollars to the United States in exchange for SDRs, thus again ensuring that a deficit led to a loss of reserves — i.e., that asset settlement was achieved. Conversely, in the event of a US surplus, the Substitution Account would have sold SDRs to the United States to the extent that there was a decrease in global official holdings of dollars, thus again leading to asset settlement. So long as the Substitution Account was holding dollars, this would have enabled asset settlement to be achieved without any interference with the reserve composition policies of individual countries. Had the Account's holdings of dollars become exhausted, it would have been necessary to revert to a designation procedure as under the previous approach.

Chapter IV of the *Reform Report* was concerned with the future role of the various reserve assets — reserve currencies, gold and SDRs. It was pointed out that, if asset settlement were adopted, there would be a progressive decline in the proportion of reserves held in reserve currencies, since all future reserve growth would be in SDRs.* The main feature of the chapter was its discussion of the way in which this process might be hastened by the creation of a Substitution Account in the Fund. This would have been a special account empowered to accept reserve currency balances from members and to issue SDRs in exchange — the sort of operation long advocated by Robert Triffin. A substitution operation of this type would have been necessary either to give any hope of reintroducing traditional 'on-demand' convertibility, since otherwise the United States would have been confronted with the risk of being at any time faced with impossible demands for the conversion of the large outstanding stock of dollar balances (the 'dollar overhang', which vastly exceeded its own reserves), or for two of the three methods of introducing asset settlement. (The exception was asset settlement achieved through designation.) The chapter noted that substitution would raise questions about the terms on which the balances acquired by the Substitution Account would be serviced and amortized by the reserve centres, but did not attempt to offer solutions. It also noted the existence of an alternative way in which the threat to US liquidity posed by the existence of the dollar overhang might be overcome — through bilateral agreements under which some dollar holders might agree to the transformation of short-term into long-term claims ('funding' [5]). Finally, the chapter contained a schizophrenic discussion of gold, which mentioned possibilities varying

---

* It is necessary to qualify this statement to the extent that secular growth in the need for working balances might make it appropriate to allow some increase in reserve currency holdings in the future. This would have involved a departure from strict asset settlement.

5. Prior to the C-20 it was commonplace to refer to 'funding' dollar balances into, e.g., SDRs. C-20 terminology was to distinguish funding (of bilateral short-term into bilateral long-term claims) from substitution (which involved the transformation of bilateral short-term claims into a short-term claim of the reserve holder on the IMF and a long-term claim of the IMF on the reserve centre). Consolidation — the elimination of short-term claims on the reserve centre so as to increase its liquidity — might be achieved through either funding or substitution.

from a rise in the official price of gold to the possibility of channelling some monetary gold — perhaps from the IMF's own stocks — on to the private market; and by a discussion of the yield on the SDR, which raised the possibility of increasing the interest rate so as to encourage a greater desire to hold SDRs.

Chapter V was entitled 'The Problem of Disequilibrating Capital Movements' — the official name for the vast speculative flows that plagued the adjustable peg. It reviewed the official list of remedies — wider margins, harmonization of interest rates, controls, dual foreign exchange markets, restraining official reserve holders from joining the speculative bandwagon, and short-term credits.

The final chapter was devoted to the interests of the developing countries in international monetary reform. These countries had already established their own forum, the Group of 24, or G-24, (consisting of eight nations each from Africa, Asia and Latin America), to coordinate their position in international monetary negotiations. The chapter reflected their view that the recent disorders in the international monetary system had jeopardized their interests, and that a reformed system should make greater provision for the transfer of resources to developing countries — notably by introduction of the link.

The *Reform Report* was warmly welcomed by most Governors at the 1972 Annual Meetings of the Fund as providing the agenda for the forthcoming negotiations of the C-20. There was, however, one country that did not join in the general acclaim: the United States. George Shultz, Secretary of the Treasury, unveiled a new US plan for reform of which only the vaguest hints had appeared in the *Reform Report*, in the form of the attention paid to the possibility of using 'objective indicators' to guide changes in par values. The centre of the US plan was the use of reserves as objective indicators, not of the need for exchange rate changes *per se*, but of the need for adjustment in one form or another, with the choice of adjustment technique to be left to the discretion of the individual country whose reserves were deviating from their norm. Convertibility, of the traditional on-demand variety, would have been restored as the *quid pro quo* to acceptance of the indicator system, once the US liquidity position permitted.

The 1972 Meetings did not produce much else in the way of substantive discussion. Personality issues loomed larger than economic ones. In particular, the decision of the United States to veto the reappointment of Pierre-Paul Schweitzer for a third term of office as Managing Director of the IMF — leaked by the French shortly before the Meetings — provoked a series of almost passionate tributes to his work, which were always warmly applauded. However, when Anthony Barber followed his tribute with the observation that one characteristic of a great public servant was his ability to recognize when his usefulness was at an end, it became apparent that the US veto was not going to be contested. The search for a new Managing Director was then set in motion: but it was 10 months before an acceptable candidate willing to take the job was found, in the person of H. Johannes Witteveen, an economist and former Dutch Finance Minister. The other personality questions concerned the C-20. The chairmanship of the Committee itself — i.e., the Ministers — was easily settled, with Ali Wardhana, the Indonesian Finance Minister and retiring chairman of the Board of Governors, being a natural candidate who commanded general assent. The key post, however, was Chairman of the Deputies. Here there was a knife-edge contest between C. Jeremy Morse of the Bank of England, who was supported by most of the Europeans, and Rinaldo Ossola of the Banca d'Italia and chairman of the G-10 Deputies, who was sponsored by the United States. Jeremy Morse was eventually elected.

The C-20 had its first meetings at both Ministerial and Deputy level during the Annual Meetings. They were concerned solely with procedural questions, such as the election of the chairman and determination of the number of advisors and observers who might be present. The preparations for the attempt to negotiate a fundamental reform of the international monetary system were therefore complete.

The Committee of Twenty: September 1972 – June 1974

There was a 2-month interval between the procedural meetings of the C-20 and the first working meeting of the Deputies in late November. The time was occupied by the preparation of working papers, particularly by the 'Bureau', which consisted of the chairman and four vice-chairmen of the Deputies. The vice-chairmen were selected with the aim of making the Bureau reasonably representative in terms of both geography and doctrine. They were: J. H. Frimpong-Ansah, of the Bank of Ghana; Alexandre Kafka, the long-serving Brazilian Executive Director in the Fund; Robert Solomon, of the United States Federal Reserve Board, who played a major role in organizing the inter-central bank cooperation of the 1960s; and Hideo Suzuki, of Japan. The Bureau was serviced by a staff of one — the chairman's personal assistant, Eddie George of the Bank of England — which must give it the unique record in the history of international organizations of having been understaffed. It was also, of course, able to call on the services of the IMF staff, and to some extent did so, but the bulk of the work was done by the members of the Bureau themselves.

The Deputies generally met at 2-month intervals. Meetings typically lasted 3 days, although their length varied from 1 to 5 days on particular occasions. Half of the Deputies' meetings were followed by Ministerial meetings, which typically lasted 2 (rather short) days. Meetings of the C-20 were attended by far more than 20 people. There were usually about 180 in the room at meetings of the Deputies, of whom about 70 were entitled to speak. Each of the 20 IMF constituencies had two Deputies, and their Fund Executive Director was also present in his own right and entitled to participate in discussion. Each constituency was entitled to appoint a further five persons as advisers, who did not have the right to speak. Then there were the members of the Bureau, plus the chairman's personal assistant; two members of the IMF staff with Deputy status, plus a further three or four at the adviser level; observers accorded the right to speak from six international organizations — the EEC, UNCTAD, OECD, GATT, the IBRD and BIS; and several members of the IMF staff providing supporting secretarial services. Numbers were even greater at ministerial-level meetings, where the above cast was present in a supporting role to the 20 principal ministers ('Members'), who were each also accompanied by two 'Associates' accorded the right to speak (often central bank governors or, in multi-country constituencies, Finance Ministers from the smaller countries). The Managing Director of the IMF participated in meetings of the Ministers, and the other international organizations were also represented at a more senior level. Large as these numbers were, they did not approach the number involved in the Bretton Woods conference in 1944 — some 730 [6] (although this included the full secretarial, interpreting and supporting staff, who might have added another 100 or so to the C-20 total). There was, incidentally, an overlap of one person between those participating in the C-20 and those who had attended the Bretton Woods conference: J. J. Polak, who in 1944 had been a junior member of the Dutch delegation, was in 1972 Director of Research of the IMF and therefore one of the two Deputy-level IMF representatives at the C-20.

International negotiations are generally based on extensive documentation, and the Deputies' meetings were no exception. Deputies would submit documents as the occasion arose — sometimes basically analytical, sometimes outlining new (or not so new) proposals. The main documents around which discussion was centred during the earlier meetings of the Deputies were, however, 'annotated agendas' prepared by the Bureau. These were intended to

6. J. K. Horsefield, *The International Monetary Fund 1945-65*, IMF, Washington DC, 1969, Vol.I, p.89.

structure the discussion to draw attention to the points that required resolution. The annotated agenda would generally describe the state of play so far as agreement over aims was concerned; outline the alternative proposals in circulation; sometimes offer a certain amount of analysis relevant to the choice between these proposals; and pose questions which it was hoped that Deputies would answer. A large part of the meetings were occupied by Deputies declaring their views on these annotated agendas, section by section. Their contributions varied from direct answers to the questions posed to discursive philosophical contributions, from serious analysis to repititious statements of aspirations, and from brisk challenges to other Deputies to attempts to synthesize compromise solutions. What struck someone accustomed to the interplay of seminars or academic conferences was the rarity of contributions in the latter categories; indeed, the proceedings were aptly characterized by Jeremy Morse on one occasion as a 'multilateral monologue'.

A meeting of the Deputies therefore produced a series of declarations of national positions which sometimes clarified where countries stood, sometimes educated the participants, and occasionally resulted in new ideas or a feeling that the general will had crystallized. The Bureau then had the unenviable task of trying to distil these contributions so as either to form the basis for a new annotated agenda for discussion at a subsequent meeting (hopefully narrowing the area of disagreement), or else to draft a text that was intended to express a set of agreed views. The main text discussed was the *Outline of Reform* (hereafter referred to as the *Outline*). As the meetings continued, the discussion of texts came to occupy an increasing part of the time. A comparison between the *First Outline of Reform*,[7] which was published before the 1973 Annual Meetings in Nairobi, and the final *Outline* published at the conclusion of the C-20's work in June 1974,[8] must raise some doubts about whether this time was well expended. The *First Outline* indicated the existence of disagreement on a wide range of issues; the final version had no fewer than ten annexes added to amplify these disagreements, but revealed that disagreement had been eliminated on only two long-term issues: first, the (Ministerial) C-20 had decided to perpetuate itself in the form of a Fund Council (para. 31); second, the Fund would create a new facility — the Extended Fund Facility — 'under which developing countries would

---

7. The *First Outline of Reform* appears in the IMF *Survey*, 8 October 1973.
8. The final *Outline* appeared in the IMF *Survey*, 17 June 1974, and was reprinted in *International Monetary Reform: Documents of the Committee of Twenty* (hereafter 'C-20 Documents'), IMF, Washington DC, 1974.

receive longer-term balance of payments finance' (para. 30).

At one time or another the C-20 also set up 'technical groups' to consider important disputed issues in more depth, or at least at greater length, than was possible in the C-20 itself. These groups were chaired by a member of the Bureau and contained one representative of each constituency — often Executive Directors or their Alternates — and of the Fund, plus speaking observers from those of the international organizations that chose to participate, plus one or two advisers from each constituency. Their working methods were less ponderous than those of the C-20 itself, but they were even more prone to spend their time drafting texts expressing disagreement rather than seeking to analyse subjects with a view to reaching agreement. The groups were concerned with objective indicators (two groups, one with the title 'Adjustment'); the link, and the more general subject of facilitating resource transfer to developing countries; intervention and settlement; disequilibrating capital flows (ironically set up immediately after the C-20 had endorsed the adjustable peg that is their necessary and sufficient condition); and liquidity and consolidation. [9]

When the C-20 first started work there was a rather general hope that the programme of following the restoration of a par value system by complementary basic reforms in the rest of the system would in due course succeed. However, disillusion began to set in quite soon. The strains in the Smithsonian exchange rate structure (even excluding sterling, which was already floating) began to erupt during the second substantive meeting of the Deputies, in Paris in January 1973, with the introduction of a dual exchange market by Italy, followed by a float of the Swiss franc. Before the Deputies met again the second devaluation of the dollar had occurred, failed and been succeeded by the advent of generalized floating. Undeterred, 3 weeks later the first substantive meeting of the C-20 Ministers agreed on one thing: that the reformed system should be based on 'stable but adjustable par values' — i.e., that the system that had just collapsed should be reinstated.

There was then a phase during which it became evident that progress was slower than had been hoped, but in which many still believed that the objective of a comprehensive reform incorporating a resurrected adjustable peg was ultimately realizable. There was a flurry of optimism that the negotiations were getting somewhere in July 1973, when it seemed that a mutation of the US indicator proposal involving a set of reserve ceilings which countries would have been penalized for exceeding, through the imposition of negative interest rates, might provide a basis for agreement. But these hopes were

9. The reports of the technical groups are reprinted in the *C-20 Documents*, op. cit.

dashed at the next meeting of the Deputies in early September, with the result that the *First Outline* presented to the Annual Meetings reflected disagreement on all the major issues — except for the exchange rate regime. A minority view was that generalized floating was permanent, and hence that the C-20's endorsement of the adjustable peg demonstrated that the Committee was too out of touch with reality to justify the hope that it would produce a comprehensive workable reform. The minority retained the hope that agreement would be reached that would lead to real reform on certain specific issues, mainly regarding the supply of reserve assets, but they believed that the question of fundamental importance involved adapting the system to enable the world to live with a generalized float. This required agreements in two areas: (a) changing the basis of valuation of the SDR (which was previously defined with reference to par values, and hence *de facto* attached to the dollar under a system in which par values had become meaningless), and (b) developing guidelines for internationally responsible national management of floating exchange rates. Since these were regarded as primarily relevant to the transitional period pending introduction of the reformed system being designed by the C-20, principal responsibility for them was remitted to the Executive Board, with the C-20 maintaining an interest in the progress of discussions there — particularly as these impinged on the valuation of the SDR under the reformed system.

Between the Nairobi Annual Meeting in September 1973 and the C-20 Ministerial meeting in Rome in January 1974 there was a pervasive feeling of the futility of the reform exercise, coupled with a refusal to admit failure. The *First Outline* was greeted in Nairobi with a reaffirmation of the need for a comprehensive reform, and the Committee called for an accelerated work programme to achieve agreement by July 1974. It was decided that this would best be promoted by intensive work in technical groups, but — with the exception of the work on symmetrical intervention systems in the Technical Group on Intervention and Settlement — these groups did not achieve a great deal. Meanwhile in the outside world there were such exogenous shocks as the October War, the Arab oil embargo, and a quadrupling in the price of oil.

It is difficult to identify any analytical reason for the shape of the international monetary system being dependent on the price of a particular commodity, even of the most important commodity in world trade. Any satisfactory system needs to make provision for the orderly adjustment of current account positions in response to disturbances; for the accumulation of financial assets by countries in current account surplus; for the elimination of the incentive to disequilibrating capital movements; and for the channelling of flows of financial capital to areas where investment opportunities exceed local savings. These needs were emphasized, but they were not created, by the oil price increase. Nevertheless, the quadrupling of the oil price provided a convenient alibi for abandoning — or, officially, postponing — the quest for a reformed system. The final phase of the C-20's work was therefore dominated by concern to reach agreement on a number of issues of immediate importance. The first success lay in the agreement reached at Rome to base the valuation of the SDR on a basket of currencies, thus providing the world with a unit of account and the central banks with a reserve asset well adapted to a world of generalized floating. It was carefully specified that this decision applied only to the interim period pending establishment of the reformed system, and was without prejudice to the valuation technique to be adopted when that day arrived. (This reservation has had some effect in discouraging subsequent use of the SDR by the private sector, but the utilization of the 'new SDR' has already proved so extensive [10] that the future has in practice been heavily prejudiced.) This was followed in June by the adoption of the Guidelines for Floating that the Executive Board had worked on; the agreement to institute a 'trade pledge' — i.e., a Declaration that those members of the Fund who chose to sign it would pledge themselves not to impose additional trade restrictions without a prior finding by the Fund that they had a balance-of-payments need; the introduction of a temporary 'oil facility' to assist those members of the IMF most affected by the oil price increase; and reforms in the decision-making organs of the Fund, involving the ultimate creation of a Ministerial Council (modelled on the C-20) and the immediate creation of an Interim Committee (to take the place of the Council until the necessary amendments to the IMF Articles could be made) and a 'Development Committee' (a joint Ministerial Committee of the IMF and IBRD to supervise the transfer of real resources to developing countries). In parallel with this concern with immediate steps, the C-20 continued to revise the *Outline* that was supposed to describe the shape of the reformed system that would be introduced when the world had settled down by eliminating inflation and major payments disequilibria. As already noted, however, the final version of the *Outline* revealed virtually no progress in resolving disagreed issues, and was notable chiefly for the listing of alternatives in the annexes.

10. By late 1975 the 'new SDR' had emerged as a significant unit for denominating bonds in the offshore market, been adopted for the expression of dues in the reopened Suez Canal, been adopted by the IATA for future use in denominating air fares, and provided the unit to which the currencies of Burma, Guinea, Iran, Jordan, Kenya, Malawi, Qatar, Tanzania and Uganda were pegged.

In comparison with the initial objective of writing a new monetary constitution for the world these results were meagre. There was no agreement on a set of rules for assigning adjustment responsibilities, no design of a viable adjustment mechanism, no introduction of an SDR standard, no substitution and no curb on the asymmetries. These facts explain the use of the word 'failure' in the title of this book.

Postscript to the C-20: June 1974 - January 1976

The outcome of the C-20 was, in effect, a decision to learn to live with the non-system that had evolved out of a mixture of custom and crisis over the preceeding years. This non-system was, however, illegal under the IMF Articles, which required each country to maintain and defend a par value. It was therefore necessary to amend the IMF Articles in order to legalize existing practices, and thereby restore legality to the operation of the Fund. In addition, there were various matters, concerned with gold and the provision of conditional liquidity by the Fund, that needed immediate attention. The 18-month period following the end of the C-20 was therefore spent in achieving agreements on this very limited range of 'immediate steps'. Agreement was finally reached at the meeting of the Interim Committee in Jamaica in January 1976.

The two most contentious issues involved the exchange rate regime and gold. The agreement ultimately reached on gold, which in most essentials was achieved at the time of the IMF Annual Meetings at the end of August 1975, is outlined and discussed in Chapter 6. The negotiation of a new Article IV, concerning the exchange rate regime, was eventually remitted to the United States and France to hammer out between themselves, which they did in the course of the summit conference at Rambouillet in November 1975. The flavour of the new Article IV is well conveyed by Section 2 (b):

> Under an international monetary system of the kind prevailing on January 1, 1976, exchange arrangements may include ...
> (iii) other exchange arrangements of a member's choice.

The Article is sufficiently liberal to allow a country to peg its currency if it wants to, to anything it chooses (except gold) - any other currency, or a composite of several currencies, including the basket SDR, or by mutual pegging, as in the European snake - within any margins it chooses; to allow it to change the peg gradually, as under the crawling peg, or by large steps, as under the adjustable peg; or to allow it to let its currency float, intervening as and when it pleases, subject only to the restraints on aggressive intervention provided by the Guidelines for Floating. The French aversion to floating was reflected merely in (a) an agreement for more consultations and greater cooperation in reducing erratic exchange rate fluctuations, and (b) a provision allowing 85 per cent of the total voting power of the Fund to vote to reinstate the adjustable peg (but with the right for countries to continue floating even after a general return to a par value system). Since there is no reason to expect more consultations and cooperation, in the absence of a framework of rules, to have much effect, and since the possibility of mustering an 85 per cent majority for restoration of the adjustable peg can safely be disregarded, the agreement was a complete victory for the United States. Cynics have, however, suggested that French diplomatic sensibilities were mollified by France's being given the responsibility of conceding to US wishes. Whether it was wise to couple the inevitable and overdue legalization of floating with such a complete abandonment of a framework of international rules is a subject considered in Chapter 8.

The period under review also saw a series of steps to increase access to conditional liquidity in the Fund. These comprised establishment of the Extended Fund Facility, renewal of the oil facility for a second (and final) year, liberalization of the compensatory financing facility, an average increase of 33.6 per cent in the size of quotas, and an agreement to increase temporarily (until the quota increases become effective) the size of each credit tranche by 45 per cent. The IMF was not, however, the sole source of increased conditional liquidity: at the initiative of the United States, the OECD agreed to create a Financial Support Fund (popularly known as the 'safety net') totalling $25 billion to aid OECD members who might experience difficulty in financing their oil deficits by other means. Whether this omission of the developing countries marks a first move toward the establishment of antagonistic regional blocs, as has been feared in some quarters ever since the demise of the Bretton Woods system (though usually with different-shaped blocs being envisaged), remains to be seen.

The comprehensive revision of the IMF Articles finally announced in April 1976, while this book was in proof, dealt with a number of other matters as well. Adequate support for the immediate introduction of the planned IMF Council did not exist early in 1976, so the amendment instead contained an enabling provision allowing the Council to be established if and when an 85 per cent majority can be mustered. In addition to various administrative changes, the amended Articles also allow some liberalization in the rules governing use of the SDR.

What emerged after the C-20 cannot be described as an international monetary 'system', in so far as the word system implies a well-defined set of rights and obligations. Countries are free to do in large measure as they please, with regard not only to their exchange rates but also to the volume and composition of the reserves that they hold and the methods that they use to effect payments adjustment. One country, at least, seems happy enough with a non-system in which the dollar is once again unrivalled and the pretensions of the IMF to conduct a world monetary policy have been brought to nought, leaving the Federal Reserve unchallenged. US Secretary of the Treasury William Simon even compared the results of the Jamaican meeting of the Interim Committee to those of the Bretton Woods conference. The rest of the world did not subscribe to the view that Jamaica was one of the foundation stones of the new international economic order, but on the other hand the advent of floating exchange rates has made acquiescense in a dollar-centred system markedly less irksome than a full dollar standard would have been, for the system no longer imposes obligations to follow US monetary policy, to finance US deficits involuntarily or to risk importing US inflation. A comparison of the relative merits of the non-system legalized at Jamaica and the type of consciously designed system being sought by the C-20 is provided in Chapter 8.

4

National positions and national interests

This chapter describes the positions adopted by the major participants in the reform negotiations and attempts to explain national positions on the basis of real or perceived national interests. Many elements enter into a country's national interests, and there is no point in venturing a comprehensive taxonomy; suffice it to observe that economic well-being is one such element which is of particular and obvious importance in economic diplomacy, but that other elements — such as national self-respect and harmonious relations with other countries — were also relevant in the context of the reform negotiations.

As recounted in previous chapters, the events leading up to and following the breakdown of the Bretton Woods system tended to produce a polarization between the United States on the one hand and the Europeans and Japanese on the other hand. In addition, the developing countries had increasingly come together to form a coherent pressure group in international economic affairs during the 1960s, and by 1972 felt bound together by common interests, shared emotions and institutional ties through UNCTAD and the Group of 24 (G-24). It is therefore convenient to treat most of the participants in one or another of these groupings. There remain, however, three significant participants — Canada, South Africa and Australia — that did not fall into any of the three groups; all of them exhibited views on at least one major issue that lay well outside the mainstream of C-20 thought, so they are treated in a final section entitled 'The Heretics'.

In examining the reasons for the national positions adopted in the course of controversial negotiations, one inevitably tends to focus on areas where there is a conflict of interests between countries. It is worth emphasizing at the outset, therefore, that most countries believed (though with varying intensity) that they shared a common interest in the maintenance of a cooperative international economic system, incorporating liberal trading policies, the maintenance of an international capital market, the provision of development finance, the avoidance of competitive payments policies, the minimization of global cyclical fluctuations, the absence of erratic exchange rate variations, orderly methods of payments adjustment, and the provision of reserves through a fiduciary reserve asset. It was the fear that the progress made in realizing these objectives during the quarter-century of the Bretton Woods system would be jeopardized by its breakdown that provided the motive force behind the reform exercise. And when one comes to consider whether it is worth seeking to construct a reformed system in the future, one essentially has to ask whether these objectives are in fact threatened by the existing 'interim' arrangements.

The United States

The key to understanding the position adopted by the United States in the reform negotiations is to recognize that it was believed in Washington that the US deficit was essentially the result of the desire for surpluses in the rest of the world.[1] This view had been given considerable intellectual status in the 1960s by the writings of the dollar standard school, and the facts that now seem to many (including the author) to refute it — notably the increase in the US deficit following the Vietnam involvement and its explosion following the relaxation of US monetary policy in 1970 — were then too recent for their significance to have been fully absorbed.[2] The reluctance of other countries to concede as big a dollar devaluation as the United States wished during the pre-Smithsonian negotiations was interpreted as providing confirmation of the rest of the world's attachment to a state of permanent surplus, rather than as a reflection of the recession then in process. US officials did not, however, share the other view of the dollar-standard school: that the state of the US balance of payments could be regarded with indifference. They wanted to see a surplus restored — to safeguard US jobs, to end the US-baiting for which a deficit provided an ideal pretext, to permit capital exports and to have the financial strength to restore some form of convertibility to placate

1. This view comes across clearly in paragraphs 4-7 of the basic US negotiating document entitled *The U.S. Proposals for Using Reserves as an Indicator of the Need for Balance-of-Payments Adjustment* (hereafter referred to as *The US Proposals*). This was published as Appendix A.5 to the 1973 Report of the Council of Economic Advisers in the *Economic Report of the President, 1973*, US Government Printing Office, Washington DC, 1973.
2. I have to confess that as late as the autumn of 1972 I wrote that the question as to whether the US deficit was demand-determined or supply-determined was still an open one: J. Williamson, 'International Liquidity — A Survey', *Economic Journal*, September 1973, p.707.

their foreign partners. And they were convinced that the asymmetries in the previous system precluded the United States' achieving a surplus, whatever actions she might take.

The special situation of the United States led to other respects in which her attitudes differed markedly from those of other countries. First and foremost, the dollar was the major reserve currency. This fact did confer advantages on the United States — the ability to borrow cheaply to finance past deficits, as analysed in the literature on seigniorage; the ability to finance future deficits without first stock-piling low-yielding reserves, as neglected in the literature on seigniorage; the freedom in foreign policy (and especially its military extension) conferred by this lack of a financial constraint of the customary type; the ability to avoid adopting costly adjustment measures; and the political influence given by an unconstrained ability to lend to other countries suffering a run on their currency. It was, therefore, hardly surprising that the United States was hesitant about proposals likely to circumscribe the role of the dollar. Indeed, some Europeans thought that the United States had become so accustomed to freedom from foreign financial constraints as to make it unlikely that she would really agree to arrangements that involved reducing the dollar to the status of an 'ordinary' currency, and hence proposals made by the United States that claimed to be doing this were prone to be treated with suspicion. Second, the fact that the dollar was the major intervention currency meant that the United States herself undertook very little intervention, and, as long as the dollar was *de facto* inconvertible, that her reserves did not change as a result of runs into or out of the dollar. Hence the financial losses that central banks normally suffer as a result of successful speculation on a forthcoming parity change were almost entirely avoided by the United States, being borne instead by the central banks of the other countries, which had to buy expensive dollars before a dollar devaluation and sell them more cheaply afterwards. Since much of the speculation was undertaken by the multinationals and most multinationals are US-based, it is even possible that the United States had a financial interest in parity changes being preceded by speculative runs. Be that as it may, she certainly did not have the same fear of intensifying speculation as other countries did, and this was — at least under existing arrangements — based on real self-interest. Third, the United States economy was less open than most others; the theory of optimum currency areas[3] would therefore suggest that she would have relatively little interest in the maintenance

3. See in particular R. I. McKinnon, 'Optimum Currency Areas'. *American Economic Review*, September 1963.

of fixed exchange rates and a correspondingly large interest in ensuring that necessary adjustments were undertaken with the aid of exchange rate changes.

The US plan for a reformed system was first outlined by Secretary of the Treasury George Shultz at the 1972 Annual Meeting of the IMF, and presented in full to the first working meeting of the Deputies in November 1972.[4] Its centrepiece was the proposal to introduce a 'reserve indicator system' under which countries would be obliged to adjust when their reserves passed certain specified points. The operation of such a system would require that each country be allocated a reserve norm: it was recognized that the selection of norms would be difficult and contentious. Various suggestions as to how norms might be allocated were advanced — e.g., in proportion to IMF quotas or past reserve levels — but without expression of a preference for any particular method. The sum of countries' norms was envisaged as being roughly equal to the total of reserves in existence. The reserve norm would be surrounded by two 'warning points', and, further removed, by an 'outer point' and a 'low point'. If a country's reserves passed one of the warning points there would be a strong presumption that it should adjust, though the means by which adjustment should be achieved were to be left to the discretion of the individual country. If its reserves moved toward the outer point or low point, it would be expected to apply adjustment measures 'of progressive intensity', and, if its reserves reached these critical levels, the country would become subject to 'pressures' if a programme of adjustment deemed adequate by the IMF were not in place. Certain ideas as to possible pressures were put forward — the loss of scheduled SDR allocations, an authorization for other countries to impose surcharges on the country's exports, or the imposition of a tax on excess reserve holdings — again without the expression of a definite preference for particular forms of pressure.

The US proposals envisaged a restoration of convertibility of the dollar into primary reserve assets (meaning, in practice, SDRs) once the US liquidity position were strong enough and a reserve indicator system were in operation. Convertibility was, however, to be circumscribed by the introduction of 'primary asset holding limits' (PAHLs) through the indicator system.[5] Each country would have a PAHL set at a fixed proportion above its norm, and if its reserves exceeded its PAHL it would cease to be eligible to convert additional

4. *The US Proposals, op.cit.*
5. The PAHL was originally called a 'convertibility point', but was renamed after it had been pointed out that this was a misnomer for the point where convertibility rights disappeared.

reserve accruals into primary reserve assets. (The United States also proposed that reserve centres should be accorded the right to limit other countries' holdings of their currencies, which led to the unanswered conundrum of what a country with reserves above its PAHL and denied permission to hold more reserve currencies was supposed to do. Presumably the answer was that it had to float.) The PAHL proposal was merely one indication of the gulf separating United States from European views on the subject of convertibility. Another was the US insistence that 'in a reformed system holdings of foreign exchange should be neither banned nor encouraged'.[6] A third was the deliberate refusal to use the term asset settlement, while arguing against the concept on the ground that ' ... fluctuations in [foreign exchange] holdings could add some elasticity to the system as a whole in meeting sudden flows of volatile capital'.[7]

There was a third important element in US thinking, which, perhaps mistakenly from the standpoint of diplomacy, was less emphasized than indicators and convertibility. This was the introduction of multicurrency intervention (MCI), which was proposed on the ground of greater symmetry — specifically, on the ground that it would permit the dollar to have the same degree of flexibility within the margins as was previously present between any other pair of currencies. A more important but less emphasized consequence of MCI would have been that it would have enabled the dollar to float without thereby destroying the system of pegged exchange rates between all other currencies.[8] A system of MCI is one in which each of the major currencies has its value in relation to each of the others stabilized by direct intervention in each of the exchange markets. The version of MCI that the United States preferred was that of 'ceiling intervention', in which each participant undertook to intervene by buying any other

6. *The US Proposals, op.cit.*, p.130.
7. *Idem.*
8. In August 1971 there was no way in which the Europeans could maintain pegged exchange rates between themselves while allowing the dollar to float, precisely because at that time virtually all intervention was in dollars. The following year the members of the EEC began intervening in each other's currencies in order to maintain their rates closer to their parities against one another than resulted from uncoordinated dollar intervention. This arrangement was known as the 'snake in the tunnel', since the European currencies were held close to one another and tended to fluctuate together (in a snake) within the dollar intervention points (which constituted the tunnel). In March 1973 the snake broke out of its tunnel, but because intervention was being undertaken in each other's currencies and not merely in dollars it was possible to maintain pegged rates within Europe while allowing the dollar to float. (At that time the members of the snake were Belgium-Luxembourg, Denmark, France, Germany, the Netherlands, Norway and Sweden.)

participant's currency whenever its own currency was at the ceiling against that other currency — i.e., at parity plus the margin.

Indicators, on-demand convertibility and MCI were the three central elements in the reformed system as envisaged by the United States. The operation of such a system may be described briefly. When sufficient pressure on the payments position of one country participating in the MCI group developed to push its exchange rate to the margin as against some other participant, the surplus country would intervene by purchasing the currency of the deficit country. It would then decide whether to retain this currency in its reserves (assuming that the deficit country did not veto this), or whether to demand conversion into primary reserve assets by the deficit country. In either event continued reserve gains by the surplus country and continued reserve losses by the deficit country[9] would ultimately bring their reserves to levels at which the indicator points would be breached and *both* countries would be obliged to initiate adjustment actions (at least if they were reasonably equal in size, though many Europeans feared that in practice the United States would escape pressure simply by virtue of the size of her permitted reserve fluctuations relative to theirs). If, as the United States always emphasized should be the case, the sum total of all countries' norms was set equal to the total quantity of reserves in existence, there was argued to be a presumption that the pressures on both deficit and surplus countries would be more or less equalized, in the sense that at any time one might expect to have roughly as many countries (on a weighted basis) in both categories being subjected to pressures. In the event of a speculative capital flow causing reserve movements which the IMF judged to be reversible rather than demanding adjustment, the indicator could have been overridden and the surplus country could have provided the deficit country with the extra liquidity it needed simply by refraining from requesting conversion for the time being.

There is no denying that these proposals had a comprehensive scope and a degree of originality that was in striking contrast to the concentration on a limited number of points of direct national concern practised by other countries (Italy excepted). Despite the overt concern with the achievement of a consistent system, however, the US proposals were clearly motivated by a concern to promote what were conceived as US national interests. The reserve indicator system was

9. One of the open questions about an indicator system was whether it should be based on gross or net reserves. Under a system based on gross reserves, the deficit country would, contrary to the statement in the text, have escaped adjustment pressure if the surplus country had chosen not to convert.

as obviously a response to Washington's 1970s-style fear that the rest of the world was conspiring to impose a permanent deficit on the United States as her vetoing of bancor had been a response to her 1940s-style fear that the rest of the world was set on exploiting her real resources by imposing on her a permanent surplus of terrifying size. On-demand convertibility seemed certain to preserve an important reserve role for the dollar, especially if the yield on the SDR were kept low and the SDR remained valued in terms of the dollar. And MCI was designed to increase the flexibility of the dollar exchange rate and to ensure that the United States in future had the freedom to float or to vary its par value. The cost of adopting MCI, from the US standpoint, would have been that it would have ended US immunity from the financial penalties of successful speculation on par value changes. One can wonder whether this consequence was fully appreciated when the reserve indicator proposal was adopted, since one result of an indicator system would surely have been the provision of improved information from which the speculators might have profited.

Another distinctive attitude of the United States was her insistence that balance-of-payments policy should properly be directed at the preservation of overall balance, as reflected in reserve changes, rather than the achievement of a particular target for the current account. No doubt some would explain this position by the fact that the United States, as a capital-abundant country, was almost certain to be a capital exporter, so that overall balance would imply a current account surplus. But it may also have reflected the general attachment to the principles of a market economy of the US Administration. Whether the policy of free capital movements indicated by *laissez-faire* was in fact in the national interest of the United States is a debatable question. In general there is a presumption that capital-exporting countries are able to improve their own welfare, at the cost of that of other countries, by restricting the export of capital, since private capitalists tend to export capital up to the point where the marginal private product of investment at home is equal to that of investment abroad, whereas national welfare maximization requires that the marginal social product of domestic investment be equated to the marginal private product of investment abroad. Because of the existence of profits taxation and of the effect of a greater capital stock in raising wages, there is a presumption that the marginal social product of investment exceeds its marginal private product (although where investment creates pollution there is a factor operating in the opposite direction that may be important in particular instances). Hence it may seem odd that the United States should have placed so much stress on the achievement of capital mobility. (There is a Marxist explanation of the phenomenon,

which would attribute US policy to the fact that it reflected the
interests of the capitalist class rather than those of the nation as a
whole.)

There was one other respect in which it was difficult to see how the
United States furthered any serious national interest by the stand she
took in the C-20. This concerned her adamant opposition to the link.
The reason always given was that the link would tend to undermine
confidence in the SDR. It may well be true that there were one or two
important potential SDR creditors who were suspicious of the SDR on
account of its lack of 'backing', and whose suspicions would have
been aggravated by the link. But such solicitude for the SDR was
unconvincing when accompanied, as it was, by opposition to change in
the basis of valuation and improvement in the yield of the SDR. One
possible motive for US opposition to the link was the financial one: that
more SDRs for developing countries would have meant less
seigniorage for the United States. The sum potentially involved was,
however, so trivial, especially in comparison with the shortfall of the US
aid programme below the internationally-agreed target of 1 per cent of
GNP, that it is very difficult to believe that it justified the loss of
goodwill among the developing countries. It is also possible that the
United States objected to the loss of the power of patronage provided
by the ability to disburse aid. Or the Administration may have feared
Congressional opposition to the erosion of its authority over aid implicit
in the link.

Europe and Japan

If the main aim of the United States in the reform negotiations was to
achieve a system with a broad symmetry of obligations between
surplus countries and deficit countries, the main aim of the 'Europeans'
was to achieve a measure of symmetry between 'reserve centres' (by
which was meant the principal reserve centre, the United States) and
other countries. A situation of monetary dependence, such as was
implied by a dollar standard, was unacceptable for broad political
reasons of national self-respect, because of the resulting inequality of
power. In the past the mechanism establishing United States
obligations in the system had been (official) convertibility, and it was
therefore natural that the restoration of some form of convertibility
should have been a major objective. In some quarters there was still a
tendency to treat convertibility as a symbol without a clear concept of
its economic significance, but this was less true in Europe than in the
United States. In general the Europeans accepted the intellectual case
for seeking asset settlement, rather than on-demand convertibility, that

had been argued in the *Reform Report*. This was one result of the general mistrust of a reserve currency system that was engendered by the way the Europeans had found themselves locked in to support of the dollar during the 1960s.

The Europeans accepted the fact that the dollar overhang presented a problem to any rapid resumption of convertibility by the United States. This was, indeed, one of the reasons for favouring a system of asset settlement rather than on-demand convertibility. But even with asset settlement (unless it were achieved through designation) there was a need for a measure of consolidation of the dollar overhang, and so the Europeans tended to favour the creation of a Substitution Account in the IMF and some also favoured funding. The Europeans also accepted the fact that, in the reformed system, convertibility would be into SDRs rather than gold; indeed, this was one of the few points that had been taken for granted by everyone since the shape of a long-term reform was first discussed at the 1971 Annual Meetings.

There was also a fair measure of agreement among the Europeans on a number of the proposals being advanced by other countries. Except for Germany, they were willing to concede the link to the developing countries. Most of them were strongly critical of the US indicator proposal, less because of opposition to the general philosophy of strengthening the obligation on surplus countries to play their part in the adjustment process than because of dislike of particular features of the proposal, which served to reinforce a general suspicion that the indicator proposal was a way of getting the rest of the world to make the adjustments needed to keep the US balance of payments in order. In the first place, they intensely disliked the PAHL proposal, because of the fear that in practice it would enable the United States to escape adjustment pressures when she was in deficit and the principal surplus countries were prevented from converting. A reserve indicator system would still have put pressure on the reserve centre in deficit provided that it was based on net rather than gross reserves, but the Europeans were sceptical of the possibility of developing consciously designed pressures as potent as that of reserve depletion. Second, the idea of providing 'elasticity' through variations in reserve currency holdings was regarded as naive, since the natural reaction of a country making an unconstrained portfolio choice would be to get rid of the currency of any country that needed credit as quickly as possible in case it were devalued. Elasticity would therefore be perverse — unless, at least, there were either political arm-twisting to persuade countries not to convert at times when the deficit country was short of liquidity, or else the PAHL came into operation. The Europeans were anxious to excise political arm-twisting, which they felt had not been conducive to harmonious relations in the past, and they therefore argued that the necessary elasticity be provided through multilateral credit facilities, for example within the IMF. And they were certainly not attracted by reliance on the PAHL, since it would only be the deficit of an extremely large financial power that would be likely to be large enough to push other countries above their PAHLs. Third, most of the Europeans retained a desire to preserve (or, after March 1973, to restore) a par value system, and they were very conscious of the fact that this would be made more difficult by the presence of an indicator mechanism because of the assistance that such a system would give to speculators in predicting forthcoming par value changes.

Although the Europeans shared considerable interests, their position was far from monolithic. It is therefore appropriate to examine the main strands of thought in the principal countries.

The country that displayed the greatest concern for the development of a consistent position in the mainstream of thought, rather than being preoccupied by particular national concerns, was undoubtedly Italy. The Italians had invented the 'third approach' to asset settlement — the idea of using the dollars in a Substitution Account as a buffer stock — in the hope of overcoming the developing countries' resistance to asset settlement on the ground that it interfered with freedom of reserve composition, and they sought to promote, amplify and modify this approach, as occasion demanded, in the C-20. They were enthusiastic supporters of a substitution operation to reduce the dollar overhang. When the United States revealed her proposals for a reserve indicator system, the Italians countered with an alternative proposal, which proposed using the cyclically adjusted basic balance rather than the level of reserves as a presumptive indicator (on the grounds that reserve changes could be manipulated too easily, and in any event contained important random elements that should not be allowed to influence adjustment). Despite this concern for the system as a whole, however, the Italians were not immune from the desire to protect their particular national interests when the occasion demanded. This was illustrated most clearly by their pressure to 'mobilize gold' during the later stages of the C-20 negotiations, notwithstanding their long-standing commitment to enthroning the SDR. The fact was, however, that Italy was confronted with a chronic payments deficit as a joint result of capital flight, domestic production difficulties and the increase in the price of oil, and as a result she came close to exhausting her currency reserves and borrowing possibilities. The one asset left was a vast stock of gold acquired during the years of heavy surplus in the mid-1960s. The prospect of having to sell this off on the private market, which would inevitably have depressed the gold price, was obviously far less attractive than being able to sell gold to other monetary authorities at the market price. (The compromise eventually reached by the G-10 during the final meeting of the C-20 was to allow the use of gold as collateral for loans at a market-related price, which enabled Italy to raise a substantial additional loan from Germany.)

Despite the fact that their economic position made them the dominant European power and would have enabled them to play the leading role in the negotiations from the European side, the Germans chose to adopt a position based very much on their particular national concerns. In the German view, the great failing of the Bretton Woods system was the inflationary bias that it had developed in its later years, and the prime object of reform was to eliminate this bias. This German concern is readily understandable in view of the fact that they were more determined — and perhaps also found it easier — to prevent the domestic generation of inflation than other countries, but had seen their efforts regularly undermined by the importation of inflation from abroad. Their concern with inflation led to a preoccupation with the establishment of effective control over the volume of global liquidity. This meant not only establishing a system of asset settlement so as to prevent any future US deficit leading to an expansion of global liquidity, but also restricting the freedom of reserve holders to switch into 'non-traditional' reserve assets. It is worth pausing to analyse why the Germans wished to limit the freedom of reserve composition, since this was one of the more important subsidiary issues in the reform negotiations.

'Non-traditional reserve assets' are defined as Euro-dollars and those European currencies that have begun to be held in reserves in recent years, principally the DM but also the Swiss franc, the French franc and others. A switch of reserves by some third country out of dollars into one of these non-traditional reserve assets leads to an expansion of global liquidity. For example, a switch from dollars to DM leaves the reserves of the third country (and also US liabilities) unchanged, but increases German reserves by the sum switched, thus expanding global liquidity (not to mention making it difficult to prevent an increase in the German money supply). With a switch into DM the Germans could at least try to offset the expansionary impact of the reserve switch — although they resented the reserve-currency role forced upon them, since they did not need the extra liquidity it offered them in the short run, found themselves subjected to a financial loss as the yield they paid on DM tended to exceed that earned on the dollars they acquired, and believed that in the long run the operation of a secondary reserve currency was liable to land a country in an exposed liquidity position from which the only certain defence was the maintenance of 100 per cent reserves against reserve liabilities.[10] With a switch into some other non-traditional reserve asset the expansionary potential was far less likely to be offset. This was particularly true of a switch from US Treasury Bills to the Euro-dollar market, which led to a direct increase in the lending potential of the Euro-market. The borrowing would typically be undertaken by the residents of some fourth country, the central bank of which would thus acquire an increase in dollar reserves, which it in turn would place either in the United States or in the Euro-market. To the extent that these funds were placed in the United States, there would be a once-over increase in international liquidity as a result of the reserve switch (as in the case of a switch into DM). To the extent, however, that the reserve gain was placed back in the Euro-market, there would be a further increase in the lending potential of the Euro-market and a process of multiple credit expansion would occur.[11] In order to curtail this multiple expansion (the 'carousel effect', as it was called), the central banks of the Group of Ten had in 1971 agreed to avoid future increases in their placements in the Euro-markets. But the developing countries had become increasingly conscious of the possibility of raising the yield on their reserve portfolios by diversifying into the Euro-market and the new reserve currencies, and there had therefore been a continued expansion in the proportion of Euro-dollars in reserves during the 1970s. This provided yet another example of the destabilizing implications of a system with multiple reserve assets. Hence Germany set it as one of her main objectives in the reform to secure curbs on portfolio choice adequate to ensure future control of international liquidity.

10. These German attitudes towards the reserve-currency role (and also to extensive private foreign holding of DM) explain the somewhat unorthodox version of funding that ther Germans indicated they would be willing to undertake during the C-20. This would have involved Germany swapping some of her short-term dollar assets for long-term assets with a mobilization clause. Mobilization would have been permitted in the event of a reflux into dollars of the funds (either private or official) that had been shifted from the dollar to the DM during the years of weakness of the dollar. Such a solution would have been financially attractive to Germany in so far as the interest rate on the funded debt exceeded the short-term rate, as well as setting an example of funding that might have persuaded other countries to follow her lead and thus contributed to the German objective of curtailing international liquidity. Critics argued that funding with a mobilization clause was a contradiction in terms, and represented a German attempt to have her cake and eat it too.

11. Indeed, central bank redepositing appears in practice to be the only significant source of multiple credit expansion in the Euro-market, though even this does not result in a Euro-dollar multiplier much in excess of unity, because of interest-arbitrage leakages from the market. J. Hewson and E. Sakakibara, 'The Euro-Dollar Multiplier: A Portfolio Approach', IMF *Staff Papers*, July 1974.

Germany also remained opposed to the link. Her objections to the link were based on its possible inflationary implications, as regards both the greater first-round impact on aggregate demand of a given volume of SDRs if these were allocated to countries expecting to spend them rather than hold them, and the pressure for greater SDR allocations if these were going to provide aid.

The French had traditionally led the resistance to monetary domination of Western Europe by the dollar, and this fact inevitably gave them an important role in the C-20. Their aim continued to be that of curbing the dollar, though their lingering love affair with gold and their strong attachment to pegged exchange rates tended to impede their pursuit of this objective by the most direct and obvious means. The attachment to gold was understandable in financial terms: French gold reserves were large, as was the hoarding of gold by the private sector. But Anglo-Saxons never seem to have succeeded in divining just what it is that motivates the almost theological aversion to flexible exchange rates of the French (an aversion that is nevertheless not held with sufficient fervour to have prevented the franc being allowed to float out of the snake when market pressures developed in January 1974), although one factor is, no doubt, the desire of the French Treasury to strengthen its power position *vis-à-vis* the spending ministries. The French belief in pegged exchange rates, which would have been threatened by intensified speculation, and the potential effect of the PAHL in obliging countries to accumulate dollars involuntarily and so enable the United States to escape adjustment pressures, were probably the major reasons for their particularly critical reaction to the US indicator proposal. It was not that the French were unsympathetic to the general aim of trying to ensure that surplus countries played a proper part in the adjustment process: after all, they faced a perennial dispute as to who should initiate adjustment whenever they got out of line with their German neighbours. Indeed, it was the French who initiated the compromise proposal for a reserve ceiling beyond which reserves would have to be deposited in a special account in the Fund, where they would carry a negative interest rate.

Britain had a long history of involvement at the centre of international finance, which was reflected in the fact that her IMF quota was still easily the second largest (after that of the United States). Mr. Barber's initiative at the 1971 Annual Meeting was followed by an active role in getting the reform negotiations started, but during the negotiations themselves the British played a relatively minor role. This may have been partly as a result of the appointment of an Englishman as Chairman of the C-20 Deputies, partly because two decades of economic failure had sapped British self-confidence, and partly because the British were torn between loyalty to their new partners in the European community and their instinctive sympathy for a number of the positions being espoused by the United States. The US position in 1972 did, after all, look remarkably like the British position of 1944: both called for penalties to force surplus countries to adjust, no circumscribing of the reserve-currency role and ample international liquidity.

One respect in which a direct national interest led to a distinctive emphasis in British policy concerned the topic of substitution. If a Substitution Account were to have been created, it would have enabled holders of sterling as well as dollars to substitute SDRs for their currency holdings, and would thus have enabled Britain to dispose of the reserve currency role that she had so zealously defended at the end of the war and through the 1950s but had become so disillusioned with during the 1960s. And this role would have been ended in a way that did not carry the uncomfortable burden of having to earn a current surplus of a size adequate to repay the sterling balances in the short run. The British also made an important contribution in the form of the invention of a symmetrical intervention system based not on multicurrency intervention but on SDR intervention without private holding of SDRs. This had previously been considered a contradiction in terms, since market intervention is achieved by exchanging one's own currency for the intervention medium, but it was pointed out that SDR intervention could be achieved without the private sector holding SDRs provided that market participants were required simultaneously to sell the SDRs they acquired to the central bank of a second country in exchange for its currency. This proposal was examined in the report of the Technical Group on Intervention and Settlement and is discussed in the Appendix to Chapter 5.

Most of the smaller European countries tended to be conservative in their outlook. The Iberians were so conservative as to be no more than marginal participants. Both Austria and Belgium had an attachment to par values and monetary discipline and retained a respect for gold. Perhaps surprisingly, in view of their fame for progressive domestic economic policies, the Scandinavians also tended to adopt a conservative stance, although they did not have any particular attachment to gold, which is perhaps not surprising since they did not own much of it — as the other smaller West European countries (Austria, Belgium, the Netherlands, Portugal and Spain) all did. The Dutch shared a belief in monetary discipline with the other smaller European countries, but they were far more open-minded on the exchange rate question. The common interest of the smaller European countries lay in their continuing desire to contain inflation and their common difficulty in achieving this in an inflationary world with economies as open as theirs were. Hence the priority they attached to the restoration of international monetary discipline. And, since this depended on the achievement of an agreed reform, one can understand why the Dutch in particular made major efforts to establish agreed European positions that gave some hope of providing a basis for compromise with the United States. [12] Despite the agreement on broad aims between the Europeans, this was far from easy when it came to hammering out common positions on specific issues.

The Japanese played a more modest role in the reform negotiations than might have been expected in view of their emergence as one of the three major economic powers in the (non-communist) world. Japanese economic expansion had been based on export-led growth for years, and there was a widespread belief in Japan that an undervalued currency was desirable in order to perpetuate her outstanding growth performance. This was reflected in the decision in August 1971 to keep the Tokyo foreign exchange market open for 2 weeks at the old parity, which cushioned Japanese exporters from the immediate penalties of appreciation by enabling them to cover outstanding contracts at the previous rate. (Japan was able to limit speculative profits almost entirely to her own nationals by virtue of her still-stringent exchange controls over foreign holdings of yen.) She reluctantly agreed to revalue the yen at the Smithsonian Conference, and again agreed reluctantly to float in February 1973, but she nonetheless remained among the most dedicated opponents of exchange rate flexibility. The attraction of pegged exchange rates appears to have been the (questionable) belief in the desirability of having an undervalued currency, coupled with confidence in her ability to make any fixed rate an undervalued rate in due course. The Japanese were also among the most hostile critics of the reserve indicator proposal, which was perhaps not surprising in view of the fact that during the first year of the C-20 negotiations they were under intense pressure from the United States to adjust away their surplus, and therefore tended to interpret the reserve indicator as a mechanism that would strengthen the US hand in any similar future confrontation (which was, after all, what the United States hoped it would achieve). As a major creditor country which expected to remain that way, Japan also had a strong interest in the SDR being a high-yielding asset. She

---

12. The lack of rigidity in Dutch views on the exchange rate question was well exemplified by the 1974 Per Jacobsson lecture of the Dutch Deputy, Conrad Oort. See C. J. Oort, *Steps to International Monetary Order*, Per Jacobsson Foundation, Washington DC, 1974.

pursued this interest by supporting the 'strong SDR', interpreted first (especially when the yen was the strongest currency) as an SDR that appreciated with the strongest currency, and subsequently as an SDR defined on the basis of the 'asymmetrical basket' (see Chapter 6).

The developing countries

The developing countries had no doubt that what they wanted out of the reform was above all a greater transfer of real resources to promote development. Since the cause of underdevelopment is a lack of real resources and underdevelopment is an unsatisfactory state of affairs, this was a highly rational objective. Moreover, the reform negotiations were a logical occasion on which to pursue this objective. Not only had the United States taken the lead in seeking to link the reform of other aspects of the international economic system (notably trade liberalization) with the question of monetary reform, but the seigniorage from SDR creation was the only obvious source of income that could be redistributed through an international decision rather than requiring the charity of individual national legislatures.

The primary aim of the developing countries was, therefore, the establishment of a link between SDR creation and development assistance. This aim was pursued unremittingly, and considerable diplomatic skill and patience were exercised in lining up the hundred-odd developing countries that were members of the Fund in a united front, articulated through the G-24. Not only did the developing countries achieve agreement on the principle of the link, but they also reached a decision on the form of the link that they preferred; namely, that the basis of SDR allocation be changed so as to allocate a greater proportion of newly created SDRs to developing countries than they would have been entitled to on the basis of allocation in proportion to quotas, with the least developed countries entitled to a still more generous share than the other developing countries.[13] The only bargaining counter that the developing countries used to promote the link was the implicit threat to refuse to ratify any reform that did not include the link, and this had no great bargaining value until such time as the industrial countries had agreed on a reform that they were anxious to see translated into an amendment of the IMF Articles.

13. The alternative proposal was that a proportion of newly created SDRs should be allocated to development finance institutions (the World Bank, International Development Association, and the regional development banks: the African Development Bank, the Asian Development Bank, and the Inter-American Development Bank).

The developing countries also pursued other proposals that might have stimulated resource transfer. After the failure of the Technical Group on the Link to make any progress, they pressed for, and succeeded in securing, a Technical Group on the Transfer of Real Resources with wider terms of reference. The proposals considered by this group at the instigation of the developing countries included an obligation on developed countries to avoid cutting aid in the course of remedying a deficit, but to increase aid when in surplus if they were not already achieving the aid targets;[14] use for development finance of the payments made by reserve centres to amortize their debts to a Substitution Account; and improved access to capital markets. In addition, the developing countries gave a cautious welcome to the proposal for an 'Extended Fund Facility' that would allow them under certain circumstances to draw on the IMF for longer periods and in greater sums than permitted under normal Fund rules — though their welcome was qualified by the proviso that the facility was to be regarded as a complement to, rather than a substitute for, the link. And, when the subject of gold began to be discussed at the tail-end of the C-20, the developing countries were obviously attracted by proposals to allow the IMF to sell its gold on the private market and to use the profit over the official price for purchase of the obligations of development finance institutions. The only one of these proposals that won acceptance in the course of the C-20 negotiations was the Extended Fund Facility. However, the developing countries secured a second success in this area with the agreement to create the Development Committee as a regular forum for the specific purpose of supervizing the process of, and proposals for, resource transfer, which opened the possibility of gaining further concessions in the future. And, after the C-20 finished work, agreement was reached to sell one sixth of the IMF's gold and to use the profits for development finance (see Chapter 6).

There were two other areas of debate where the developing countries displayed interest and tended to adopt a common position. The first was the exchange rate regime, where most of them supported retention of the adjustable peg quite forcefully. Even those developing countries that had themselves adopted a floating rate or crawling peg argued for retention of the adjustable peg by the developed countries. The arguments used to support this preference ranged from unproven

14. The aid targets recommended by the United Nations are that the gross flow of financial resources to developing countries amount to 1 per cent of GNP, and that official development assistance (ODA) amount to 0·7 per cent of GNP. The OECD Development Assistance Committee has recommended that ODA have a concessional element of at least 84 per cent.

and theoretically implausible deleterious effects on their terms of trade to the effect of adding yet another source of variation in their environment on their need for reserves and the willingness of their industries to participate in the foreign trade sector. Subsequent investigation has revealed that the effect on their need for reserves, at least, is negligible.[15] However, in so far as the developing countries were prepared to shift their reserves around in anticipation of par value changes, they had a more rational reason for supporting retention of the adjustable peg than they cared to admit: the hope that they could get in on the speculative profits that the system generated.

The other area in which the developing countries tended to take a common stand concerned the freedom of reserve composition. In recent years an increasing number of developing countries have adopted more aggressive portfolio management policies, which have involved both a shift into non-traditional reserve assets and a willingness to shift between reserve assets in the light of expected yields (which include, of course, the effects of exchange rate changes). They valued the additional income yielded by these policies, and displayed great reluctance to consider surrendering their freedom in this direction in the interests of stabilizing the system. Whether they would have been willing to see their freedom circumscribed had they been offered a *quid pro quo* such as the link in return is a hypothetical question.

The developing countries were, however, no more a monolithic bloc than the Europeans were. The most important subset of countries with important interests distinct from those of the majority were the oil exporters. Even before the quadrupling of oil prices in late 1973, they were looking forward to a lengthy period as major creditor countries. They had, therefore, a strong interest in the existence of reserve assets with an attractive yield, and in avoiding limits on reserve holding such as would have been implied had they been subjected to a reserve indicator system. The United States was well aware of the need to exempt the oil exporters from her proposed indicator system: her initial proposal envisaged the creation of special 'investment funds' under which oil exporters could hold official funds for long-term investment purposes provided that they observed 'certain criteria with respect to

15. J. Williamson, 'Generalized Floating and the Reserve Needs of Developing Countries', in D. M. Leipziger, ed., *The International Monetary System and Developing Nations*, Agency for International Development, Washington DC, 1976. The paper proved that the percentage increase in reserves needed to maintain the same level of security against reserve depletion in the presence of generalized floating was almost certainly less than 1 per cent for all developing countries.

term, size and nature of the holdings'.[16] The oil exporters remained suspicious of the conditions that other countries might attempt to impose upon them in return for the privilege of having investment funds excluded from the indicator system, but negotiations never got to the point of testing whether these suspicions could be overcome.

Even excluding the oil exporters, there was a broad spectrum of interests among the developing countries. At one extreme lay a number of 'newly-industrializing' countries that have in recent years passed the point of 'take-off'. These are countries like Brazil, Korea, Mexico Singapore and Taiwan, which have based their development strategy principally on a policy of export promotion and therefore have a strong interest in the preservation of a liberal international economic order. Many of these countries attached great importance to freedom of reserve composition and relatively little to the link. At the other extreme lay the least-developed countries of the Indian subcontinent and the greater part of Africa between the Sahara and the Zambezi, which were still overwhelmingly dependent on primary commodities for export revenue. They therefore had a natural interest in schemes for commodity price stabilization, but, perhaps because of their commodity boom in progress at the time of the C-20, coupled with the usual myopia, there was little pressure for the inclusion of commodity agreements within the ambit of the C-20 negotiations. The main exception was Sri Lanka, whose exports crop — tea — had not benefited from the commodity boom. In an effort to promote interest in commodity agreements, the Sri Lankan Deputy, Lal Jayawardena, unearthed and circulated Keynes' abortive war-time proposals for a comprehensive scheme of commodity agreements financed by the IMF.[17] But the main thrust of the least developed countries' policy was to secure an increase in aid through the link. Between the two extremes of the newly industrializing and the least developed there lay both middle-income countries whose progress had faltered, such as Argentina and Chile, and low-income countries which had started to make economic progress and established their international creditworthiness, such as Egypt, Indonesia, the Ivory Coast, Kenya and Malaysia.

Considering the range of interests to be accommodated, the measure of success that the developing countries achieved in forging a common position was not unimpressive. Their solidarity was demonstrated in a way that surprised many in the West when most of

16. *The US Proposals, op.cit.*, p.170, para.28(e).
17. These papers were subsequently published. See J. M. Keynes, 'The International Control of Raw Materials', *Journal of International Economics*, 1974(4).

those developing countries that suffered a financial loss from the oil price increase refused to join with the West in condemning the action of the Organization of Petroleum Exporting Countries (OPEC).

The 'Heretics'

Three significant participants in the C-20 negotiations did not fall into any of the groups of countries considered above. Apart from the fact that at one time they were the three great dominions of the British Empire, which is presumably a coincidence, their only common characteristic was that in one respect or another they stood outside even such consensus as the C-20 achieved.

The first of these countries is Canada, whose heresy was to believe in floating. The Canadian dollar had floated from 1950 to 1962, and Canada initiated the trend that climaxed in generalized floating by again floating in 1970. Academic opinion is virtually unanimous in concluding that, apart from the gross mishandling that led to the end of the first float in 1961-62, Canada's floating exchange rate served her well.[18] (However, there is still some doubt as to the extent to which a one-to-one relationship with the US dollar provided a psychological parity that resulted in speculation being more stabilizing in the Canadian case than can be expected generally. It is therefore proper to observe a certain caution in using Canadian experience to dismiss fears that floating exchange rates may prove to be pretty volatile.) The Canadian authorities endorsed the academic view regarding the success of their floating rate, and they recognized that the extent of capital market interdependence with their dominant neighbour ruled out any degree of monetary independence under a fixed rate regime. They were determined not to be bullied back into the adjustable peg — either by the Smithsonian realignment, by the decision to base the reformed system on 'stable but adjustable par values', or by an over-restrictive set of IMF Guidelines for Floating. The issue of floating aside, the Canadians played their traditional international role of bringing a sympathetic, fair-minded, honest and constructive presence to the conference table.

The second 'heretic' is South Africa, whose heresy was to believe in gold. The outstanding economic fact about the South African economy is its dependence on the gold mining industry, which in 1974 provided

18. See, for example, P. Wonnacott, *The Floating Canadian Dollar*, American Enterprise Institute, Washington DC, 1972, or R. M. Dunn, *Canada's Experience with Fixed and Flexible Exchange Rates in a North American Capital Market*, Canadian-American Committee, Washington DC, 1971.

11 per cent of GDP and 45 per cent of export revenue. It is therefore entirely unsurprising that South Africa should favour an important monetary role for gold, since this can hardly help but raise the price at which she can sell her principal export product. What is surprising is not that South Africa should have pursued this natural interest, but that she should have reconciled herself to the SDR to the extent of joining the Special Drawing Account. In fact this was a perfectly rational step: given that her own non-participation would in no way jeopardize the future of the SDR, she had the same incentive as any other country to become a participant. And the economic future of the gold mining industry seems reasonably assured even in the absence of a commodity stabilization programme for gold on the part of the world's monetary authorities, so that South Africans can be sufficiently relaxed on the subject to appraise their interests rationally.

The final 'heretic' is Australia, whose heresy was the desire to be allowed to do her own thing unencumbered by any international restraints. Australia is probably the only country in the world of any size that would have been perfectly happy living on a dollar standard (with the possible exception of the United States). Australia felt herself to be a small country that threatened no one, did not seek to mould the rest of the world to her convenience, but merely asked it to leave her alone, confident of her ability to adapt to the world as she found it. This philosophy was reflected in her opposition to reserve indicators, and especially to any idea of pressures being triggered by indicators; her indifference to arguments about asset settlement; and her reluctance to hold SDRs unless they offered a competitive rate of return.

The Australian position is one that essentially denies that formal international organization serves any serious social function. An acid test of the validity of this thesis is to ask whether the world would lose anything if it were composed entirely of countries with Australian 'Stone Age' attitudes. When one recalls that Australia revalued in 1973 at the height of the world boom and devalued in 1974 in the midst of world depression, accompanying her revaluation by import liberalization and her devaluation by increased tariffs, one may feel that the restraints supposedly involved in membership of the IMF and GATT could usefully be strengthened rather than dispensed with.

5

Adjustment

'There will be a better working of the adjustment process', proclaimed paragraph 4 of the *Outline of Reform*, in a declaration of faith that many observers felt to be optimistic in the light of the prescriptions that followed. But, however inappropriate expressions of faith may seem in a document that was supposed to describe agreed proposals, the aspiration for a better working of the adjustment process was universal. The failure to secure prompt adjustment during the 1960s was recognized to have been the proximate cause of the breakdown of the Bretton Woods system, as well as the cause of significant resource misallocation and disruption of domestic stabilization policies. Hence a major objective of the reform exercise was agreed by all to be that of securing an improvement in the adjustment process.

The present chapter is devoted to an examination of the substantive issues that arose in the course of the discussions in the C-20 on the subject of payments adjustment. As noted in Chapter 1, there are two distinct aspects to this topic. The first concerns the question as to which country has the responsibility of initiating adjustment action, and when; the second concerns the techniques that should be used to effect adjustment when adjustment is desired. There is a vast and rich academic literature on the latter subject: it embraces *inter alia* Meade's analysis of the role of exchange rate changes in resolving 'dilemma' situations, the assignment problem, the monetary theory of the balance of payments and the analysis of the welfare costs of securing adjustment through payments controls. In striking contrast, the question of determining the circumstances under which adjustment is called for has received no more than spasmodic and incidental attention in the academic literature: the overwhelming majority of writers have been content simply to assume a target of 'external balance'. Where this has been spelt out at all it has generally been interpreted as a zero reserve change, despite the fact that countries with inadequate or excess reserves can hardly be expected to subscribe to this objective.[1] It was in fact the question of adjustment responsibilities that generated the major controversies in the C-20. This reflected a widespread feeling that the failure to secure adjustment in the 1960s was not only, and perhaps even not mainly, a result of the absence of an effective crisis-proof adjustment technique, but was to a major extent attributable to the ambiguity and disagreement as to the assignment of responsibility as to which country should initiate adjustment.

It is therefore appropriate to examine in some detail the question of adjustment responsibilities, and the first half of the chapter is devoted to this topic. But, if academic economists have traditionally ignored this question, it is equally true that the C-20 dismissed the question of adjustment techniques with a lack of controversy that was hardly justified by the intellectual merit of the prescriptions embodied in the *Outline*. The second half of the chapter is therefore devoted to the more traditional aspect of the topic of adjustment. An appendix deals with the distinct but related issue of the intervention system.

Adjustment responsibilities

There was a very general desire among participants in the C-20 to reconstruct international monetary relations on a more symmetrical basis than had characterized the Bretton Woods system, especially in its later stages when the world had found itself on a reluctant dollar standard. Both the United States and the Europeans had come to the conclusion that the asymmetries inherent in a dollar standard were detrimental to their interests : the United States because of a belief that this imposed a more or less permanent deficit upon her, and the Europeans because of a belief that the loss of monetary autonomy was

---

1. The main exception concerns the literature on optimal reserves, which was surveyed in J. Williamson, 'International Liquidity — A Survey', *Economic Journal*, September 1973, Section II.1. The optimal reserves literature has in recent years been becoming increasingly concerned with the interaction between liquidity and adjustment; see, for example, L. Nybery and S. Viotti, 'Optimal Reserves and Adjustment Policies', *Swedish Journal of Economics*, December 1974. The lack of economic analysis of the principles that welfare economics would indicate to be relevant in determining payments objectives, coupled with the importance that the subject assumed in the reform negotiations, prompted an attempt on my part to fill the gap; see J. Williamson, 'Payments Objectives and Economic Welfare', IMF *Staff Papers*, November 1973. Much of the analysis in the first half of this chapter is based on that paper.

at best offensive to national self-respect and at worst obliged them to import inflation. It is, of course, true that any search for complete symmetry between nations as diverse in their economic size and characteristics as the 126 then-members of the IMF would have been doomed to failure, if only because the private market does not deal as freely in Brazilian cruzeiros as in US dollars. But the C-20 never embarked on a futile search for an illusive total symmetry: the concern was for symmetry in certain crucial respects, most notably with regard to adjustment obligations.[2]

The proposals
Even within the field of adjustment obligations, however, different countries had radically different perceptions of the important asymmetries that required correction. The critical asymmetry to the United States was that between deficit and surplus countries, while to most other countries it was the asymmetry between the reserve centre and the rest of the world that was crucial. Hence the United States was led to devise the reserve indicator proposal described in the previous chapter, while the Europeans regarded asset settlement as the key element of a more symmetrical system.

There was, of course, no contradiction between these two proposals: they were addressed to different asymmetries, and it would have been possible to construct a system that incorporated both. Indeed, in vital respects the proposals were strikingly parallel, for both proposals rested on the presupposition that a country's adjustment obligations should be determined by its stock of reserves. This is by no

194172

2. The chief academic critic of the search for symmetry was R. N. Cooper, 'Eurodollars, Reserve Dollars, and Asymmetries in the International Monetary System', *Journal of International Economics*, 1972(2). His demonstration that total symmetry was inconceivable, in the absence of far more drastic reforms (with far greater cost in terms of disruption of the efficient operation of private markets) than those contemplated by the C-20, was convincing on most — though not all — points. (One erroneous argument was that satisfaction of the equal value principle required that the SDR be valued at par in terms of one currency: the error in this emerges in the discussion of the valuation of the SDR in the next chapter.) The demonstration was fundamentally irrelevant, however, since those asymmetries shown to be inherent were of only marginal relevance to the search for symmetry in adjustment obligations undertaken by the C-20. Marina v. N. Whitman ('The Current and Future Role of the Dollar: How Much Symmetry?', *'Brookings Papers on Economic Activity*, 1974 (3)) has since criticized the search for symmetry in adjustment obligations, on the ground that US leadership in evolving a pattern of post-oil-price-increase current account objectives is essential, but conditional on her showing greater flexibility in adapting her payments targets than other countries can be expected to show (p.581). I confess that I do not understand the logic of the latter assertion.

means a trivial measure of agreement. When the reserve indicator proposal was first introduced into discussion, it was countered by the suggestion that the cyclically adjusted basic balance, rather than the reserve level, should be used as a presumptive indicator of the need for adjustment. It was argued that the use of reserve levels as indicators of the need for adjustment was wrong, both because reserves reflected a host of transitory factors stemming from the state of the cycle and reversible capital movements, and because of the concentration on reserve stocks rather than on payments flows. It was ironical that those who used these arguments were generally strong supporters of asset settlement, despite the fact that the purpose of the latter was to extend the discipline exerted by the threat of depletion of the stock of reserves to the country that had previously been exempt from such discipline. A consistent supporter of the use of basic balances as indicators of the need for adjustment should have sought to weaken the reserve constraint rather than to extend its application.

The mere fact that the two proposals both involved determining adjustment obligations on the basis of reserve stocks does not, however, imply that this is a sensible thing to do. The first and most fundamental question that needs to be asked is whether reserve stocks provide a logical basis for the exertion of payments discipline. This question has two parts: (a) stocks versus flows, and (b) reserves versus some other payments aggregate. After that it is natural to consider whether payments discipline should apply to surplus as well as to deficit countries, and whether there is a case for exempting reserve centres from its application. All these issues emerged to some extent and at some time during the C-20 discussions, most explicitly in the discussions of the two technical groups on indicators, but the following sections will attempt a more analytical treatment than these issues received in the C-20.

Stocks versus flows
The main objection to a stock-based indicator recorded in the *Documents of the C-20* was that advanced by Germany in the Technical Group on Adjustment (paras 6-8) to the effect that a system based on reserve stocks relative to norms was likely to prove inflationary since countries would claim extravagant norms, the IMF would create enough SDRs to equate the world total of reserves to the sum of norms, and many countries would then be unwilling to hold reserves as large as their norms and would thus impose unwanted surpluses on the

responsible minority. Such fears may not have been unreasonable, but it is possible to conceive of mechanisms to safeguard the system against such an inflationary bias: for example, by allocating countries' obligations to service SDRs in proportion to their norms, or by revising norms in the light of actual average reserve holdings.

There is, however, a far more fundamental question, which may have underlain the initial Italian counterproposal for a flow indicator, although it was never discussed explicitly. This is the question whether stocks or flows (or both) are significant for economic welfare. Tradition, no doubt based on the primacy of income flows in Keynesian analysis, has ascribed exclusive importance to flow imbalances. A payments deficit was regarded as a bad thing because it meant that a country had an excess of domestic investment over domestic saving that could not be justified by a productivity of the investment sufficiently high to attract an autonomous capital inflow from the rest of the world (and vice versa for a surplus); the flow imbalance, therefore, reflected an international misallocation of resources. If, because of a series of historical accidents, a country ran a large cumulative imbalance, that was unfortunate; but it provided no reason for seeking a large cumulative imbalance in the opposite direction, which would merely have created a new set of distortions. This argument seems to me to be untenable in view of the importance that contemporary theory attaches, for compelling theoretical and empirical reasons, to portfolio (stock) equilibrium. A cumulative payments imbalance, which is reflected in a deviation of a country's reserves from their optimum level, is necessarily associated with a deviation in either the country's capital stock or its claims to wealth ownership (except perhaps in the case where a country suffers simultaneously from a major departure from full employment and a payments deficit). A surplus, for example, means that absorption is below the level indicated by autonomous capital flows: either capital accumulation is lower, or savings are higher, than is compatible with payments balance. In either event, a perpetuation of flow imbalance leads to a stock disequilibrium: either the country ends up with a smaller proportion of the world capital stock than is consistent with the maximization of world income, or else it ends up with an above-equilibrium wealth-income ratio. The new theories of the consumption function teach that individuals in such a situation would reduce their savings; the corollary is that nations in such a state should reduce their savings. It follows that a stock disequilibrium, reflected in a deviation of reserves from an appropriate norm based on welfare-maximizing calculations of the character analysed in the literature on optimal reserves, should be reversed by a future flow imbalance of opposite sign to that which caused the stock disequilibrium.[3]

To argue that an appropriate distribution of stocks is necessary for the maximization of global economic welfare is not, however, to argue that flows can be disregarded. Indeed, the existence of diminishing marginal utility to the flow of consumption, and of increasing costs as the rate of investment rises, provide reasons for expecting welfare to be reduced by sharp flow imbalances (at least on current account) even where these do not lead to cumulative (stock) disequilibria, or where they serve to correct stock disequilibria. A rationally managed country will therefore seek to avoid both excessive flow imbalances and stock disequilibria. It follows that an appropriate payments target might be formulated as an underlying current account target (C^*) which suffices to transfer the underlying capital outflow (denoted K) determined by considerations of efficient resource allocation ('thrift and productivity'), as well as making a contribution to restoring reserves (R) to an appropriate target level (R^*). Algebraically, the payments target may be expressed:

$$C^* = K + \alpha(R^* - R) + (\mathring{R}^* - \text{SDR allocations}).\qquad(1)$$

The optimal reserve level, R^*, and the speed of adjustment, α, are determined simultaneously by an optimizing analysis of the character developed in the literature on optimal reserves.* The final term in the equation covers the need for secular growth in the level of reserves.

The fundamental question that should arise in deciding whether to base an indicator structure on stocks or flows is, therefore, which of these could best encourage countries to pursue a mutually consistent set of adjustment policies satisfying equation (1). The answer to this question would seem to depend upon the role that the indicator is supposed to fulfil: in particular, upon whether it is supposed to diagnose when adjustment is needed, or whether it is supposed to define a country's adjustment obligations. The difference between a

---

3. Such a criterion does, of course, require a number of glosses in its application. For example, stock disequilibrium may occur without being reflected in reserve statistics: consider a country that undertakes large-scale official foreign borrowing (or adopts other capital account policies with similar effects) in order to sustain consumption at a level higher than is consistent with the maximization of intertemporal welfare. Or consider a country (Germany 1975?) whose economic structure is so dependent on exports that any attempt to reduce savings — i.e., the current account surplus — rapidly might result in excessive microeconomic dislocation; it is conceivable that the second-best policy, given the existence of adjustment costs, involves acceptance of a current account surplus and encouragement of a capital outflow for a lengthy period ahead.

*It is possible that a truly optimum policy would involve α varying with the size of the deviation of R from R^* rather than being constant.

'diagnostic' indicator and a 'definitional' indicator is fundamental, even though it was sufficiently elusive to have been overlooked throughout the C-20 negotiations. A diagnostic indicator states that adjustment actions should be taken when certain threshold points are breached. A definitional indicator states that adjustment policy should be continuously guided by the objective of avoiding certain thresholds being breached. If one is seeking a diagnostic indicator, it is not clear that a flow indicator would be particularly useful, but there is a compelling reason for believing that a stock indicator would be unsatisfactory: the fact that a country hitting a reserve ceiling would be induced to adjust in order to create a deficit to eliminate its excess reserves, but then not expected to take any further adjustment action until it hit another indicator point at the minimum level, when it would have to adjust to create a surplus, and so on, would build an unnecessary and costly element of instability into the system.[4] If, on the other hand, one is seeking a definitional indicator, then a stock indicator which encourages a country to adjust when its reserves deviate from $R*$, and penalizes it if its reserves get so far away from $R*$ as to breach an indicator point, seems *a priori* a reasonable way of encouraging countries to adjust in a manner consistent with equation (1). And, if the sum of the $R*$s is equal to the world level of reserves, a structure of definitional indicators might impart an element of consistency in payments objectives as sought by the United States.

It was unfortunate that the United States' representatives did not draw the distinction between a diagnostic indicator and a definitional indicator or seek to provide a theoretical underpinning for their proposals similar to the foregoing. Indeed, *The US Proposals* was even ambiguous about whether it was proposing a stock indicator or a flow indicator: it spoke of ' ... a system in which disproportionately large gains in reserves for a particular country indicate the need for adjustment measures to eliminate a balance-of-payments surplus ... ' (para. 2) and a past failure ' ... to provide adequate inducements to achieve and maintain balance-of-payments equilibrium ... ' (para.3). Since 'surplus' and 'payments equilibrium' are flow concepts, and the word 'indicator' had always been used before in the diagnostic sense, this invited the interpretation that the United States retained the traditional preoccupation with flow equilibrium in the balance of payments, and was suffering from the delusion that a cunning new way of diagnosing its absence was to study the integral of past flow imbalances. The fact that the US representatives explicitly argued that

4. See P. B. Kenen, 'Floats, Glides and Indicators', *Journal of International Economics*, 1975(2).

indicator points would encourage countries to adjust before those points were breached, and that the object of the exercise was to impart a broad consistency to payments objectives, would seem to imply that they did indeed envisage indicators defining the limits within which a country had an obligation to maintain, through adjustment policies, its reserve level. But if this was clear to the US representatives, their language did not make it clear to others, who thought they were arguing about diagnostic indicators. Thus the IMF staff undertook a study of how well various indicators might have been expected to perform on the basis of historical experience, which did not suggest that any of them were particularly promising.[5] But this conclusion was relevant only if indicators were envisaged as filling a diagnostic role; and it is hardly surprising that indicators should leave something to be desired in this capacity, because adopting any one indicator necessarily means discarding other relevant information. If one is seeking to diagnose whether adjustment is needed to achieve any well-defined ends, it is almost tautological that a comprehensive assessment can be expected to out-perform any indicator. The real problem was that the United States wanted to set up a system to help define the ends, but did not say so sufficiently explicitly, so that endless time was wasted on a wild goose chase debating the relative merits of assessment versus indicators in fulfilling purposes that were conceived quite differently by the different participants. So far as the definitional question of specifying adjustment obligations is concerned, a stock indicator appears appropriate.

Reserves versus basic balances

A second question is whether it is more appropriate to base international constraints over payments disequilibria on the stock of reserves, or on some other payments aggregate that endeavours to exclude transitory elements from its scope, such as the basic balance (perhaps cyclically adjusted). There can in principle be no doubt that it is irrational to expect a country to undertake adjustment measures when it is faced with disturbances, whether caused by seasonal, cyclical or speculative factors, that are going to be reversed in due course: the fundamental reason for holding reserves at all is precisely that of enabling a country to avoid the adjustments that would be needed to maintain continuous flow balance. But this is in no way inconsistent with the idea that countries should have an appropriate idea of a normal level of reserves, and should gear their adjustment policies towards securing a return to that norm when for some reason their reserves

5. The study is noted in the report of the Technical Group on Indicators, para. 31.

deviate significantly from it. The models of optimal reserve holding demonstrate this quite clearly: countries are pictured as simultaneously selecting a target reserve level (R^*) and an adjustment coefficient (α) which describes the speed with which they should aim to restore their reserves toward R^* when they deviate from target as a result of random disturbances. Hence, provided that reserves are allowed to fluctuate enough to fulfil their principal social function of permitting the stabilization of certain other economic variables, such as output, absorption and exchange rates, the fact that many transitory and reversible disturbances are reflected in reserve changes does not constitute a case against basing adjustment obligations on reserve levels. Moreover, there is a real danger that a policy that emphasized the avoidance of adjustment in response to transitory disturbances would have the practical effect of reinforcing the natural reluctance of governments to initiate adjustment action except when the need had become overwhelmingly obvious. There is much to be said for reversing the onus of proof (as suggested in *The US Proposals*), so that a reserve deviation would signal a need for adjustment unless it could be convincingly established that a payments reversal was already in prospect.

Symmetry

I conclude from the foregoing discussion that the stock of reserves provides the most appropriate basis on which to determine a country's adjustment obligations, as assumed implicity in both the reserve indicator proposal and the asset settlement proposal. The next question to ask is whether there is a logical case for seeking symmetry in the adjustment obligations imposed on countries: first, as between surplus and deficit countries; second, as between reserve centres and other countries. The answer to both questions is closely bound up with the issue of whether total adjustment costs will be reduced if all countries can be expected to initiate adjustment. There are several reasons for arguing that they will.

First, consider the case where two countries have an imbalance that results from the conjunctural situation. Which country should adjust to minimize total adjustment costs depends on the state of overall global demand; with excess demand it is desirable that the deficit country adjust, while in a recession it should be the surplus country. Hence any automatic exemption of one country from an obligation to consider initiating adjustment, because it is a surplus country or a reserve centre, may lead to inappropriate measures. Second, consider an imbalance that results from a cost discrepancy and that therefore calls for an exchange rate change to correct it. With floating rates it may not matter much which country takes the initiative, in so far as any initiative at all proves necessary; but with any sort of par value system it is easier if the country that is out of line with the majority is the one expected to make the change. Third, consider the implications of the fact that the business cycle generally shows a high degree of international synchronization. Limited reserves serve to ensure that during a world cyclical upswing some countries are obliged to curtail demand by a shortage of reserves, thus limiting the inflationary movement and contributing to world economic stability; if some countries are exempted from a reserve constraint, this built-in stabilizer is weakened. Similarly, an obligation on surplus countries to adjust when their reserve level becomes excessive could be expected to build in a defence against global deflation.* Fourth, consider the implication of allowing one country to undertake complete and automatic sterilization of reserve flows (which is a logical corollary of exempting a country from a reserve constraint). The result is that any change in monetary policy in that country produces a magnified effect on the world money supply — in contrast to the situation in a normal country, where a monetary expansion partly leaks out abroad and is partly neutralized by foreign sterilization. Given that monetary authorities make mistakes, there is much to be said for the more cautious policy of partial sterilization.

There therefore exist a series of cogent intellectual arguments for seeking to place symmetrical adjustment obligations on all countries, quite apart from the US fear that in the absence of such symmetry other countries would pursue a mercantilist search for surpluses that would inevitably end up with her carrying a large residual deficit. The economic factors are reinforced by a consideration of the politics of the situation. If, as argued in Chapter 2, the lack of a clear assigment of responsibilities for initiating adjustment was one of the root causes of the breakdown of the Bretton Woods system, then a new system needed to include such an assignment; but it is highly doubtful whether countries would ever agree to a set of formal rules that were not seen to apply to all.

On these grounds one can construct a case both for some form of reserve indicator system and for asset settlement. The case for the indicator system is, however, the weaker of the two, in as much as reserve movements already provide a discipline of sorts. The threat of reserve depletion already exists to discipline deficit countries (except, of course, for those reserve centres that escape pressure owing to the absence of asset settlement), while reserve accruals also exert some

---

*This is the international analogue of the familiar argument for a fixed rate of monetary growth as ensuring that the monetary sector acts as a built-in stabilizer.

pressure for adjustment. Apart from the fact that complete sterilization of reserve inflows is often difficult, so that reserve accruals have an expansionary impact, there is the fact that rational countries do not wish to impoverish themselves by investing an excessive portion of their wealth in low-yielding reserves. There is, therefore, little more reason for supposing that an international monetary system is incapable of operating without an indicator system than there is for supposing that a central bank is unable to influence domestic monetary conditions unless the cash balances of all individual agents are subject to norms, warning points, lower points and outer points. But perhaps there is slightly more reason: the fact is that the world economy, unlike most national economies, is dominated by a very small number of agents, who may therefore indulge in strategic reasoning ('if we don't adjust then A will be forced to') that would be better eliminated. In any event, both at Bretton Woods and during the C-20, the principal country that thought of itself as a deficit country placed major emphasis on securing pressures to force surplus countries to adjust, which suggests that major deficit countries have a psychological need for reassurance that their adjustment efforts will be reinforced rather than thwarted by the policies being pursued in surplus countries.

In contrast, the asymmetry between the primary reserve centre and other countries was obvious and unchallengeable, and there was no basis for doubting that the way to end it was the introduction of asset settlement. The United States nevertheless chose to oppose asset settlement — while expressing a willingness to restore the traditional on-demand convertibility when circumstances permitted. The reason given was that asset settlement would deprive the system of a useful element of elasticity. If, for example, a significant part of the vast outstanding stock of privately held dollar balances should have been switched out of dollars, the United States would have been in no position to provide primary reserve assets to the central banks of the countries into which the balances were switched. It would therefore have been most convenient if in these circumstances the central banks that acquired dollars should have decided to hold on to them rather than convert them. However, the idea that if convertibility were a reality — rather than purely nominal, as a tight set of PAHLs would have implied — central banks would have voluntarily held on to a currency being unloaded by the private sector was singularly implausible. Theory and empirical evidence[6] alike lead to the conclusion that the elasticity in a reserve currency system will be perverse in the presence of

6. The evidence is summarized in Williamson, 'International Liquidity — A Survey', *op.cit.*, Section II.2.

convertibility and the absence of political arm-twisting. Asset settlement is therefore better regarded as protection against the operation of perverse elasticity than as the impediment to constructive elasticity portrayed by the United States. Any necessary element of 'elasticity' in the settlement system is better provided through multilateral credit facilities, in which the debtor country contracts debt denominated in a neutral unit such as the SDR, as proposed by the advocates of asset settlement.

Problems with the reserve indicator proposal

Nothing more needs to be added on the technical aspects of the operation of a system of asset settlement, since this is not a field in which the C-20 made any intellectual progress over the analysis of the *Reform Report* recorded in Chapter 3. (Indeed, it could be argued that replacement of the clear and concise term 'asset settlement' by locutions such as 'the more mandatory system [of settlement]' and 'the future convertibility system' was a mark of intellectual regression.) There is, however, a great deal more to add on the details of the reserve indicator proposal, since it was the details rather than the principle that provoked most of the antagonism to the proposal. These details concerned the width of reserve bands, the effect in triggering speculation, the question of whether indicators were to be based on net or gross reserves, PAHLs and pressures.

As already stated, the principal social function of reserves is that of fluctuating in a way that contributes to the stabilization of such other variables as output, absorption, prices and exchange rates. A system that pinned countries down to avoiding any significant reserve fluctuations would therefore destroy the purpose of holding reserves at all (except in so far as an unusable reserve stock somehow engendered confidence). Various passages in *The US Proposals* tended to suggest that the United States was envisaging such narrow bands for reserve fluctuations as to curtail severely this central and legitimate purpose of reserve holding. For example, ' ... the indicator points [should be defined] so as to get "enough" elbow room for *some* fluctuation in reserves to meet transitory payments imbalances ... ' (para.27, italics supplied). More specifically, it was proposed that each country be assigned a 'low point' which ' ... might approximate a level of reserves considered to be close to the minimum level ordinarily necessary to maintain confidence and to guard against extreme emergencies' (para.24(a)). If reserves remained below this point for a specified time period, 'definite adjustment pressures would be anticipated'. This seemed harmless only if one believed that adoption of the indicator system would not make deficit countries adjust more rapidly than previously: but, unless the system were thus redundant in its effect on deficit countries, it was surely reasonable to anticipate that 'the level ordinarily necessary to maintain confidence' would rise once the level that previously sufficed for that purpose were designated the point at which a country became subject to pressures to adjust. The effect of having a low point would therefore have been to freeze a part of the reserve stock and thus limit the usefulness of reserves in fulfilling the function for which they are held. The moral is obvious: the existing system already contains an implicit low point at the level of zero reserves, and to raise that point would serve no constructive purpose. The logic of this view was accepted by the Technical Group on Adjustment (para.45).

Another aspect of the indicator proposal that caused much apprehension was the effect that a reserve indicator system would have in stimulating speculative capital flows. The initial proposals for 'objective indicators' had been advanced by academic economists in the context of providing automatic or presumptive rules to determine small parity changes in a crawling-peg system. In this context the fact that the indicator would make prediction of parity changes easy was unimportant — indeed advantageous, in so far as there is a presumption that the provision of correct information to the market will increase the efficiency of microeconomic decision making — because anticipated parity changes could be offset by interest rate differentials without violating the conditions for asset market equilibrium. But, as Peter Kenen emphasized,[7] the combination of indicators that made it clear when major adjustment actions could be expected and 'stable but adjustable par values' was not a happy partnership. It could, of course, be counterargued that there were in any event going to be speculative flows under an adjustable peg, which is true, but those with a great attachment to pegged exchange rates did not find this an adequate reason for accepting an innovation that could not help but aggravate the problem. The most that they might have found acceptable was a simple upper limit on the reserve accumulation permitted before a financial pressure commenced, which would have left the problems faced by deficit countries unchanged and have left surplus countries with a similar need to try to implement adjustment measures in anticipation of recognition of their necessity by the market. In other words they might have accepted something that was clearly a definitional indicator, but they could not live with something that was believed to be a diagnostic indicator.

7. P. B. Kenen, 'After Nairobi — Beware the Rhinopotamus', *Euromoney*, November, 1973.

Another contentious detail of the reserve indicator proposal concerned whether indicators were to be based on gross or net reserves. The United States did not formally commit herself to a position on this issue. However, the Europeans took it as axiomatic that if a difference between a gross and net indicator were to exist — which it would not have under a system of asset settlement (except for base levels) — then the system should be based on net reserves, and the United States refused to endorse this position despite her opposition to asset settlement. The reason that a gross reserve indicator was unacceptable to the Europeans in the absence of asset settlement is easy to see. Consider what would have happened in the circumstances of the speculative crisis of February 1973, which occurred just before this topic was first discussed. Because of the inconvertibility of the dollar, the vast shift of funds from the United States to Germany produced a large gain in gross reserves by Germany and no fall in the gross reserves of the United States: the system would therefore have placed the entire obligation to initiate adjustment on Germany. Of course the United States could reply that this would no longer be the case once convertibility was restored, and that in any event the same possibilities of evading adjustment obligations would be open to other deficit countries under the multiple-currency system they were espousing if the creditors were prepared to refrain from requesting conversion. But these replies hardly provided reassurance. One of the unattractive features of the early 1960s that the Europeans wanted to prevent re-emerging was the political tension caused by the reserve centre pressing its partners to refrain from conversion even though they judged this desirable on grounds of portfolio management, and hence they wanted to minimize the impact on the other party of the decision whether to convert (or, better still, to eliminate the decision altogether by making conversion mandatory). And the countries that would not have been members of the MCI group were naturally indignant at the prospect of being excluded from a source of credit available to the select few.

PAHLs (primary asset holding limits) provided another bone of contention. The problem as seen by the United States was as follows. Suppose that 50 per cent of the world reserve stock were composed of SDRs and 50 per cent of dollars, and that the sum total of all countries' norms was equated to the stock of reserves. Then any net conversions of dollars into SDRs would have tended to exert adjustment pressures on deficit countries — more particularly, on the reserve centre — without the indicator mechanism producing a corresponding pressure on surplus countries. To limit this pressure, the United States proposed to place an upper limit on the quantity of SDRs that any individual country might hold. To Europeans this seemed a clumsy, inaccurate and lopsided way of providing the protection against conversion of outstanding dollar balances that they recognized to be necessary and had proposed to ensure through the provisions of asset settlement, which (according to the 'third approach') would have been provided through a Fund Substitution Account issuing the additional SDRs that were being demanded and in turn holding a claim on the United States corresponding to the dollars that were being converted into SDRs.

The final contentious detail of the reserve indicator proposal concerned the set of pressures that were envisaged. It was not the idea of pressures on surplus countries that was objectionable, at least to the other industrial countries; as already noted, the French at one stage proposed that reserves above a certain point be required to be paid into a special account that would bear a negative interest rate. It was rather the idea of providing a whole menu of pressures from which the IMF would have to choose — loss of future SDR allocations, charges on excess or deficient reserves, the deposit of excess reserves in an account bearing a negative interest rate, graduated charges on drawings from the IMF, ineligibility to borrow from the IMF, constraints on official borrowing, authorization of discriminatory exchange controls, and publication of an IMF Report (a particularly terrifying form of pressure in the eyes of some countries) — that appeared guaranteed to maximize tensions.[8] It is one thing for a country to commit itself in advance to abide by certain rules, which may include specified penalties in well-defined circumstances; it is quite another to expect it to acquiesce gracefully in the discretionary decision of an international body to mete out punishment. It is difficult enough to get the IMF to say anything even mildly critical of a major member; the idea that the Executive Board, or even the new ministerial-level Council that was proposed, would suddenly start voting to impose a particular pressure on a particular member appeared unrealistic. And criminology has taught that the effectiveness of deterrence depends far more on the certainty than on the severity of retribution.

This completes the review of the important issues that emerged in the course of the C-20's attempt to legislate a framework of international rules governing countries' overall adjustment obligations. Although no agreement was reached on any of the substantive issues — as opposed to such procedural issues as the creation of the Ministerial Council in the IMF to supervise the adjustment process, and agreement on the range of issues that the IMF should take into account

8. The list of proposed pressures appears in the report of the Technical Group on Adjustment, paras.56-68.

in reviewing the adjustment process — the discussion was not without potential value. Participants in the discussions ended with a far better appreciation of the interests that other countries were concerned to safeguard and the range of possible methods of constructing safeguards, and if at some future date the reform effort is resumed there will be a more satisfactory base from which to start seeking a solution that might win general acceptance.

Overall balance versus current account targets
It is worth adding that there is another dimension to the question of adjustment obligations that played a much smaller role in the C-20 discussions than had been anticipated by some observers.[9] This involves the question of the structure of the balance of payments — i.e., whether countries should have national targets and/or international obligations separately for the current and capital accounts, or simply for the overall balance (the change in reserves). The United States had a clear view that countries should only have targets regarding their reserves and not as regards the composition of their balance of payments. This reflected the general American ideological disposition in favour of market mechanisms : capital flows should be essentially unrestricted, or at least the international community should avoid pressing countries to restrict capital mobility, and current account adjustment should then aim to secure a balanced overall account — i.e., to secure a flow of real resources to transfer the financial flow. The Europeans were far more inclined to adopt a target for their current account surplus, and to use capital controls in an effort to make the capital account adjust to the current account, rather than vice versa. This difference in philosophy was not, however, as sharp as it appears in the preceding portrayal. The reason is that the European current account targets were generally chosen with a view to covering the out-flow of aid and a 'normal' level of long-term capital exports, while the primary role of capital controls was generally that of trying to suppress presumably reversible movements of short-term capital. Provided that the current account target is modified in the light of the desired underlying capital flow, the European approach is also consistent with the aim of ensuring that in the long run the current account adjusts to transfer real resources on the basis of relative international conditions of thrift and productivity. The question is one of whether it is worth risking some distortion in the underlying capital flows in order to suppress some of the speculative froth, which is a question of

9. See in particular M. V. Posner, *The World Monetary System: A Minimal Reform Program*, Princeton Essays in International Finance No.96, Princeton, 1972.

judgement rather than principle. In so far as there was a difference of principle it was resolved by a *modus vivendi* in which countries were to be allowed to control capital flows if they so wished, except for capital exports to developing countries, but would not have international obligations to control them if they did not so wish.

Adjustment techniques

The battery of weapons that have been used by governments over the years to influence payments flows may be classified into four general categories: (*a*) financial policies, of which special importance attaches to monetary policy; (*b*) exchange rate policy; (*c*) current account controls; and (*d*) capital account controls. As noted in Chapter 1, the Bretton Woods system had been as ambiguous about the question of what techniques were supposed to be used to secure adjustment as it had been in assigning the responsibility to initiate adjustment. Current account restrictions were largely proscribed; capital controls were permitted but necessarily insufficient; exchange rate changes were allowed in circumstances of 'fundamental disequilibrium', but countries proved reluctant to make them except as a last resort; and financial policies were principally assigned to the pursuit of domestic full employment objectives. During the 1960s the logic of the commitment to full employment became apparent. So long as countries committed themselves to full employment targets that produced different national rates of inflation (and irrespective of the importance one attaches to cost, demand and expectational factors in generating inflation), exchange rates would have to alter to neutralize the differences* in inflation rates. The 1970 IMF report, *The Role of Exchange Rates in the Adjustment of International Payments*, marked official though reluctant acceptance of this fact, coupled with the declaration that periodic discrete changes in par values remained the appropriate method of changing exchange rates. The C-20 endorsed these views without any essential change. The question that arises is whether it was right to do so.

Current account controls
It has long been widely agreed among economists that there is no case for varying controls on current account transactions as a method of

---

*Strictly speaking one should speak of inconsistent rather than differential inflation rates, since differential productivity growth in different sectors or different income elasticities of demand for the exports of different countries may require slightly different national inflation rates to preserve payments balance.

securing payments adjustment. This consensus[10] rests on the presumption that interferences with the market mechanism must be expected to reduce the efficiency of resource allocation. There is, of course, no doubt that particular controls may serve a legitimate purpose in countering instances of market failure or in altering the international distibution of income (as, perhaps, when a developing country imposes an optimal tariff or export levy), but — quite apart from the advisability of insisting that the onus of proof be on those wishing to introduce restrictions — recognition of this fact does nothing to justify the use of controls for purposes of securing payments adjustment. If a control is worthwhile on these grounds, then it is legitimate irrespective of the state of the balance of payments : there is no reason for supposing that from a global standpoint changes in current account restrictions ever constitute a first-best policy. From a national standpoint, of course, controls that throw the bulk of the cost on foreigners (such as raising tariffs below the optimal tariff or cutting aid) may be highly attractive, which is precisely why it is important that their use be outlawed by effective international agreements, and that payments difficulties not be admitted as a legitimate excuse for violating these obligations. The C-20 played its part in reinforcing the existing international agreements to this effect (*Outline*, para.14), with the addition of a rider that controls adversely affecting the interests of the developing countries be deemed particularly undesirable (para.16).

Capital controls

Capital account restrictions are more widely used and less widely condemned as instruments of balance of payments policy, and this was reflected in the *Outline* (para. 15):

'Countries will not use controls over capital transactions for the purpose of maintaining inappropriate exchange rates or, more generally, of avoiding appropriate adjustment action. Insofar as countries use capital controls, they should avoid an excessive degree of administrative restriction which could damage trade and beneficial capital flows and should not retain controls longer than needed....'

Some economists are prepared to condemn all capital

10. The latest dissentients from this consensus are the Cambridge Economic Policy Group in the *Economic Policy Review*, No.1, 1975. Their case was refuted by W. M. Corden, I. M. D. Little, M. fg. Scott, *Import Controls versus Devaluation and Britain's Economic Prospects*, Trade Policy Research Centre, London, 1975.

controls with the same conviction that current account controls are customarily censured, on the ground that they impede global economic efficiency.[11] Others including the author, believe that there are important distinctions on the lines hinted at, though hardly elucidated with analytical insight, in the above quotation. The essential question to be asked in seeking to discriminate between 'beneficial' and 'disequilibrating' capital movements is whether global welfare would rise as a result of a real transfer corresponding to the potential financial flow. There is a presumption that a net flow of long-term capital from one country to another is stimulated by the attraction of a higher expected rate of return in the recipient country, which (unless tax obligations are unequal in the two countries) is likely to be a reflection of the higher productivity of investment in the recipient; hence world welfare is raised by ensuring that the financial flow leads to a real transfer so as to effect an international reallocation of physical investment. In contrast, there is no presumption that a flow of short-term capital motivated by the hope of realizing a speculative gain on an exchange rate change implies anything about the desirable international distribution of capital formation, and it would therefore be foolish to allow such flows to influence the current account. Whether such flows are better suppressed or financed is a question of expediency.

Irrespective of one's view on whether capital controls should be used to assist the financing of basic imbalances, or at least to avoid an intensification of the problem of financing such imbalances, they cannot provide a substitute for a mechanism to secure current account adjustment. This is because it is the current account surplus or deficit that measures the extent to which the country is lending real resources to, or borrowing real resources from, the rest of the world, and this real transfer should be made on the basis of criteria of efficient resource allocation. To use capital controls to make the capital account adjust to the current account and avoid current account adjustment is to allow real transfers to be determined by whatever series of historical accidents happen to have influenced the current account.

Financial policies and exchange rate policy

The central question in selecting an adjustment mechanism therefore concerns the relative role to be assigned to financial policies on the one hand and exchange rate changes on the other. Throughout the 1960s a

11. For example, A. Gutowski, 'Flexible Exchange Rates versus Controls', in F. Machlup, A. Gutowski, F. A. Lutz, eds, *International Monetary Problems*, American Enterprise Institute, Washington DC, 1972.

preponderant plurality of interested economists had campaigned for a much greater role for exchange rate changes, principally on the ground that independent national monetary policies were impracticable in anything but the short run under fixed exchange rates, and that such policies could play a valuable role in permitting output to be stabilized at a full employment level. If, for example, it were necessary to remedy a payments deficit, the cost in terms of lost output would be far less if a devaluation were implemented to produce a switch of expenditure (both at home and abroad) toward the country's goods, and deflationary fiscal/monetary policies were introduced only to the extent necessary to release resources for the balance of payments, than if deflation alone were relied on, which would initially imply a deflation of output several times as large as the desired improvement in the trade account (although the size of the necessary deflation would diminish over time as the increased unemployment slowed inflation and so produced a change in competitiveness that ultimately provided a substitute for devaluation). Not only would adjustment be less painful if deficit (surplus) countries were relieved of the necessity to travel down (up) the Phillips curve from their normal position, but their normal (preferred) positions might yield different national rates of inflation on account of differences in national 'tastes' for unemployment versus inflation, or differences in the position of the Phillips curve in different countries; such systematic differences in national rates of inflation could be accommodated provided that their external effects were neutralized through exchange rate changes.

In the early 1970s, just as the official world was being convinced of the necessity of allowing prompt exchange rate changes, something of a reaction against flexible exchange rates began to set in among academic economists, especially those of a monetarist persuasion. This reaction rests on two distinct intellectual bases. The first, which is, in my view, the less convincing, is the notion that the traded goods produced by different countries are such close substitutes that exchange rate changes cannot lead to changes in the relative prices of goods supplied by different countries. Instead, exchange rate changes are supposed to cause almost immediate proportionate changes in domestic price levels which offset the exchange rate change: in so far as devaluation 'works', it does so by reducing the real value of the money supply and thus deflating expenditure, just as a monetary contraction would. In fact, however, the more systematic surveys of the evidence[12] reinforce the impression one gets from the most cursory

---

12. The evidence is reviewed in Marina v. N. Whitman, 'The Payments Adjustment Process and the Exchange Rate Regime: What Have We Learned?', *American Economics Review*, May 1975, Section III.

examination of the relevant price statistics: that exchange rate changes are nowhere near wholly offset in the medium run.

The second basis of the reaction against exchange rate flexibility is the importance increasingly attached to the role of expectations in the inflationary process. According to the new view, which has found increasing empirical support, it is the acceleration or deceleration of inflation from the rate previously expected, rather than the rate of inflation itself, that is determined by the pressure of demand. This implies that the welfare gain[13] through holding unemployment at a rate below the 'natural rate' (that rate where there is no acceleration or deceleration of inflation) is transitory rather than permanent. Monetary policies that produce inconsistent rates of inflation in different countries, and therefore create the need for exchange rate changes, produce only a short-term gain in output and employment at the cost of an acceleration of inflation that will be permanent unless a subsequent deceleration is bought at the cost of output deflation.

It cannot be denied that this theory erodes the case for exchange rate flexibility and the case against seeking monetary union.[14] Nevertheless, there remain persuasive grounds for retaining a belief in the value of exchange rate changes in certain circumstances. First, while the evidence for the role of expectations in accelerating the actual rate of inflation is now overwhelming, the evidence for a unitary coefficient is still inconclusive. The implication of a less than unitary coefficient is that the unemployment/inflation trade-off still persists in the long run, even though the long-run Phillips curve is steeper than the short-run one, so that some welfare gain remains from the ability to choose the long-run rate of monetary expansion best suited to the needs of the individual country. One may guess that this non-homogeneity may prove significant at low rates of inflation but will not prove to be so at high rates: that is, that a real output gain may be available in going from a long-run inflation rate of 1 per cent to a rate of 2 per cent, but not in going from 10 per cent to 20 per cent. Second, a role for expectations actually reinforces the value of exchange rate changes in securing adjustment when the disturbance affecting the balance of payments is real rather than monetary in origin. A rise in demand for exports that requires a rise in the relative price level of the

13. Some monetarists would contend that holding unemployment below the 'natural rate' would impose a welfare loss even in the short run, since the increase in employment would arise only because workers were cheated into accepting jobs that they would have refused had they known the expected real wage was going to be eroded by inflation. I still find this bit of the monetarist story bizarre.
14. For statements of the standard case against monetary integration see J. M. Fleming, 'On Exchange Rate Unification', *Economic Journal*, September 1971, or W. M. Corden, *Monetary Integration*, Princeton Essays in International Finance No.92, Princeton, 1972.

country in order to re-equilibrate the balance of payments will be more disruptive if the internal inflation necessary to accomplish this at a fixed exchange rate causes expectations of further inflation that have to be extinguished by output deflation before the economy can settle down at its new equilibrium. Third, even if inflationary expectations are the major form that cost-push factors take, it is far from clear that they are the only form: they do not, for example, offer a ready explanation for the acceleration of inflation in France in spring 1968 or in Britain in autumn 1969 (any more than does the pressure of demand or the rate of monetary expansion). A world in which particular countries suffer such cost-push impulses is one in which there remains room for exchange rate changes to remedy their payments consequences with minimal disruption, on the lines previously described. Fourth, 'mistakes' in monetary policy, domestically or in the rest of the world, may be remedied less disruptively with the aid of exchange rate changes, for similar reasons. Fifth, the attempt to peg exchange rates does not always lead governments into the coordination of monetary policies that is in the last analysis essential, but instead into a series of controls and restrictions that are destructive of economic welfare. Finally, from the standpoint of an individual country (one thinks of Germany), it only makes sense to think of repegging its exchange rate when it is convinced that its partners will follow a monetary policy consistent with its particular national needs. It is therefore only after the perceived needs of different countries have been brought into line that a repegging of exchange rates could be expected to succeed.

Consideration of the preceding list of circumstances in which exchange rate flexibility is valuable suggests that the 'new case' for fixed exchange rates is a case that is relevant only to countries that are unlikely to suffer differential real shocks or cost-push impulses, and that are able to agree on strong institutional coordination of their monetary policies. It is therefore a case that is highly relevant to European monetary integration,[15] but of only hypothetical relevance to the relations between Europe, the United States, Japan and the developing countries. It is, of course, precisely these wider relationships that are at issue in choosing an adjustment mechanism for the IMF world; and it is clear that the C-20 was correct in

15. I have argued elsewhere, however, that even in this context it does not entirely dispose of the danger that monetary union would intensify regional problems, in as much as the associated labour market integration might prompt an equalization of real wages unjustified by productivity levels; but that this danger might be a blessing in disguise if it provoked regional policies, with an egalitarian end result. See J. Williamson, 'The Impact of European Monetary Integration on the Peripheral Areas', in J. Vaizey, ed., *Economic Sovereignty and Regional Policy*, Gill and Macmillan, Dublin, 1975.

recognizing that in this world fixed (as opposed to temporarily pegged) exchange rates were simply not a serious option.

The choice of an exchange rate regime

The choice therefore lay between alternative regimes in which exchange rates would change. The choice of a regime was, indeed, the central question that faced the C-20 in legislating an adjustment mechanism. It could, admittedly, have been supplemented by an attempt to organize *ex ante* coordination of monetary policies in the IMF, on the lines that have been suggested by Ronald McKinnon;[16] but this possibility simply did not appear on the agenda of the C-20 negotiations. In choosing an exchange rate regime it was not particularly helpful to portray the choice, as was sometimes done, as that of selecting a point on a spectrum with completely fixed exchange rates at one end and freely floating rates at the other. The issue was not so much one of the degree of flexibility as the form that the necessary flexibility should take; whether this should be by the adjustable peg or crawling peg, or by free or managed floating. Indeed, it is not particularly clear which of the three intermediate exchange rate regimes — the adjustable peg, the crawling peg and managed floating — is supposed to be the most or least flexible. Managed floating may in practice produce smaller exchange rate variations than the adjustable peg: think of the relative variation of the Canadian dollar and the DM against the US dollar during the period June 1970 to March 1973. The crawling peg implies a limitation on the size of par value changes that may be made at a particular point in time, and is in that sense a less flexible system than the adjustable peg; but on the other hand the crawling peg demands that par values be adjusted far more frequently, so that in that sense it is a more flexible system. Not only is it unclear which regimes are more or less flexible; it is not clear how greater flexibility is supposed to be measured. By the realized degree of exchange rate variation? By the time that must elapse before countries face the facts of life about the inconsistency of the monetary policies that they are pursuing? By the extent to which the adjustment rules of the gold standard are followed?

The selection of an exchange rate regime is therefore not fruitfully approached by posing the question 'more or less flexibility'. It is more profitable to consider the particular advantages and disadvantages of the five potential regimes. Of these five, fixed exchange rates have

16. R. I. McKinnon, 'Sterilization in Three Dimensions: Major Trading Countries, Euro-currencies, and the United States', in R. Z. Aliber, ed., *National Monetary Policies and the International Financial System*, University of Chicago Press, London, 1974.

already been dismissed as infeasible on a worldwide basis in the preceding section. The other textbook case, freely floating rates, also remains of academic interest alone. First, governments themselves undertake international transactions of a non-negligible size, and so, unless they bind themselves to effecting their transactions according to some automatic timing rule, they will inevitably find themselves judging when is an advantageous time to make payments, and therefore to a limited extent managing the rate. Second, free floating cannot sensibly be defined simply by the absence of intervention, but requires also the non-use of other policy instruments (official foreign borrowing and lending, trade and exchange controls, fiscal and monetary policy) with a view to influencing the exchange rate, and even the best-intentioned government is in practice likely to find it impossible to exclude external calculations from its mind when determining such policies. But, even to the extent that free floating is feasible, it is highly questionable whether it is desirable. It is now well established that speculative activity is essential to the dynamic stability of the foreign exchange market, [17] but experience since March 1973 (particularly during the summer of 1974) demonstrated dramatically that speculation in a floating regime can be dangerous to the private sector. This perhaps explains why, contrary to the hopes of many advocates of floating, exchange rates in the floating period have proved to be so volatile: an adequate volume of stabilizing speculation is brought forth only by large swings in exchange rates which take the rate beyond any reasonable estimate of its equilibrium zone. In these circumstances it does not require particularly finely articulated management of the exchange rate to enable central bank intervention to improve on the unaided performance of the private market.

That leaves the three intermediate exchange rate regimes. Of these, it has already been argued at length in Chapter 2 that one, the adjustable peg, is inherently inconsistent with a high degree of capital mobility, for the quite fundamental reason that one cannot have asset market equilibrium when there are opportunities of riskless capital gains available every time that a par value change becomes necessary. Despite this, the C-20 plumped for restoration of the adjustable peg without any serious consideration of the alternatives. Why it did this will be examined in Chapter 7. Suffice it to note here that the addition of 'floating rates in particular situations' to the list of legitimate exchange rate practices does nothing to provide the crisis-free method

---

17. The pioneering paper was A. J. C. Britton, 'The Dynamic Stability of the Foreign Exchange Market', *Economic Journal*, March 1970. The most extensive investigation is by W. E. Witte, 'Dynamic Adjustment in the Foreign Exchange Market', Ph. D. thesis submitted to the University of Wisconsin, Madison, 1975.

of exchange rate adjustment that the adjustable peg lacks. If the market anticipates that a currency with an overvalued or undervalued rate is about to be cut loose from its par value, it will have just as much incentive to switch out or in as if it believes that there is about to be a formal devaluation or revaluation.

Consider next the crawling peg. The essential feature of the crawling peg has nothing to do with the particular figures that were originally invented to illustrate how fast and frequently parities might be adjusted, nor with the formulae that, under some variants of the proposal, were supposed to determine when parities should be adjusted. The central insight is that, if the obligations to defend rigid margins that are inherent in a par value system are to be respected yet the par values themselves are to be changed without disrupting the system, it is necessary that expectations of future par value changes be able to adjust interest rates in such a way as to re-establish asset market equilibrium. This in turn implies that parity changes be small enough to avoid a presumption that a changed parity will be followed by a sudden movement in the market exchange rate. Just how small this need be is not unambiguous, but there are some guides; for example, the Brazilian crawling peg works admirably with changes in the range of 1 per cent to 2 per cent. With a band of as much as 9 per cent, which is the figure implicity considered by the C-20, there would seem ample scope for parity changes of up to 3 per cent or even 4 per cent at a time, at intervals of not more than every 2 months. The great disadvantage of the crawling peg remains the fact that where large changes in exchange rates prove to be necessary it is impossible to effect them immediately: this means that interest rate differentials have to be tied down to offsetting the anticipated exchange rate change during a lengthy adjustment period. (It would be pointless to tack the crawling peg on to the adjustable peg as an optional extra, in the manner envisaged by the C-20 in para. 11 of the *Outline*, since without a proscription on large par value changes and temporary floating market participants would still face the riskless possibility of speculative gains and could be relied on to act accordingly.)

Seven countries have used the crawling peg at some time (Argentina, Brazil, Chile, Colombia, Israel, Uruguay and Vietnam), and there is rather general agreement that it succeeded in allowing them to neutralize the external effects of their high inflation rates efficiently. It has sometimes been asserted that the favourable experience of these countries is irrelevant to the decisions facing the major industrialized nations, but no analytical reason for this assertion seems to have been advanced, and none seems particularly evident. Nonetheless, no country attempted to introduce into the C-20 a serious discussion of the possibility of basing the reformed system on the crawling peg.

The final regime is that of managed floating, defined as a system in which countries do not have any obligation to defend particular rates, but nevertheless make some attempt to manage their rates by intervention or otherwise. This is the regime that has been in effect among the major currencies, other than those in the European snake, since March 1973. The system has clearly proved its feasibility in this period. World finance continued to function reasonably satisfactorily despite the turbulence resulting from the oil price increase, and there is so far no evidence that trade has been significantly disrupted. On the other hand, exchange rates have proved to be pretty volatile — more volatile than before the advent of floating by just about any standard, and more volatile than many advocates of floating had anticipated, or than the Canadian precedent would have indicated likely. [18] This volatility occurred despite the fact that intervention was heavier in the year following floating than it had been previously, and it remained heavy even during the second year of floating.[19]

Although floating rates were reluctantly resorted to in the midst of the C-20 negotiations and proved more satisfactory than the adjustable peg that they replaced, the C-20 never discussed the possibility of adopting managed floating as the basis for the reformed system. Instead, it was felt necessary to explain that the float was not the reform. What did happen was that the IMF Executive Directors were requested to develop a set of Guidelines for Floating as a part of the immediate steps to be taken to allow the world to live peacefully with floating exchange rates during the supposedly transitional period pending the return to a par value system. A set of Guidelines was ultimately agreed by the Executive Board just in time to be adopted simultaneously with the final meeting of the C-20. Since the Guidelines were one of the two substantive acts of international monetary reform that emerged from the period of the C-20 negotiations, it is worth pausing to examine them.

The Guidelines for Floating

The Guidelines[20] aimed to provide a set of criteria for the internationally responsible national management of floating exchange rates, which the IMF would use in exercising surveillance over the payments policies of

---

18. F. Hirsch and D. Higham, 'Floating Rates — Expectations and Experience', *Three Banks Review*, June 1974.

19. J. Williamson, 'Exchange Rate Policy and Reserve Use', *Scandinavian Journal of Economics*, 1976(2).

20. The Guidelines appear in the *IMF Survey*, 17 June, 1974.

those countries that were not fulfilling their legal obligation to defend a par value. They were primarily concerned with intervention policy, but were also intended to permit the IMF to exercise surveillance over other actions that influence exchange rates, such as intervention in the forward market, official foreign borrowing and lending, capital controls, dual exchange markets, and monetary and fiscal policies, in so far as these are adopted for external rather than internal reasons. The principal aim of the Guidelines was to outlaw aggressive intervention — e.g., 'competitive depreciation' — while encouraging smoothing intervention that would contribute to orderly market conditions, and intervention designed to limit the deviation of exchange rates from a medium-run norm.

Guidelines 1 and 2 expressed the principle that a country should lean against the wind' by acquiring reserves when its currency was appreciating and selling reserves when its currency was depreciating. They suggested that a country had something of an obligation to intervene in order to smooth out erratic day-to-day and week-to-week fluctuations, and automatic permission to moderate longer run movements except where this would conflict with other Guidelines. This was the type of policy that Canada had followed in the 1950s, and that had been advocated as a general rule by Paul Wonnacott.[21] It was designed both to moderate rate movements and to preclude aggressive intervention (since the latter consists in intervention that pushes a rate in a direction opposite to that where market forces are taking it). Guideline 3 introduced the concept of a 'range of reasonable estimates of the medium-term norm for the exchange rate', which was a suitably cautious way of reintroducing the concept of a parity (defined as an effective exchange rate, however, rather than in terms of a par value in some common standard). Guideline 3(a) provided that, if a country wished to intervene other than defensively as permitted under Guidelines 1 and 2, it had first to establish a 'target zone of rates' with the IMF, and if the Fund agreed that this target lay within the 'range of reasonable estimates of the medium-term norm' then the country might intervene aggressively to push the rate toward the target zone. Guideline 3(b) allowed the IMF to take the initiative in urging a country to encourage its rate to move in a particular direction if it felt that the country's exchange rate had diverged from the range of reasonable estimates of the medium-term norm to an extent likely to be harmful to

21. The suggestion was first made in P. Wonnacott, 'Exchange Stabilization in Canada, 1950-54: A Comment', *Canadian Journal of Economics and Political Science*, May 1958, and subsequently amplified in *The Canadian Dollar 1948-62*, University of Toronto Press, 1965, Chapter 12, and *The Floating Canadian Dollar*, American Enterprise Institute, Washington DC, 1972, Chapter 6.

the interests of other countries. This was intended both to enable the IMF to persuade countries of the need for active policies if the market was failing to take a rational view (the dollar depreciation of July 1973 comes to mind as an example), and to provide a net to capture any country that sought to secure a competitive rate change by engineering or taking advantage of a temporary movement and then intervening to prevent a rebound of the rate.

The other three Guidelines contained prescriptions concerning the application of the first three. Guideline 4 was a reflection of the reserve indicator proposal. It encouraged countries to outline their objectives regarding future reserve changes, and, if these objectives were deemed reasonable by the Fund in the light of the country's existing reserve stock and the world reserve situation, countries were to be allowed to modify the application of Guideline 2 and the exchange rate norms of Guideline 3 to facilitate the achievement of their reserve accumulation objectives. For example, a country with reserves judged excessive both by itself and the Fund would be encouraged to intervene more heavily to limit depreciation than appreciation, and its target exchange rate zone might be set at a more appreciated rate than otherwise. Guideline 5 said that countries with floating rates should not use current account controls (but watered this down by adding 'like other members'). Guideline 6 recognized, though it scarcely met, the important problem posed by the fact that the interests of the issuers of intervention currencies are also affected by decisions regarding intervention. Suppose, for example, that the dollar were appreciated above its target zone, but that, because the world was in a recession, the only countries that chose to exercise their intervention rights were those whose currencies were appreciating and/or appreciated above their target zones. Guideline 6 asked countries to ' ... bear in mind ... the interests of ... the issuing countries in whose currencies they intervene', which tells an intervening country with a choice of intervention currencies to buy one that is below its target zone, rather than dollars. But, if the dollar were the only intervention currency, the net effect of other countries' interventions would be to appreciate the dollar still further. Presumably Guideline 6 exhorts other countries considering intervention to weigh the benefit to their own interests against the harm to the United States that would be caused by a further appreciation of the dollar. It is not difficult to guess the decision they would reach; which is why the Guideline hardly meets the problem.

Despite this important inadequacy, which is an example of the sort of asymmetries that it was hoped that the reform would eliminate but that have if anything been intensified by the failure to achieve a reform, the Guidelines were a major accomplishment. They demonstrate that it is possible to formulate rules that recognize that exchange rates are a matter of international concern, and that protect the legitimate international interest, within the framework of a system of floating. It is not clear that they have in fact been fully implemented, partly because the United States in particular has been averse to attempts to establish norms or target zones for exchange rates. The Guidelines nevertheless provide a ray of hope for the future that is in striking contrast to the intellectual nihilism of the C-20's endorsement of 'stable but adjustable par values'.

Appendix: the Intervention System

The intervention arrangements constituted one of the outstanding asymmetries of the Bretton Woods system and as such they provided an obvious candidate for reform in the C-20 negotiations. Most countries had adopted the practice of intervening in dollars to defend their currencies within the 1 per cent margins specified in the IMF Articles (with sterling area and franc zone countries using the pound sterling and French franc respectively as their intervention currencies), while the United States largely refrained from intervention at all and instead satisfied her obligation to defend the par value of the dollar by freely buying and selling gold at rates close to par. These asymmetrical practices had two asymmetrical consequences. First, they built up the reserve currency role of the dollar, since use of the dollar as intervention currency both necessitated central banks holding working balances in dollars, and implied that in the first instance reserve acquisitions took the form of dollar holdings, so that — given the absence of any obligation to seek settlement in primary reserve assets — it required a deliberate act to switch reserves into a medium other than dollars. Second, the dollar's intervention currency role resulted in a limitation of its intra-margin flexibility. Countries pegging to the dollar defined their margins as ±1 per cent around their dollar parity,[1] which gave them a band[2] of 2 per cent in terms of the dollar. The band between two currencies pegged to the dollar was therefore 4 per cent, since the

1. For some obscure reason the Technical Group on Intervention and Settlement chose sometimes to call par values — i.e., the central rate of a currency in terms of the numeraire — parities, and sometimes to call parities — i.e., the central rate of one currency in terms of another, which is the ratio of two par values — 'cross parities'. I retain the standard IMF nomenclature, which is unambiguous.
2. The band measures the maximum permissible exchange rate change between two currencies neither of which changes its par value and is therefore twice the margin.

maximum permissible exchange rate change between A and B occurred if A appreciated 2 per cent in terms of the dollar, while B depreciated 2 per cent. The dollar, therefore, had only half the intra-margin flexibility between any other pair of currencies. ('Pyramiding' of margins could go even further between currencies pegged to non-dollar intervention currencies: in principle the band between a currency pegged to the pound and one pegged to the French franc was 8 per cent.)

The United States made it clear from the outset of the reform negotiations that she strongly favoured eliminating the special limitation on the intra-margin flexibility of the dollar that arose from its status as the basic intervention currency. Many Americans also believed that this status restricted the freedom of the United States in taking an initiative to change the par value of the dollar. I disputed that proposition in Chapter 3; but what the dollar's intervention currency role undoubtedly did limit was the ability of the United States to float the dollar. So long as the dollar was the basic intervention currency, it could be floated only by the other countries that peg to it ceasing to defend their par values. (Thus in March 1973 the maintenance of the snake was possible only because the European countries intervened in their own currencies rather than in dollars.) The ability of the United States to float independently without thereby forcing floating on the rest of the world would almost certainly have proved crucial to a reformed system constructed according to the C-20 blueprint of convertibility plus stable but adjustable par values, since a float would have been the only US defence to a flight of privately held dollars into other currencies. (Asset settlement could have provided protection against a switch of official dollars into SDRs, but not against a switch of private dollars.)

The Europeans accepted the desirability of the United States having the same degree of flexibility as themselves, and they sympathized with the solution of multicurrency intervention (MCI) proposed by the United States. However, they had grave misgivings about the implications for settlement that MCI might have. So did the developing countries, which were suspicious of MCI precisely on the ground that it might lead to a generalization of the reserve currency role. Just as the reserve role of the dollar had grown naturally from its intervention role, so might the other currencies in the MCI group acquire a reserve role naturally unless there were specific settlement obligations precluding this result. This would have led to a multiple reserve currency system, which the Europeans rejected because of the near-impossibility of retaining control over international liquidity in such a system and because of its inherent vulnerability to 'speculative' reserve shifts between currencies, and the developing countries rejected because it threatened to produce reserve growth in the form of reserve currencies rather than SDRs. These problems would not have arisen with a system of asset settlement, but this was precisely what the United States was unwilling to concede. The general goodwill toward an MCI system could therefore not be translated into concrete agreement because of the disagreement on the crucial issue of settlement.

Just how central this issue is can be seen by considering the assertion that the choice between 'floor' and 'ceiling' intervention determines whether deficit or surplus countries bear the responsibility for initiating adjustment.[3] 'Ceiling intervention' places the onus of defending the margins on the surplus country — i.e., that one whose currency reaches the ceiling — which therefore acquires the currencies of the deficit countries. If it is unable or unwilling to convert these, reserve losses can never place adjustment pressure on the deficit countries, and so it is the surplus country that has to undertake adjustment if it is not to run the risk of exporting real resources in exchange for suspect currencies indefinitely. In contrast, under a system of 'floor intervention' it is the deficit country that has to intervene, and therefore that has to adjust when its stockpile of foreign currencies threatens to run out. This argument depends crucially on the assumption that there is no settlement: with asset settlement the surplus country presents the currencies acquired in intervention to the deficit country, which thereby loses reserves exactly as under a system of floor intervention. With asset settlement the choice between floor and ceiling intervention — or, for that matter, a system in which each country intervenes at both margins in its own market — is a technical detail of little consequence.[4] With optional or partial convertibility the question of whether the location of the intervention obligation matters is far less clearcut than in the two cases of inconvertibility and obligatory conversion; but it would seem to be at least of potential significance, especially if convertibility were to be limited by a set of PAHLs.

Compared to the question of the settlement system that accompanies it, the other details of an MCI system are secondary. Such a system presupposes a group of currencies — the Technical Group on

3. The argument is due to P. Salin, 'The Problem of Symmetry in the Process of Adjustment and the Reform of the International Monetary System', unpublished, 1972.
4. One technical argument advanced in favour of ceiling intervention was that it would avoid the necessity of participants in the MCI scheme holding working balances of a large number of other currencies and/or concluding swap agreements with a large number of other countries. The main technical argument in favour of intervention at both floor and ceiling rested on imperfections in arbitrage, especially prior to closure of markets in the afternoon or because of time differences.

Intervention and Settlement mentioned a group of some 10 to 20 — whose central banks intervene in any of the others, as occasion demands. It has sometimes been argued that it is technically inefficient to replace single currency intervention by MCI, since central banks are obliged to watch a number of rates rather than just one and to hold, replenish and dispose of stocks of a number of currencies, thus losing the economies resulting from having an international money. The experience of the snake seems, however, to have demonstrated that the economies forgone in MCI are quantitatively trivial. Under a par value system (which is the only context in which MCI was discussed) the basic obligation of members of the group is to intervene in their own market when the rate against any other member reaches the prescribed maximum margin from parity. (The Technical Group on Intervention and Settlement more or less assumed that this margin would be 4·5 per cent, which was the margin between non-dollar currencies that had resulted from the Smithsonian 2·25 per cent margins between the dollar and other currencies.) Each member may intervene at both margins in its own market, or each member may restrict intervention to one margin (the same for all countries) and rely on arbitrage from its partner's market to defend the other margin. In addition there is the problem of intra-margin intervention. This is generally felt to be desirable in order to smooth out erratic short-term payments fluctuations, but the questions arise as to when and in what currency it should be undertaken; it is clearly desirable to avoid the contrary intervention that could arise if central banks could intervene freely within the margins. Intervention at the margin has its own built-in rules: one intervenes to defend the margin in the currency against which one is at the margin. An obvious extension of this rule is to provide that intra-margin intervention take place in the currency furthest from parity on the appropriate side, but this may pose problems where the market is thin. The foreign exchange market experts seems to feel that the only practical solution is to 'concert' intervention policies — i.e., to telephone the central bank of the country in whose currency one is planning to intervene, to ensure that it has no contrary intentions. This is fine within Europe, but would involve central bankers working night shifts if Japan and Australia were in the MCI group.

The need for such 'concertation' was perhaps the principal factor limiting the prospective size of the MCI group. That raised the problem of how the non-members would defend their par values. One suggestion, thought relevant to countries still closely dependent on a single power, was that they continue to peg to a particular currency in the MCI group. Another class of idea considered more suitable for countries with diversified external economic relations, was that these countries unilaterally undertake to intervene in one or several MCI currencies with a view to defending a rate that was some sort of average of their parities against some or all of the MCI currencies. There is no point in reviewing the detailed suggestions made by the Technical Group on Intervention and Settlement (paras.15-19), since these have been rendered redundant by the definition of the SDR in terms of a basket of currencies. This provides a natural basis (already used by several countries, such as Iran and Kenya) for countries to peg to, even though they continue to intervene in a particular currency.

The Technical Group on Intervention and Settlement may not have recognized the possibility of using the basket SDR as the basis for defining margins in a system of currency intervention, but it did consider the possibility of conducting intervention in SDRs. It had always previously been assumed that this would become feasible only if and when the SDR was widely held by the private sector; after all, intervention consists in a transaction between a central bank and a private agent. Private holding of the SDR seemed a distant prospect and, to many minds, an undesirable one, since it would resurrect the possibility (that was thought to have been terminated by the 1968 Washington Agreement to create a 2-tier gold market) of shifts between currencies and primary reserve assets leading to changes in the stock of official reserves. The Technical Group on Intervention and Settlement pointed out, however, that one could allow commercial banks to arbitrage SDRs without their being allowed to hold SDRs (paras. 35-8). If a group of central banks agreed to buy and sell SDRs at par $\pm 2\cdot 25$ per cent, any deviation greater than 4·5 per cent from parity between the market exchange rates of the participants would create the opportunity of profitable arbitrage by buying SDRs from one central bank and selling them to the other. This suggestion, which originated in the Bank of England, proved popular with both the foreign exchange dealers and the developing countries. The twin attractions to the developing countries were (*a*) that it would place the SDR firmly in the centre of the system and so avoid any danger of a multiple reserve currency system emerging, and (*b*) that it would allow all countries that wished to do so to participate. Its only real drawback would seem to be its dependence on the functioning of an effective par value system: as developed by the Technical Group on Intervention and Settlement, the approach requires that the SDR be valued according to the 'par value approach' (see Chapter 6), and assumes that central banks would post prices at which they would deal in SDRs based on margins around par values. Whether it might prove possible to design an SDR intervention system for application in a world of managed floating is a question that could become of importance in the future, especially if the argument in the chapter regarding the non-viability of a par value system is correct.

6

Reserve assets

'The SDR will become the principal reserve asset ... ' declared paragraph 24 of the *Outline of Reform*, in another notable confusion of aspiration and achievement. But, as with the desire for a better working of the adjustment process, the aspiration was widely shared. Most countries, with the exception of the major gold producer, possibly some of the major gold holders, notably France, and a few of the small creditor countries that never joined the SDR scheme (such as Singapore), felt that they shared a common interest in the construction of an SDR standard. The issues involved in the creation of a fiduciary reserve asset had been extensively discussed during the 1960s, and the long debate had reached a successful climax in Rio in 1967. From then on there was a general will to build on the achievement of the Rio Agreement, and at the outset of the reform negotiations there was a rather general hope — crystallized by Anthony Barber's speech at the IMF Annual Meeting in 1971 — that major progress in this direction would be achieved.

It is relatively easy to see what is involved in a full SDR standard. The SDR would not be just the principal, it would be the only, reserve asset. For this to be literally true, either intervention must be undertaken in SDRs (with commercial banks therefore either holding or arbitraging SDRs) or else settlement must be immediate (and, of course, obligatory). The volume of international liquidity is determined exclusively by the decisions of the international community on the number of SDRs to be created. All the problems of reserve shifting caused by the existence of a multiplicity of reserve assets are swept away. The problems of managing the system are those of determining the value of the SDR, its interest rate, the volume of SDRs to be created, the terms and conditions on which conditional liquidity is to be provided, and the proportions in which newly created SDRs are to be distributed to different countries.

The problem that faced the C-20 was, however, considerably more

complex than that of designing a pure SDR standard *in vacuo*. Rightly
or wrongly (probably rightly), it was taken for granted that revolutionary
changes were out of the question, if only because central banks are
cautious institutions that would resist forced sudden changes in the
assets that they hold — especially if they were asked to restrict their
international assets to one as untested as the SDR. This meant that the
C-20 not only had to have some conception of the shape of the SDR
standard that might ultimately emerge, but also to consider the
problems of the transition to such a system. And this involved not just
arrangements to transform the existing system into a new one without
jeopardizing the legitimate interests that countries had built up in the
past, but to create an interim system that would contain pressures
making for further evolution toward the ultimate goal but would
nevertheless be viable in its own right for an indefinite period.

The first part of this chapter considers the problem of designing an
SDR to fit this demanding interim role. The second section discusses
the other controversial proposal for reform of the SDR that was
considered by the C-20 — the introduction of the link. The next two
sections consider the roles of the two other major forms of reserve
asset, gold and reserve currencies, including the possibility of
substituting SDRs for both gold and reserve currencies through a
substitution facility in the Fund. The final section deals with the
problem of the control of international liquidity, covering both the
conditions necessary for the exercise of such control and the criteria
that should guide it.

The SDR

Anthony Barber's 1971 speech at the IMF Annual Meetings had
attracted major attention because of its eye-catching proposal that the
SDR replace gold as the numeraire in terms of which par values are
expressed. At the time this seemed an eminently sensible diplomatic
proposal, in so far as it offered a way for the international community
to register its support for the principle that the United States have the
power of initiative as regards par value changes of the dollar. The C-20
had no difficulty in agreeing at an early stage that the SDR should
become the numeraire (*Outline*, para.24). It turned out, however, that
this decision was a minor embarrassment.

The problem arose because the breakdown of the par value system
in March 1973 made it imperative to reconsider a problem that had
been resolved with remarkably little controversy when the SDR was
being designed in the mid-1960s. This concerned the fundamental
question of what an SDR was; not in the sense of what it was 'backed'
by, or whether there were adequate assurances of its liquidity provided

by the obligations of other countries to accept it in the event of a balance-of-payments need (which were questions that had been very thoroughly thrashed out); but in the sense of what determined what an SDR was worth — the problem of the valuation of the SDR. In the circumstances of 1967 it had seemed natural enough to define the value of the SDR in terms of gold; gold was still thought of as the basic reserve asset, its value in terms of currencies was defined by the par value system and this value still ruled in the private market as well, and the asset being introduced was thought of as a supplement to gold. When the SDR was introduced into circulation in 1970, the par value system still survived and the dollar was still, in principle, convertible into gold by monetary authorities (although the value of gold in the private market differed from the monetary price as a result of the end of the Gold Pool in 1968), so that there were no compelling grounds for modifying the earlier decision to define the value of the SDR by reference to par values. There was, however, a problem about interpreting this decision.

When the IMF was established it was decided that all transactions with the Fund would be effected at par values, and this practice was maintained so far as the General Account was concerned until the end of 1971. Since currency exchange rates could deviate, if only slightly, from parity, the practice meant that the currency in which a transaction was effected was not a matter of indifference to the country involved: for example, if a country were making a repayment to the Fund it would prefer to repay in dollars rather than sterling so long as the pound was above its dollar parity. This was not unduly important with General Account transactions, at least as long as margins were narrow so that the financial stakes were modest, since each transaction was individually negotiated on the basis of an established set of rules. But, since a country designated to receive SDRs was to have a choice of the currency it provided in exchange, the practice would have been unsuitable for the SDR Account. The rule of all transactions being undertaken at par was therefore replaced by the 'equal value principle', which specified that users of SDRs should receive precisely the same currency value (in terms of current market exchange rates) no matter what country was designated to receive their SDRs and what convertible currency it chose to provide. This principle required that currency/SDR exchange rates be proportionate to market exchange rates at the time the transaction was effected; if, for example, the pound were 0·5 per cent above its dollar parity, then a country providing pounds in exchange for SDRs would have to provide 0·5 per cent fewer pounds than it would have to if the pound were at parity against the dollar. However, the equal value principle necessarily means question therefore arose of what is meant by 'defining the value of the SDR by reference to par values'. The answer given to this question when the SDR was introduced was to define the dollar as always being at par against the SDR. Thus the dollar/SDR exchange rate could change only through a par value change of the dollar, while (for example) the pound/SDR rate could change either because of a par value change by the pound or because the sterling/dollar exchange rate changed within the margins.

As long as margins were as narrow as they were before 1971, which currency was treated as being at par made little practical difference to the value of the SDR. The important changes in the value of the SDR were those that resulted from changes in par values. For example, had the Smithsonian parity changes been implemented exclusively by revaluations by strong currencies, as initially desired by the United States, the effect would have been to depreciate the SDR in terms of currencies in general. In fact the Smithsonian par value changes took the form of a balance between devaluations and revaluations that left the value of the SDR in terms of currencies in general (measured by trade weights) almost exactly unchanged, while the SDR appreciated 8·57 per cent in terms of the dollar. Thereafter the practice of calculating the transactions value of the SDR in terms of currency A on the basis of the (new) par value of the dollar and the dollar/A exchange rate was resumed. In view of the wider margins adopted at the Smithsonian, however, the importance of the practice of always treating the dollar as being at par was much increased. A general weakening (or strengthening) of the dollar against other currencies within the margins resulted in a significant depreciation (or appreciation) in the purchasing power of the SDR over currencies in general. The SDR underwent a further 11·11 per cent appreciation in terms of the dollar, and also an appreciation of some 4 per cent in terms of currencies in general, on the occasion of the dollar devaluation of February 1973. But, with the advent of generalized floating the following month, there was clearly going to be no occasion for any future change in the dollar/SDR rate, while the rate between the SDR and all other currencies could fluctuate without limit as a consequence of the ups and downs of the dollar. Thus the depreciation of the dollar against the snake by some 12 per cent in mid-1973 caused a depreciation of the SDR in terms of currencies in general (measured by trade weights) of perhaps 7 per cent. So long as this situation continued, the SDR was simply a dollar with a low interest rate (1·5 per cent). As such it would rapidly have become unwanted by creditors, and, although the obligations to accept SDRs could have been used to compel countries to hold SDRs against their will, the prospect of advancing the SDR towards the ultimate goal of becoming the basic reserve asset would have been non-existent.

The advent of generalized floating therefore created a pressing need to establish a new basis for valuing the SDR. This need reinforced the concern that had already been expressed by some members of the IMF Executive Board about both the non-competitive interest rate and the previous valuation basis of the SDR, and in the spring of 1973 the IMF turned its attention to these topics. The deliberations of the Executive Board were monitored by the C-20 with a view to recommending provisions for the reformed system, and Annex 9 of the *Outline* describes the four possible techniques of valuing the SDR that emerged from discussion. Since the introduction of the 'new SDR' on 1 July 1974 provided the second substantive act of international monetary reform to emerge from the period of the C-20, it is important to consider the questions involved in some detail.

Four techniques were proposed during discussion as providing possible bases for valuing the SDR in the reformed system.[1] These four techniques had differing implications as regards (a) the suitability of the SDR for use as the numeraire; (b) the ability to satisfy the 'equal value principle' — i.e., to ensure that the SDR had a unique value at every point in time; (c) the stabilization or evolution of the value of the SDR over time; and (d) the 'robustness' of the system of valuation, in the sense of its ability to function irrespective of whether or not some or all countries were failing to defend their par values. The various techniques of valuation were evaluated primarily on the basis of these four criteria. The reason that the early decision to make the SDR the numeraire for expressing par values subsequently proved to be embarrassing was that two of the proposed techniques for valuing the SDR did not guarantee that the 'transactions value' of the SDR — i.e., the currency/SDR exchange rate — need bear any necessary relationship to a country's par value in terms of the SDR. This became known as the problem of 'inconsistency' between par values and transactions values.

Of the techniques proposed as possible bases for valuing the SDR in the reformed system, the one that was closest to traditional practice was the 'par value technique'. This envisaged that the transactions value of the SDR would be set at par, or at some specified distance — e.g., half the established margin — away from par, for every currency. The treatment previously accorded the dollar would, therefore, have been generalized to all other currencies. This would have meant abandonment of the equal value principle: the SDR would have had

---

1. For another discussion of this subject see J. J. Polak, *Valuation and Rate of Interest of the SDR*, IMF, Washington DC, 1974.

broken cross rates, with all the attendant problems of the incentives created to engage in certain arbitrage transactions and to avoid other SDR transactions, and the consequent need to specify precisely countries' rights and obligations with regard to use of the SDR. The par value technique also had the limitation of only being workable at all when an effective par value system was in operation. Finally, it should be appreciated that it would have preserved the situation in which the evolution in the value of the SDR over time was dependent on the balance between devaluations and revaluations.

A second approach, that of the 'standard basket technique', involved a far more radical break with previous practice, since par values had no part to play in determining the transactions value of the SDR. This was the technique that was actually adopted. The value of the SDR was declared equal to a basket of currencies which in the event contained 40 US cents, 38 pfennigs, 4·5 UK new pence, and specified sums of 13 other currencies.* The value of the SDR in terms

* The composition of the basket is as follows:

currency	percentage weight	units of currency in one SDR
US dollar	33	0.40
Deutschmark	12.5	0.38
Pound sterling	9	0.045
French franc	7.5	0.44
Japanese yen	7.5	26
Canadian dollar	6	0.071
Italian lira	6	47
Netherlands guilder	4.5	0.14
Belgian franc	3.5	1.6
Swedish krona	2.5	0.13
Australian dollar	1.5	0.012
Danish krone	1.5	0.11
Norwegian krone	1.5	0.099
Spanish peseta	1.5	1.1
Australian schilling	1	0.22
South African rand	1	0.0082

The currencies in the basket are those with a share in world exports of goods and services that averaged more than 1 per cent in 1968-72. The percentage weights are based on these export figures, except that the dollar got a 50 per cent bonus weighting, ostensibly because of the special importance of the dollar in international finance. The actual number of currency units were chosen, to 2 significant figures, so as to approximate the desired percentage weights as closely as possible, while ensuring that the SDR value was equated to its base date value under the previous valuation technique to 6 significant figures.

of currency A can be calculated on any day by valuing the specified quantities of the 16 component currencies at their market exchange rates with currency A, and summing. An appreciation (depreciation) of any currency in the basket produces a depreciation (appreciation) of the SDR in terms of that currency and an appreciation (depreciation) of the SDR in terms of other currencies; the purchasing power of the SDR over the weighted average of the currencies composing the basket remains constant by definition. This is true whether the appreciation results from an upward float, an appreciation within the margins, or a revaluation.

The standard basket has three major advantages over its competitors. The first is that it remains operable under all exchange rate regimes:[2] it does not require the operation of an effective par value system, it does not threaten to impose on the Fund the need to decide whether the Europeans or the United States are 'really' observing their par values when both are claiming to do so but the market rates between the two are nowhere near parity (as happened in mid-1973), and it does not require the Fund to decide when floating has become generalized and some other basis of valuation therefore has to be adopted. This robustness is an eminently practical advantage, which in the end was decisive in gaining acceptance of the standard basket, at least on a provisional basis.

The second advantage arises from the fact that as well as satisfying the equal value principle, the standard basket goes furthest towards insulating the purchasing power of the SDR from capricious variation over time. Since SDRs are reserves and the purpose of reserves is to provide an inventory against payments deficits, the ideal SDR valuation from the standpoint of country A would be one that provided constant purchasing power over a given volume of A's imports. The standard basket falls short of this ideal in two respects. First, and inevitably, the SDR cannot reflect the particular needs of country A, but must be constructed on the basis of some average that will, hopefully, be reasonably appropriate for the majority of countries. Second, the SDR is defined in terms of a basket of currencies and not in terms of a basket of internationally traded goods. This alternative was considered but summarily rejected because of a widespread if questionable belief that such indexation is inherently inflationary. What the standard basket does, therefore, is to insulate the purchasing power of the SDR

2. There is one qualification: when a currency in the basket has a dual exchange market, it is necessary to decide whether to use the commercial or financial rate. In practice the IMF has used the commercial rate, which is consistent with the second but not with the third of the advantages of the standard basket discussed below.

from the effect of exchange rate changes (at least so far as a typical country whose import sources correspond to the weights of the currencies in the basket is concerned), but not from the effect of internal inflation in the countries whose currencies compose the basket. Even this limited insulation seems, however, to have provided a useful unit of account, judging by the extent to which the SDR has subsequently been adopted for this purpose by the private sector.[3]

There is a third potential advantage of the standard basket, although (mistakenly, in my view) not much weight was attached to it and it therefore does not appear in the list of criteria for evaluating different techniques given above. This stems from the possibility provided by the standard basket of eliminating capricious changes in the relative attractiveness of holding SDRs versus currencies, with their associated incentives for destabilizing shifts in the composition of reserves. The yield of the SDR in terms of a particular currency, A, has two elements: the own interest rate of the SDR, and the appreciation of the SDR in terms of currency A. If the own interest rate of the SDR is set independently of interest rates on currencies and of expected changes in the capital value of the SDR, it is inevitable that there will be variations, which may be sharp, in the relative expected yields of the SDR and of currencies, as a result of changes in national interest rates or expected exchange rate changes. But if the SDR were valued by the standard basket and the SDR interest rate were set equal to the weighted average (with the same weights) of the interest rates on the currencies in the basket, the realized yield on the SDR would be identical to the average yield on a portfolio containing the currencies in the basket held in the same proportion that they are represented in the basket. And, in so far as market arbitrage can be relied on to equate the expected yields on different currencies, the expected yield on the SDR would also be equated to the expected yield on each individual currency, thus eliminating all incentive for destabilizing switches in reserve composition. To the extent that market arbitrage is ineffective or exchange rate expectations unfulfilled, the guarantee of stability in both yield and capital value in terms of currencies in general might have been expected to constitute an attractive feature that would have induced central banks to hold SDRs in preference to reserve currencies even though the own interest rate of the SDR were somewhat lower than the average interest rate on currencies. To reflect this expectation, and to avoid the possibility of the SDR dominating reserve currencies during the lengthy transitional period when both would have to co-exist as major reserve assets, it was suggested that the SDR interest rate be set lower than the average currency interest rate by a constant

3. See Chapter 3, n.11 (p.72).

factor that was termed a 'security discount' (a term invented as the antonym to 'risk premium'). It was hoped that this procedure would keep the SDR interest rate in line with fluctuating market rates without the repeated need to reach decisions on changes in interest rates in the IMF Executive Board; such decisions are particularly difficult to reach because they inevitably involve a clear and immediate conflict of interest between debtor and creditor countries.

The standard basket does, however, suffer from the problem of inconsistency between par values and transactions values, and this proved to be a major stumbling block to its acceptance. Define the 'central transactions value' of a currency in terms of the SDR to be its transactions value when all exchange rates are at parity. Suppose that central transactions values and par values were initially equal, but that a currency that comprised 30 per cent of the basket was then devalued by 10 per cent. The par values of other currencies would of course be unchanged, while their central transactions values would rise by 3 per cent — i.e., the SDR would depreciate 3 per cent relative to these currencies. Par values and central transactions values would thus differ. This difference could grow without limit over time, and would indeed do so to the extent that there was a (weighted) preponderance of devaluations over revaluations (or vice versa) of the currencies that comprised the basket. It was felt by many that it would be perplexing to have a numeraire in which one expressed a par value that might then differ to an arbitrary extent from the price at which one transacted business in the asset that was supposedly serving as numeraire. The obvious solution was to abandon the SDR as numeraire and adopt some abstract unit of account for this purpose instead; but it was at this point that the early decision of the C-20 to adopt the SDR as numeraire posed a problem. It proved unthinkable to ask the C-20 to go back on one of the two propositions that it had actually agreed on (the other being the resurrection of the adjustable peg). So one was left with a choice between ignoring the inconsistency between par values and transactions values, which is what has actually happened; making periodic uniform changes in par values in order to bring par values in line with central transactions values; and adopting the 'base year SDR' as numeraire (just as the 1944 gold dollar previously served as numeraire) and allowing the current SDR to drift away from the base year SDR.

A third possible technique for valuing the SDR became known as the 'adjustable basket'. Under this proposal the SDR would have again been valued as a basket of currencies, but the amount of a currency in the basket would have been adjusted whenever it was devalued or revalued, or when it floated, in such a way as to prevent its change altering the central transactions value of the SDR in terms of currencies with unchanged par values. For example, in the illustration in the preceding paragraph, the 10 per cent devaluation would have led to an 11 per cent increase in the number of units of the devaluing currency in the basket, thus maintaining central transactions values equal to par values for all currencies and preventing the 'inconsistency' problem. Similarly, a currency that floated would have had its quantity in the basket adjusted day by day on the same principle, which would of course have been tantamount to dropping that currency from the basket altogether for the duration of its misdemeanour. The function of the basket is, therefore, confined to that of determining the transactions value of the SDR within the margins; the long-term evolution in the value of the SDR is determined by the balance between devaluations and revaluations, as under the par value technique. To describe this as a basket has been likened to describing two facing pieces of bread and butter as a kosher ham sandwich. The adjustable basket suffers from the same lack of robustness as the par value technique does, but, unlike the latter, it satisfies the equal value principle (and it does so without requiring that one currency always be valued at par).

The fourth possible technique proposed was that known as the 'asymmetrical basket'. Under this proposal, devaluations and downward floats would have led to a writing up in the number of units of the depreciating currency in the basket, as under the adjustable basket, while revaluations and upward floats would not have led to any change, as under the standard basket. The object of this exercise (which has been likened to an open kosher ham sandwich) was to produce a 'stronger' SDR, specifically by preventing depreciations (other than those within the margins) of currencies in the basket reducing the transactions value of the SDR in terms of other currencies. In so far as the currencies in the basket underwent any appreciations at all, the asymmetrical basket would have guaranteed that par values came to exceed central transactions values. And in so far as there were any depreciations of currencies in the basket, the asymmetrical basket would have guaranteed that the value of the SDR would have appreciated relative to its value under the standard basket. Whether this would have raised the total yield on the SDR, which is the question of interest to a wealth-maximizing central bank as opposed to a central bank intent on minimizing the number of occasions when it has to show a book loss in its accounts, would depend on whether the prospect of appreciation in terms of currencies in general would have provoked a decision to fix a lower interest rate on the SDR, and if so, whether this reduction would in fact have been offset by the occasional capricious appreciations resulting from currency depreciations. So far as robustness and the equal value principle are concerned, the asymmetrical basket is similar to the adjustable basket.

To those not steeped in the mystique of the par value system, the arguments seemed to point conclusively towards adoption of the standard basket. It was consistent with the equal value principle (as were the other basket solutions). More critical, it alone offered an unambiguous, consistent valuation of the SDR no matter what happened to the exchange rate regime; it alone was based on an economically relevant concept of stability in value over time, which offered the possibility of providing a valuable unit of account for use by the private sector and the smaller countries; and it alone offered the opportunity of adopting a formula for the SDR interest rate that was guaranteed to preserve the yield on the SDR constant relative to that on currencies in general. To pit against these substantive economic considerations were various cosmetic trivia: that a central bank might have to show a book loss on SDR holdings in terms of its own currency even though it had continued to defend its own par value unchanged; that the United States would have to make maintenance of value payments (as other countries already did) even without a change in the par value of the dollar (readers who are unaware of the intricacies of IMF accounting practices are advised not to waste time discovering the insignificance of this consideration); and that par values and central transactions values might drift apart. However, many participants in the negotiations did not take the par value system so lightheartedly; for years (until mid-1974) those who worked and conferred in the IMF were confronted daily by the inspirational words of Article IV, Section 1(a), on the way to the elevator:

> The par value of the currency of each member shall be expressed in terms of gold as a common denominator or in terms of the United States dollar of the weight and fineness in effect on July 1, 1944.

It therefore proved impossible to reach agreement on the technique to be adopted in the reformed system.

What cut the Gordian knot was the realization that a new method of valuation was an urgent necessity, not something that could be postponed indefinitely until the rest of the reformed system was introduced.[4] Since the interim period was one of widespread floating, in

4. The situation had become so unsatisfactory by the second half of 1973 that the EEC requested, and was granted, permission to circulate SDRs between participants in the snake at values related to the par values of the EEC currencies, and therefore at a significant premium over the value at which they circulated outside the snake, which was based on the par value of the US dollar. Such a 2-tier price structure would inevitably have been damaging to the SDR if it were maintained permanently. (The decision allowing the 2-tier price structure lapsed a year later after the introduction of the basket

which there was even some dispute as to whether it was the dollar and its satellites or the snake that should be considered as observing their par values, the standard basket was the only system capable of operating satisfactorily in the existing circumstances. The C-20 proved amenable to this argument of necessity, and the standard basket was accordingly agreed in principle at the Rome meeting in January 1974 and implemented (albeit with a provision for review within 2 years) on 1 July 1974 — 30 years to the day after the start of the Bretton Woods conference, the day enshrined in Article IV, Section 1(a).[5]

Simultaneously with the adoption of the basket method of valuation of the SDR, its interest rate was raised from 1·5 per cent to 5 per cent. The 5 per cent rate was not permanently fixed, but was to vary (unless the Executive Board decided otherwise) by (on average) about 50 per cent of any future changes in a composite interest rate determined as a weighted average of the interest rates on the five major currencies in the basket. This represented something of a reversion from the *Outline's* prescription for the SDR interest rate, according to which 'the interest rate on the SDR will be set from time to time by the Executive Board in such a way as to maintain an appropriate effective yield, in the light of changing market interest rates' (para.26), to the earlier conception of a rate related by formula to an average market interest rate. The explanation for this reversion surely lies in the realization of the diplomatic difficulties that would have been involved in repeatedly changing an established rate when the national interests of the various parties are diametrically opposed, as they are — at least from a short-run standpoint, which is what usually matters — in choosing how much money debtors should pay creditors. The interest rate decision actually reached in June 1974 is a classic example of the compromises needed to secure agreement in such circumstances: the final outcome lies almost exactly half-way between the rational outcome suggested by economic analysis and the *status quo ante*. The economic analysis is that already outlined in describing the rationale for the standard

5. The use of the standard basket has, of course, resulted in inconsistency between par values and central transactions values. This problem has been handled by ignoring it. Indeed, par values have not merely been inconsistent with transactions values, but with one another. For example, when Norway established a new par value, the object was to define new parities and therefore to establish new margins with her partners in the snake; when Thailand established a new par value, the purpose was to define a new parity and thence to establish new margins with the US dollar; and when Iran established a new par value, the effect was, in conjunction with the current transactions value (not par value) of the dollar, to determine the daily dollar intervention points of the rial (for the rial is pegged to the SDR). Thus the cross rates between the Norwegian krone, the Thai baht and the Iranian rial bear no necessary relation to the ratio of their par values. And it doesn't matter so long as no one thinks it does.

basket:[6] take a composite interest rate on the currencies in the basket, for which the five leading currencies are a reasonable proxy (they constitute almost 70 per cent of the basket), and deduct a security discount of, say, 1·5 per cent. Answer: 8·5 per cent initially, since the composite rate was about 10 per cent, the rate to vary one-for-one with future changes in the composite rate. *Status quo ante*: 1·5 per cent with no variation. Compromise: 5 per cent, the rate to vary one-for-two with future changes in the composite rate.

The major characteristics of the SDR that required reform in order to promote the establishment of the SDR as the basic reserve asset were those of valuation and yield, but it was also recognized that the rules governing use of the SDR might be relaxed to advantage. There was rather general support for such ideas as extending the circumstances under which willing partners could enter into transactions in SDRs without going through the designation procedure in the IMF (for example, to facilitate the settlement of interventions undertaken to keep the snake together); authorization for the General Account of the IMF to use SDRs in place of gold or currencies in any transaction (including gold tranche subscriptions on the occasion of quota increases); and enabling any official financial institutions, such as the IBRD or the European Monetary Cooperation Fund, to become holders of SDRs. These proposals were adopted in the amendments to the IMF Articles proposed in April 1976. In addition, considerable support was expressed during the C-20 for abolition of the reconstitution provision, but in the end the projected amendment to the Articles simply reduced the majority required for its abolition from 85 per cent to 70 per cent.

The link

The reforms discussed above were motivated by the desire to enhance the monetary characteristics of the SDR. This was not true of the other important reform of the SDR considered by the C-20: amendment of the formula governing the distribution of SDR allocations, or, in more familiar terms, the link. The question at issue here was not whether the monetary characteristics of the SDR could be improved, but whether the SDR scheme could also be used to advance the objective of transferring real resources for development without prejudicing its primary function of providing a monetary asset for central banks.

6. The analysis of the optimum quantity of money, which has often been appealed to in order to provide a rationale for raising the interest rate on the SDR, might suggest a slightly higher figure than the criterion invoked in the text (of making central banks indifferent between holding SDRs and competitive assets), in so far as the optimum quantity of money analysis provides no role for a 'security discount'.

Discussion of the link was largely focused on technical questions, rather than on the basic value judgement whether the international community wished to use the seigniorage resulting from the production of fiduciary reserve assets as an instrument for effecting a modest improvement in the world distribution of income. My own view is that these technical arguments are 'secondary and unpersuasive'.[7] Given the existing facts on world income distribution, those who share this view do not need to have very much in the way of an egalitarian welfare function to favour the link. The extent to which those who opposed the link did so out of a genuine belief in the technical arguments they advanced, and the extent to which these arguments were used as a front to avoid the potential income redistribution, is largely immaterial. In either event a complete discrediting of the technical arguments for opposing the link would probably have paved the way for an agreement to institute the link, for in the 1970s it is more or less taken for granted that international organizations bias their acts in favour of the developing countries when the opportunity arises, and it is doubtful whether any country would have been prepared to jeopardize its international standing by overtly challenging this presumption. It was, therefore, appropriate enough for the C-20 to concentrate its attention on the technical issues, however secondary they may be.

The primary argument of the link's opponts amounted to an assertion that the link would undermine the monetary integrity of the SDR. There are three ways in which this might occur. The way that has been most emphasized is that the essentially limitless needs for development finance might lead to SDR allocations that were excessive from a monetary standpoint. The developing countries did their best to still this fear by explicitly accepting that decisions on SDR creation should be made solely with a view to satisfying global liquidity requirements and should in no measure be dependent upon the needs for resource transfer of the beneficiaries of the link. But, while the principle was never challenged, the criteria that govern SDR allocations are so imprecise (see the final section of this chapter) that it is understandable if agreement on the principle was not in itself particularly reassuring to sceptics. The developing countries continued, after all, to press for a new allocation of SDRs even in 1972-73, when the world was positively bloated with excess liquidity by just about any standard. If they had been in a position to determine the volume of SDR

7. The phrase is that of C. F. Diaz-Alejandro, *Less Developed Countries and the Post-1971 International Financial System*, Princeton Essays in International Finance No. 108, April 1975, p.26, in commenting on my survey of these issues in 'International Liquidity — A Survey', *Economic Journal*, September 1973, Section III.3.

allocations, this would have been an important consideration; but in fact they were not. Furthermore, some critics tended to undermine this case by arguing the opposite proposition that the link would lead to inadequate SDR creation because the advanced countries would be reluctant to sanction adequate SDR allocations when they had to earn their own reserve increases through resource transfer.[8] The latter reasoning could be inverted to argue that the need to earn reserves on the part of the countries with the decisive voice in SDR creation is just what is needed to restrain inflationary issues of SDRs.[9]

A second way in which it was thought that the link might threaten the monetary prospects of the SDR also attracted much attention in the C-20. The Technical Group on the Link stated (para.6(b)) that opponents of the link believed:

> To link allocations of SDRs to the financing of economic development in addition to purely monetary requirements would be bound to arouse suspicion and concern in the international financial community, and would exacerbate the difficulties of building up confidence in the new system.

I have already voiced my conviction that the only viable method of building confidence is to construct a system with objective characteristics that deserve confidence, and that a policy of pandering to the prejudices of the financially unsophisticated will prove counterproductive in anything but the very short run. Accordingly, the idea that confidence in the SDR could be enhanced by providing it with sound backing, and diminished by the absence of any overt backing, is not worth entertaining. What is needed to engender confidence is not a more orthodox balance sheet for the Special Drawing Account, but assurance that (a) other countries will always be willing to receive SDRs when a country needs to use them, and (b) those with the responsibility of paying the interest service on SDRs will continue to do so. If the second factor is unaffected by the link, there is no reason for the first to be affected; it is, therefore, the second one that is crucial. It seems to me that the best case one can make for believing that the link might harm confidence in the SDR rests on the possibility that developing countries might be tempted to default on their interest obligations. A financial temptation to default would, after all, arise if it appeared that the present value of future interest obligations on past SDR allocations exceeded the present value of expected future SDR allocations.

8. See H. G. Johnson, 'The Link that Chains', *Foreign Policy*, Fall 1972, p.119.
9. R. L. Haan, *Special Drawing Rights and Development*, Stenfert Kroese N. V., Leyden, 1971, pp.122-7.

Although neither the IMF nor the IBRD has yet suffered a debt default, any belief on the part of potential SDR creditors that SDR debtors had a significant financial interest in default could hardly help but undermine confidence in the SDR. The argument is nonetheless unconvincing. In the first place, if there is an incentive to default with a link, there will also be an incentive to default without one.[10] Second, default would be an offence to the international community which would be bound to threaten a whole range of international economic relationships in such a way as to make it a most unattractive course of action. Third, since the present value of future SDR allocations depends positively on the difference between the SDR interest rate and the cost of alternative sources of long-term foreign borrowing, and the latter is greater the less creditworthy is a country, the developing countries in general (and those with the greatest pressure to consider default in particular) will be the countries with the greatest interest in ensuring access to future SDR allocations, and therefore with the greatest incentive to avoid default.

The third way in which a link could undermine the monetary prospects of the SDR is, in my judgement, by far the most important, though it received the least attention in the C-20, perhaps because the principal nation opposing the link shared with the developing countries a financial interest in this condition not being satisfied. It concerns the need to provide a sufficiently high yield on the SDR to make it an attractive reserve asset for central banks to hold. The higher is the interest rate on the SDR, the lower is the element of seigniorage that would accrue to developing countries as a result of the link. Once again experience was not altogether reassuring: a number of the developing countries sided with the United States in resisting the attempt to raise the SDR interest rate to a reasonable level in 1973-74. This threat to the prospects of the SDR would, however, have been by far the easiest of the three to avoid. The matter could have been dealt with once and for all by a simultaneous agreement to set the interest rate on the SDR by a formula based on the principles already described. Paradoxically the biggest danger of the link was (and perhaps still is) posed by the possibility of the United States deciding to bow to the inevitable and concede the link while still maintaining her opposition to the payment of an interest rate on the SDR competitive with that on the dollar, which would have resulted in the developing countries gaining a degree of seigniorage from the link that would have been incompatible with

10. This follows from the fact that the link would lead to proportionate changes in both the present value of future interest obligations on past SDR allocations and the present value of expected future SDR allocations.

the SDR displacing the dollar as the principal reserve asset. Once such seigniorage gains had been experienced, it would have been far more difficult to gain the consent of the developing countries to a subsequent rise in the interest rate, however obvious it might become that this were necessary.

Various other technical arguments, both for and against the link, have been adduced and were once again rehearsed in the report of the Technical Group on the Link. They concerned such subjects as whether the link would facilitate the adjustment process by allowing a larger sum total of current account surpluses to be shared out between the developed countries, whether the increased first-round spending of SDR allocations that would result from the link would have inflationary effects or could be expected to be neutralized by demand-management policy, and whether the link would in fact increase the total flow of aid or whether it would provoke offsetting cuts elsewhere (the question of 'additionality'). There is also one consideration suggested by the analysis in the next section that has not to my knowledge been recognized explicitly up to now: it concerns the fact that a link would reduce the present value to the typical developed country of replacing gold by the SDR, and might therefore make such replacement less likely.

My own view remains that these technical arguments are unpersuasive. But they are certainly not unambiguous; and, in the absence of the unambiguous refutation of the technical arguments against the link, there remained scope for the maintenance of opposition to the link. Accordingly, strong disagreements on this subject persisted up to the last minutes of the C-20, when the developing countries won a compensation prize in the form of an agreement that the subject should reappear on the agenda of the new IMF Interim Committee at an early date.

Gold

The extent of agreement reached by the C-20 on the perenially controversial topic of gold was recorded in para.28 of the *Outline*:

> Appropriate arrangements will be made for gold in the reformed system, in the light of the agreed objectives that the SDR should become the principal reserve asset and that the role of gold should be reduced. At the same time it is also generally recognized that gold reserves are an important component of global liquidity which should be usable to finance balance of payments deficits ...

The objectives were therefore conceived as being to reinstate gold as a reserve asset, which it had effectively ceased to be since August 1971 (for the distinguishing characteristic of a reserve asset is as much that it is used in transactions between central banks as the medium-of-exchange function is the distinguishing characteristic of money), while ensuring that gold became a progressively smaller part of the reserve stock. There was, however, no agreement as to what these objectives implied as regards any of the three decisions that needed to be made: first, as to whether an official price should be retained; second, as to what transactions between central banks should be permitted; and, third, as to what arrangements should be made for the sale of monetary gold on the market.

The *Outline* simply went on to record three alternative proposals that had been advanced. The first was to maintain the *status quo*, which allowed central banks to use their gold only by selling it to other central banks at the official price, which was out of the question, or on the market, which meant — except for small holders such as Uruguay — forcing down the price against themselves. A supplementary proposal of particular relevance to this case was the establishment of a gold substitution facility within the IMF to buy gold from members in exchange for SDRs at a market-related — i.e., near-market — price and subsequently dispose of the gold gradually on the market. This would have done something to assure the liquidity of gold holdings, though the sums that could have been assured quickly would inevitably have been limited unless the IMF were to be exposed to a considerable risk of financial loss through the market price falling between the time the IMF bought gold from a member and the time it was sold on the market. The second proposal would have involved abolition of the official gold price and permission for monetary authorities to buy and sell gold on a voluntary basis at mutually acceptable prices, while retaining the right of central banks to sell (but not buy) gold on the market. The third alternative would have added the right of central banks to buy gold on the market. This was close to the proposal actually accepted 15 months after the C-20 finished work, in August 1975, except that that was accompanied by an undertaking of the G-10 that the combined gold holdings of the Ten plus the Fund would not be increased for at least 2 years, and by agreement that the Fund would sell one-sixth of its gold holdings and return — 'restitute' — another one-sixth to members, in proportion to their subscriptions, at the official price.

The C-20 did not embark on any extensive analysis of the problems posed by restoring-cum-reducing the monetary role of gold — perhaps because countries came with such long-standing, inflexible and incompatible positions as to make a meeting of minds seem improbable. Whatever the reason, it is a fact that gold was remitted to neither a technical group nor the Executive Board, as all other contentious issues of comparable importance were. (The question of adjustment techniques was not, unfortunately, a contentious issue.) There is therefore no extensive body of analysis on which one can draw, whether approvingly or critically, as there is on other issues.

The central fact about gold is that the world as a whole had an interest, and recognized that it had an interest, in seeing gold replaced by the SDR. For reasons discussed in Chapter 2, deriving from the greater possibility of exercising rational control over the supply of SDRs, the lower cost of supplying SDRs and hence the possibility of paying a competitive rate of interest on SDRs, the SDR provided a more satisfactory reserve asset at a lower real cost. On the other hand, the acceptability of the SDR — as of any monetary asset — rests essentially upon assurance that it will remain acceptable to others in time of need, and the possibility of a complete breakdown in world monetary order which would destroy this assurance cannot be entirely excluded. Many countries, therefore, desired to retain a stockpile of gold as an insurance against major disaster. But this did not give them an incentive to guarantee that they would always accept gold, and unless the bulk of the major potential creditor countries (say at least three of OPEC, the United States, the EEC and Japan) had been prepared to give such an undertaking, gold's status as a reserve asset was bound to remain at best questionable.

The second major fact is that, while the world as a whole had a financial interest in seeing the SDR supplant gold, this was not true of every individual country. Certain countries had large stocks of gold relative to their share in SDR allocations and would therefore have benefited financially through a remonetization of gold accompanied by an equivalent reduction in the size of future SDR allocations. Countries defend their national interests much as birds defend their territories : they instinctively defend what they have more vigorously than they attack what others possess. That tended to rule out any strategy that would have meant making the major gold holders significantly worse off than they would have been in the absence of any agreement. And the *status quo* tended to be measured by the valuation that the private market placed on gold holdings.

The third major fact is the nature of the gold market. It is a market dominated by speculation in a way that no other market is. Against an annual production now under 30 million ounces, there is a stock of some 1 billion ounces of monetary gold in the vaults of central banks (some 15 per cent owned by the IMF), and an unknown, but certainly substantial, stock held by private hoarders. As in any asset market where current flows are small relative to stocks, the current price is dominated by expectations of what the future price will be, rising or falling until the risk adjusted expected rate of return (which in the case of gold is equal to the expected rate of appreciation of the gold price minus carrying costs) is equal to the rate of return available on other assets. But in the gold market future price expectations are crucially dependent on what is expected to happen to the stock of monetary gold. If, at one extreme, monetary gold was ultimately to be revalued to a new and sufficiently high official price, which central banks would support by buying in the market, then the appropriate current price would be the future official price less a discount factor reflecting the time that will elapse till the new price is fixed, the carrying cost of gold and the rate of return available on alternative assets. If, at the other extreme, monetary gold were all released immediately on the market, the current price would be driven down to a level such that it would from then on be expected to appreciate at a rate equal to the return available on alternative assets plus the carrying cost of gold, while the large hoards were slowly absorbed by the excess of consumption over production provoked by the low price. The difference between the current prices implied by these two extreme cases is unknown (and, indeed, unknowable, since the price implied by the first case would depend on the actual new official price adopted) but undoubtedly substantial, which implies that the gold price is heavily dependent on speculators' expectations of the future monetary role of gold.

Given these three basic facts, it was perhaps inevitable that an agreement on the future of gold would take the form of a bargain that on the one hand did something to increase gold's usability, and on the other provided for a start in disposing of the stock of monetary gold on the market. Even this was not an easy bargain to strike: anything that increased the usability of gold reserves meant going back on the progress that had already been made in demonetizing gold, and was therefore unpalatable to the countries that had taken the lead in this cause, while the fact that major gold holders tended to define their interests by reference to a market price that was based on the assumption that monetary gold was unlikely to be released for private use made them reluctant to agree to such release. No agreement was, therefore, reached during the period of the C-20. In the following year, however, two developments paved the way to an agreement. First, the two auctions of token sums of gold by the United States demonstrated the thinness of the gold market and the unwillingness of the opponents of gold to see a prolongation of the speculative bubble in the gold market. Second, the post-oil-price-increase financial plight of the non-oil developing countries led to a search for new sources of cash that could be tapped by the international community to help these countries, and the big stock of redundant gold owned by the IMF provided an obvious target.

Agreement was reached in outline on 31 August 1975, at the time of the IMF Annual Meetings, and completed in detail at the Jamaica meeting of the Interim Committee in January 1976. It was decided, first, to abolish the official gold price and with it all monetary uses of gold in the IMF; second, to permit central banks to buy gold at any price they cared to, thus allowing inter-central bank transactions at mutually acceptable prices; third, to sell one-sixth of the stock of gold held by the IMF, with most of the profits resulting from the excess of the market over the official price to be used to help finance the new Trust Fund being established to aid the poorest of the developing countries; and, fourth, to 'restitute' a further one-sixth of the Fund's gold to members. The permission for central banks to trade at mutually acceptable prices must do something to restore the liquidity of gold, though only time will tell how much. The agreement to start disposing of monetary gold, while limited initially to 2·5 per cent of the total stock of monetary gold and with the possibility that some or indeed all of this gold will be purchased by central banks, brought an initial fall in gold prices that suggested that the gold market had got the message that it will be expected gradually to absorb the stock of monetary gold. What this agreement leaves open are crucial problems concerning the measurement and control of international liquidity and these are considered in the final section of the chapter.

Reserve currencies

The *Outline* stated that a reduction in the role of reserve currencies, as well as the role of gold, was an agreed aim of the reform. It was recognized by all that currency holdings would continue to be a necessary element of reserves unless and until a system of SDR intervention was introduced; the argument was about currency holdings in excess of working balances. At one extreme lay the long-standing Triffin-like proposals for substituting SDRs for all existing holdings of reserve currencies in excess of working balances. It transpired even during the discussions of the *Reform Report* that this approach was infeasible, not just because the United States had not reconciled herself to a loss of the dollar's reserve currency role, which she imagined would provide her with a useful element of elasticity even after the restoration of convertibility, but also because the developing countries placed a high value on maximizing the yield on their reserve portfolios, which meant holding reserve currencies, including the non-traditional ones, and switching between reserve assets. (A not unimportant subsidiary motivation for the developing countries wishing to continue holding currencies in reserves was the ability of such holdings to act as collateral for commercial bank loans.) At the other extreme lay the US proposal for restoring convertibility into SDRs when circumstances permitted, with a voluntary once-for-all substitution operation easing the way to this restoration. In between lay the 'third approach' to asset settlement of the *Reform Report*, according to which a continuing Substitution Account would have been created in the IMF and would have engaged in regular transactions with the reserve centres to ensure that asset settlement was achieved whatever the portfolio decisions of individual countries. The *Documents of the C-20* focused on the latter two proposals, which were described respectively as a system of on-demand convertibility and 'a more mandatory system' (of settlement).

Both approaches envisaged the creation of a Substitution Account in the Fund. This would have been an account that was empowered to issue newly created SDRs in return for the deposit of officially held balances of dollars, sterling or other reserve currencies. Controversy centred around three points.

First, the Indians in particular queried the desirability of any substitution operation at all. Their argument rested on the supposition that countries had well-defined preferences regarding reserve composition. If this were so, any increase in the proportion of the reserve stock held in SDRs would help satisfy countries' limited appetites for SDRs and make them less enthusiastic about new SDR allocations, and to the extent that the measurement of global reserve needs was imprecise this could be expected to curtail the new allocations that were sanctioned. Since the Indians wanted as much seigniorage from SDR allocations as possible, they were led to oppose substitution.

Second, there was the disagreement between the United States and the Europeans as to whether substitution should be once-for-all or continuously available. The United States was anxious about the opportunity that a continuously available substitution facility would have provided for countries to shift reserves out of the dollar into SDRs when the dollar was weak. Although it was not envisaged that the Substitution Account would engage in reverse substitution — i.e., paying out dollars or other reserve currencies in exchange for SDRs — countries could have achieved the same end product by holding on to the dollars that they acquired in intervention when they were in surplus. Shifts in reserve composition would therefore have been possible; and, if the United States' debt to the Substitution Account had been SDR-denominated, the capital losses corresponding to other countries' successful speculation would have been borne by the United States. It was suggested that this problem might be met by introducing a delay period of, say, 6 months, that would elapse before 'old dollars' — those not acquired in current intervention — would be converted into SDRs by the Substitution Account. The real answer is, however, that precisely the same opportunities and costs would have arisen in any system in which the dollar was genuinely convertible. The Substitution Account provided a mechanism for shielding the United States from the liquidity effects of perverse elasticity, but not, without the delay period, from its financial effects.

The United States, however, thought that it would be nice if the Substitution Account also insulated her from some of the financial problems of running a reserve currency in a world of convertibility, and that raises the third issue: the question of the terms on which reserve centres should service their liabilities to a Substitution Account. In particular, the United States would obviously have found it agreeable if the Substitution Account had held on to the dollar assets surrendered to it by those seeking substitution into SDRs, rather than that these be transformed into SDR-denominated claims. To most other countries it seemed axiomatic that debts to an international organization that expressed all its other assets and liabilities in its own internationally based unit of account should be denominated in that same unit. Not only was this necessary to relieve the IMF of the problems associated with the operation of an account that would otherwise have been exposed to capital gains and losses, but there would seem to be something of a principle at stake. I do not share the view that the US inflation of the late-1960s can plausibly be explained by a conscious or subconscious attempt on the part of the US authorities to exploit the seigniorage potential of the reserve currency role of the dollar.[11] Nevertheless, however unlikely one may judge it to be that a particular country will not abuse the privilege of unilaterally writing down the value of its debts by depreciating its currency, the fact remains that denominating a debt in its own currency does give it that option, and international relations can only be complicated if other countries are exposed to financial losses as a result of the debtor not taking what they regard as sufficiently vigorous action to defend the value of its currency.

It would also seem to be easier to solve the problem of determining

11. The view is associated particularly with R. A. Mundell, 'The Optimum Balance of Payments Deficit', in E. Claassen and P. Salin, eds., *Stabilization Policies in Interdependent Economies*, N. Holland, London, 1972.

the interest rate that reserve centres should pay on their liabilities to a Substitution Account if those liabilities were denominated in SDRs. The natural procedure is then to base this interest rate on the SDR interest rate. Presumably it would be something higher: whether that 'something' should be a nominal service charge or a significant premium reflecting the long-term nature of the Substitution Account's assets is a question on which views could be relied on to differ on predictable lines, and on which a compromise somewhere in the middle would no doubt ultimately emerge. Then there is the question of amortization. There was little opposition to the principle of amortization in the C-20: it seemed to be generally agreed that the logical end result of substitution was that one generalized the seigniorage that previously accrued to the reserve centre, which could be accomplished by the reserve centre gradually amortizing its debts to the Substitution Account and the IMF offsetting the contractionary impact on global liquidity by allocating an equal volume of new SDRs. However, to the extent that the Substitution Account needed to retain a float of reserve currencies to effect asset settlement with the reserve centres, amortization would not have been possible.

It was, however, widely felt that a more important problem than that of substituting SDRs for 'old' dollar balances was that of preventing the future growth of official holdings of currencies. Had that been accomplished, and assuming that gold were not remonetized, the growth in the demand for reserves could have been expected to be such as to make the SDR the principal reserve asset within the space of a historically short time span — perhaps no more than a decade or so. There was rather general support in the C-20 for the aim of preventing future growth in reserve currency holdings. (It was, of course, recognized that, in the absence of a switch to SDR intervention, the growth in the need for working balances would ultimately require a modification of the principle that reserve currency holdings should not expand; this qualification is assumed to be recognized in what follows.) But, as so often in the C-20, agreement on aims was not translated into agreement on means.

A traditional view of the problem might have been that establishment of asset settlement would have been a necessary and sufficient condition to prevent any future growth in reserve currency holdings. The United States, however, claimed that it was not necessary. The growth of reserve holdings in the Euro-markets meant that it was not sufficient. And on top of that, the growth of OPEC wealth led to great doubts as to whether asset settlement was any longer feasible.

In place of asset settlement, the United States proposed 'Fund surveillance over the longer-term trend of currency reserves and ultimately ... some form of action by the Fund on a discretionary basis if that trend is found to be excessive' (*Outline*, Annex 5). This action would have amounted to a Fund recommendation that currency reserves be reduced, which would have been implemented through the issuing countries requesting other countries to limit their holdings of the reserve currencies, supplemented by the right of the Fund to issue equivalent requests as regards reserve placements in the Euro-markets (*Outline*, Annex 5, Section B). Even assuming that it would have proved possible to gain agreement that countries would have respected requests of the issuing country to limit their holdings of its currency, and even assuming that issuing countries could have been relied on to pass on the recommendations of the IMF, there must be some doubt as to whether such a procedure would have proved effective. The trouble arises from the excessive reliance placed on discretionary Fund decisions in situations where countries have established interests to defend. It is one thing to agree in advance to abide by certain quasi-automatic procedures (such as designation) that can be seen as the price necessary to achieve a collectively desired goal (such as asset settlement). It is far harder to take a detached view of whether the trend of reserve currency holdings is proving to be excessive in the knowledge that such a finding is almost certain to result in a requirement that one change one's reserve composition in a manner that one would rather avoid, or that one will be required to deprive oneself of some credit that is proving rather useful, when the benefits corresponding to these immediate and tangible costs are distant and abstract. And there are always any number of special circumstances that can be pleaded in any particular instance to rationalize a refusal to vote for what one would rather not do.

Even if there is any reason to doubt that asset settlement is a necessary condition for avoiding future growth of currency reserves, there can be no doubt that it is not a sufficient condition. Since the mid-1960s Euro-currency holdings had been becoming an increasingly important component of reserves (Table 6.1). Central banks, like other holders of international money, were attracted by the higher interest rates generally available on Euro-dollars than in New York. And the attraction of the Euro-markets was even greater where the new reserve currencies were concerned, since exchange control regulations were often designed to preclude official holdings of these currencies in the domestic markets of the countries concerned.

Table 6.1
The growth of Euro-currency reserves (SDR billion)

	1965	1970	1972	1974
Reserves held in Euro-markets	1·5	10·3	21·0	38·0
Total currency reserves	24·4	44·3	95·2	124·7
Percentage of currency reserves held in Euro-markets	6·4	23·2	22·1	29·7
Percentage of total reserves held in Euro-markets	2·1	11·4	14·8	20·8

SOURCE: IMF, *Annual Reports*, 1973, Tables 9, 13; 1974, Tables 10, 15; 1975, Tables 11, 15.

The importance of the Euro-market in the context of controlling global liquidity stems from the fact that it permits a growth of currency reserves without an official settlements deficit on the part of a reserve centre. Suppose, for example, that country A, which holds its reserves in New York, has a deficit with country B, which holds its reserves in London in the Euro-dollar market. This creates no official settlements deficit for the United States, but the transfer of funds to London permits the Euro-market to extend a loan to country C, which finds itself with a reserve increase when the loan is converted into domestic currency. If country C holds its reserves in New York, the process ends with a once-over increase in global reserves; but if country C holds its reserves in the Euro-market, there is a further multiplier expansion. Although the multiplier process is limited by interest arbitrage flows, the point remains that one cannot prevent the growth of currency reserves unless additional reserve placements in the Euro-markets are precluded. This fact was recognized in the C-20, and the proposal was advanced (*Outline*, para.23(c)) that the Fund should be given the power to limit currency placements in the Euro-markets. The proposal was not agreed; but, in view of the new twist that the reserve currency system has taken in recent years, it is difficult to see how international control over the total volume of international liquidity can be established until this or some similar proposal is accepted.

Realization of the multiplier effects of central bank deposits in the Euro-markets prompted the G-10 central banks to agree in 1971 to refrain from further increasing their deposits in the Euro-markets. The G-10 lead was not, however, followed by the developing countries, which were not only attracted by the higher yields available in the Euro-markets, but, in so far as they were conscious of the result, welcomed the fact that additional deposits expanded the lending potential of the market, to which they were increasingly turning as borrowers. It is, therefore, essentially the developing countries, together with some of the advanced primary producers, whose consent will be needed if the Euro-gap over the control of international liquidity is to be plugged. This provides them with a bargaining counter that has yet to be exploited.

The final problem with the prescription of asset settlement as the key to preventing the future growth of currency reserves is that it fails to recognize the special nature of the reserve holdings of a limited group of countries — pretty well confined to the high-income, low-absorptive-capacity oil exporters (Kuwait, Libya, Qatar, Saudi Arabia and the United Arab Emirates). These countries are exporting depletable resources and, unlike the other members of OPEC and unlike other mineral exporters, they have very limited prospects of ever building up a subsequent substantial export trade in any alternative product. They therefore need to invest their current account surpluses in such a way as to yield a permanent stream of interest income to sustain consumption when their oil resources are depleted. But, unlike the major capital exporters of the past, the export of capital is largely effected by the direct acquisition of foreign assets on the part of the monetary authorities, and often these authorities display a preference for liquid assets that conform to the statistical definition of reserves. If, however, they were counted as contributing to the official settlements deficits of the reserve centres in a system of asset settlement or as pre-empting a part of a fixed total of Euro-currency assets that had to be shared around among all central banks, the stock of reserve assets available to all other holders would quickly diminish. A world liquidity shortage would ensue if the total stock of reserves were essentially fixed and an ever-increasing proportion were absorbed by this limited group of countries seeking long-term investments. It would be appropriate to counter such a shortage by SDR creation; but, as long as the countries in question declined to acquire SDRs on a substantial scale (which they would certainly have done as long as the interest rate remained uncompetitive), this would have led to a steady diminution in the stock of reserve currency claims available to all other countries.

The neat and logical solution to this problem would be to persuade these countries to change their investment practices and place long-term investments in long-term assets, which would probably be in their own best interests anyway. However, the international facts of life do not provide much scope for the rest of the world to bring pressures on these countries to pursue their enlightened self-interest. Unless and until they decide to do so, there seems no choice but to treat the reserve holdings of this group of countries essentially as though they were privately rather than officially owned. (This was the solution envisaged for the operation of any reserve indicator system in the report of the Technical Group on Adjustment, paras 46-50, and pretty much what was envisaged for the operation of the settlement system in the report of the Technical Group on Intervention and Settlement, paras 72-6.)

The control of international liquidity

One of the major tasks of the reform was widely agreed to be that of establishing control over the volume of international liquidity with a view to ensuring that this volume varied in future in a manner consistent with the needs of stable growth in the world economy. The SDR agreement had provided the power to safeguard the world against the danger of a liquidity shortage, but, as events from 1970 on had demonstrated forcefully, this power needed to be supplemented by mechanisms to prevent the unintended creation of excess reserves. When the decisions on SDR allocations for the first 'basic period' (1970-72) were reached in 1969, it had been necessary to estimate the probable growth in reserves from sources other than SDRs. The estimates made were almost all under SDR 5 billion[12] as against the actual out-turn of SDR 61·6 billion between 1970 and 1972. This surely demonstrates that, if reserve growth is ever to be determined collectively in the IMF, an essential precondition is that control be established over forms of reserves other than SDRs.

In the conditions of the early 1970s this appeared as primarily a problem of controlling the currency component of reserves. The steps necessary to this end have already been discussed in the previous section: they amount to the establishment of asset settlement (qualified, by necessity, by the exclusion of the five OPEC members whose economies lack significant alternative sources of wealth) and the imposition of international control over the aggregate volume of reserve placements in the Euro-markets. The Europeans and Japanese were willing, and indeed anxious, to see these steps taken. The United States, however, resisted asset settlement, and the developing countries resisted the imposition of controls on placements in the Euro-markets. Accordingly no agreement was reached, and the currency component of international reserves is still under no effective international control.

12. IMF, *International Reserves: Needs and Availability*, Washington DC, 1970, pp.500-1.

The other major reserve asset is gold. At one time, around 1971-72, it seemed that gold posed no problems in terms of the control of international liquidity, since the 2-tier market in conjunction with the modest premium of the market price over the official price served to prevent any significant additions to or subtractions from the stock of monetary gold. However, the sustained speculative boom in the gold market in 1973-74 (which at its peak in December 1974 carried the market price to almost five times the official price of SDR 35 per ounce) brought a realization that constancy in the physical stock of monetary gold did not imply constancy in the value of gold reserves. Once one started to wonder what the appropriate valuation of gold was from the standpoint of measuring reserves, the answer was far from obvious. As argued earlier in this chapter, gold had really ceased to be a reserve asset in anything but name after August 1971 (at least until August 1975): the only major official use of gold in this period was the German gold-collateral loan to Italy in the summer of 1974, and the fact that gold was used as collateral is the clinching proof that it was not serving as a reserve asset. However, it is equally true that the reason that gold was unusable was that it was too valuable to be used, and it does seem somewhat paradoxical to omit an asset from a country's reserve stock on the ground that the price at which it was previously valued is an underestimate of its true value.

The reason that it is considered important in the first instance to control international liquidity is because countries' reserves influence the readiness of their authorities to pursue expansionary, non-restrictive policies and to see their currencies appreciate. This suggests that the correct question to pose when seeking to assess the impact on global liquidity of the gold price increase is whether the wealth effect stemming from the increase in value of the stockpile of gold outweighs the pure illiquidity effect imparted by the inability to realize gold stocks without sustaining a loss by comparison with what the gold is felt to be worth (its market value). In this case, however, the correct question does not suggest the correct answer. This would pose a devastating problem if global reserve policy were being conducted according to a Friedmanian rule of a constant rate of expansion in the reserve stock: even if everyone agreed that the correct rate of expansion were x per cent per annum, that would not help much if one could not make up one's mind whether the existing reserve stock were about SDR 150 billion (as it was at the end of 1974 excluding gold) or SDR 350 billion (the figure corresponding to a market valuation of gold holdings). My own preference, under the regime that existed from August 1971 to August 1975, would have been to exclude gold from the measure of reserves, since it was not really a liquid asset, and instead to treat it as one of those additional considerations, such as the stock of private international liquidity and the availability of conditional liquidity, that are judged to be relevant in influencing the need for expansion or contraction in the reserve stock proper.

However, reserve creation policy is, in practice, conducted on something much closer to a discretionary basis (see below), and so long as that remains the case the problem of measuring reserves is not of overwhelming importance. What is crucial, however, is the possibility that variations in the market price of gold produce variations in how liquid monetary authorities regard themselves as being. Even before August 1975 it seemed doubtful whether it was legitimate to disregard this factor. The decision to allow central banks to buy gold from one another at mutually acceptable prices must make this practice even less acceptable. If it turns out that central banks have no difficulty in finding others willing to acquire large gold stocks at near-market prices whenever they desire to dispose of gold to finance a deficit, then gold will once more qualify as a reserve asset and the problem of reserve measurement will be solved, since the market price at any point in time will provide an appropriate measure of the value of gold. What will remain is the far more serious problem of loss of control over the volume of international liquidity, which will henceforth vary capriciously with the state of speculative sentiment in the gold market. Re-establishment of control over international liquidity would then seem to demand abandonment of the dogma that no attempt should be made to stabilize the market price of gold, at least to the extent of increasing the rate at which monetary gold is released to the market when the market price rises at more than a predetermined rate.

Despite the fact that the C-20 made no progress in establishing control over the volume of liquidity, there is some interest in the subject of the principles that should be used to exercise control to the extent that control is feasible, if only because liquidity can be increased through SDR allocations even though it cannot in practice be reduced when necessary despite the theoretical power of the IMF to cancel SDRs. Although the C-20 established a Technical Group on Global Liquidity and Consolidation, which was instructed to examine the method of estimating global reserve needs and reaching decisions on SDR creation, the *Outline* ultimately recommended that 'the Fund will continue to follow the existing principles as set out in the Articles of Agreement' (para.25). Existing Fund procedures involve an annual review of the adequacy of international liquidity, which is published each year in Chapter 2 of its *Annual Report*. The review is based upon an analytical approach first revealed in detail in the proceedings of a conference convened by the IMF in 1970 for the specific purpose of considering the problem of determining global reserve needs.[13]

The predominant standpoint at that conference was to follow the pioneering papers of J. Marcus Fleming[14] in viewing reserve creation as a policy instrument in the hands of the international authorities, which should be set with the aim of maximizing a world welfare function. The maximization is, of course, subject to a set of constraints imposed by the positive way in which the world economy operates, including the reaction patterns of the various national governments. In principle this requires that one should give a precise specification of the world welfare function, as well as construct and estimate a positive model that predicts how national governments would react to changes in reserve ease and how the international economy would respond to these variations in national policies. The obvious infeasibility of following this ideal procedure does not mean that the approach is incapable of generating operationally useful guidelines. Virtually any positive theory of the behaviour of national governments will lead to the prediction that greater reserve ease will generate more expansionary demand-management policies, and/or fewer restrictions, and/or more revaluations and fewer devaluations. The optimum rate of reserve growth is characterized by beneficial effects in the form of higher employment and fewer restrictions being equal at the margin to the untoward effects of inflation and the resource misallocation implied by larger reserve flows.

Each year, therefore, the survey of the adequacy of international liquidity contained in the IMF's *Annual Report* includes a review of developments in the demand-management and balance-of-payments policies of member countries with a view to gleaning conclusions about the degree of reserve ease prevailing in the world.[15] Inflation, export restrictions, restrictions on the inflow of capital, a lack of reserve borrowing and revaluations provide evidence of reserve ease, while their opposites provide evidence of reserve stringency. The trouble is, of course, that the various indicators generally give conflicting signals. If one is bold, like a monetarist, one may simply declare, on the basis of an analogy with domestic monetary theory and an act of faith that denies the possibility of cost-push, that the existence of inflation

13. *Idem*. The subject is also reviewed in my survey article, *op.cit.*, Section III.4.

14. J. M. Fleming, 'International Liquidity: Ends and Means', IMF *Staff Papers*, December 1961, and *Towards Assessing the Need for International Reserves*, Princeton Essays in International Finance No.58, Princeton, 1967.

15. This was, at least, the practice until 1975, when the review of the adequacy of international liquidity was largely confined to an analysis of the impact of specific recent developments, notably the advent of generalized floating, on the demand for and supply of reserves.

demonstrates that reserve growth is excessive.[16] But more cautious men believe that curtailing reserve growth just because there is inflation might lead the world to a morass of restrictions, or competitive devaluations, while doing little to restrain inflation. They therefore insist on viewing the entire picture, despite the ambiguities that result.

The IMF customarily supplements its analysis of symptoms of reserve stringency and ease by a 'quantitative' approach, consisting of a study of the evolution of the ratio between reserves and a series of variables that may plausibly be supposed to be related to the demand for reserves: the old favourite, imports; sometimes measures of the variability of payments balances; and money supplies. A comparison of the present reserves/imports ratio with that prevailing in earlier periods when the state of liquidity seemed reasonably satisfactory (say, the first half of the 1960s) is not without interest, although it is somewhat difficult to interpret in view especially of its reliance on the SDR 35 an ounce valuation of gold. But, at the end of the day, there remain ample grounds for differences of view as to whether liquidity is tight or easy; and most countries' representatives naturally choose the interpretation consistent with their countries' national interests or traditional prejudices.

Various suggestions were made in the Technical Group on Global Liquidity and Consolidation about changes in approach that might be worthwhile. The Canadians urged exploration of a Friedmanian commitment to a long-run plan for SDR creation at a steady rate, suggesting specifically that a rolling 5-year plan would be preferable to the existing system of 5-year 'basic periods'. This suggestion was not endorsed, perhaps because of the feeling that, especially while the total level of international liquidity was not under control, it was necessary to rely on discretionary decisions based on the evolving symptoms of reserve ease and stringency. The Italians proposed that there be a presumption that SDR allocations be some fixed proportion of the growth in the value of world trade; departure from this presumptive rule would have been possible with sufficient support, but the weighted majority needed to gain acceptance would have increased progressively as the rule was departed from in either direction.[17] There are, however, serious drawbacks to such a rule, in as much as it might build in inflationary pressures if the initial level of reserves were excessive and the rule provided for reserves to grow almost

16. See, for example, H. G. Johnson, *Inflation and the Monetarist Controversy*, N. Holland, Amsterdam, 1972, p.87.
17. The idea stems from the Keynes Plan and was endorsed *inter alia* by Triffin in *Gold and the Dollar Crisis*.

proportionately with trade,[18] or eventually to build in deflationary pressures if the agreed proportionate relationship were lower than that which was in fact necessary to satisfy the induced increase in the demand for reserves. The United States saw the reserve indicator system providing the key to this problem, as to most others: consultations on reserve norms would provide information on countries' reserve aims, and the level of reserve creation should be such as to enable all countries to satisfy their aims simultaneously in so far as they were prepared to accept the obligations stemming from their aims being formalized into norms. Most other countries doubted whether the discipline of the indicator structure would or should be so severe as to overcome the traditional objection to the procedure of creating enough reserves to satisfy countries' declared objectives: namely, that this provides an incentive for countries to lie, in as much as an unrealistically high declared reserve objective by a deficit country leads to additional reserve creation that tends to shift the burden of adjustment on to surplus countries. The developing countries were concerned to see more explicit attention paid to the distribution as well as the level of global liquidity, on the argument that a high total of liquidity had less expansionary consequences if it were concentrated in a limited number of countries than if it were more evenly spread. This was the only proposed innovation that has so far won any acceptance: the Fund's *Annual Report* for 1974 at least sought to study whether distribution (relative to a measure of need) had become more unequal in recent years, by constructing a modified version of the Lorenz curve. (It found that distribution had become less equal, but not dramatically so.)

The determination of global reserve needs, and the implied need for reserve creation, is therefore a subject on which ample scope for differences of views persists. My own view is that there is not much potential for fundamentally changing present procedures, except to the extent that it would be possible to place more attention on those 'symptoms' of reserve ease and stringency that are used more particularly as instruments of payments policy, and correspondingly less on those 'symptoms' that are also used importantly for internal purposes. This suggests — in direct contradiction to the monetarist view — that one should pay relatively little attention to inflation and deflation, since countries' demand-management policies are influenced by other considerations than the state of reserve ease, and, at least under a par value system, far more attention to — in particular — the

18. The analogy between a rule governing SDR creation which aimed at stabilizing the reserves/imports ratio and the real-bills doctrine has been drawn by L. Girton, 'SDR Creation and the Real-Bills Doctrine', *Southern Economic Journal*, July 1974.

balance between revaluations and devaluations. I have, indeed, argued that, if the exchange rate regime were the crawling peg, so that exchange rate changes were a regular part of the accepted response to dissatisfaction with the rate of reserve accumulation, it would be appropriate to treat the revaluation/devaluation balance as the sole criterion for changing the rate of SDR allocation.[19] With the adjustable peg it would not be feasible to go this far, because exchange rate changes occur too irregularly and erratically to serve as the sole indicator. It might nonetheless be appropriate to devote more attention to them than has been done in the past. With widespread floating in its present form this criterion would not be available, but an analogous criterion could be devised for the modified system outlined in Chapter 8.

By comparison with the initial objective of making major progress toward the construction of an SDR standard, the outcome of the C-20 can only be judged disappointing. Gold was only partially reinstated, but its ability to create problems was not ended. Reserve currencies were not brought under any control whatsoever. Control over international liquidity was not, therefore, established, and the prospects for further SDR allocations remain correspondingly bleak. Agreement was not reached over the formula that should govern the distribution of any future SDR allocations. The yield on the SDR was not raised to a point where it is competitive with that on currencies. The one real achievement was the change in the basis of valuation of the SDR, which not only gave it a distinct identity based on sound theoretical underpinnings, but made it, for the first time, a useful working instrument of international finance. But even this achievement was compromised by its provisional nature, which has proved a stumbling block to more widespread adoption of the basket SDR as a unit of account by the private sector.

19. J. Williamson, *The Choice of a Pivot for Parities*, Princeton Essays in International Finance No.90, Princeton, 1971, p.19.

7

The causes of failure

As everyone knows and has been recalled in some detail in previous chapters, the C-20 did not succeed in its mandate of designing a new monetary system for the world. The present chapter examines why it failed. Five explanations have been offered, more or less explicitly, in one quarter or another, and are examined in this chapter.

The state of the world

The official explanation offered for the abandonment of the quest for a comprehensive reform, and the substitution of a programme of piecemeal immediate measures and the hope of subsequent evolutionary reforms along an ill-defined path, was the unsettled state of the world economy. First the outbreak of intensive worldwide inflation, then the breakdown of the par value system, and finally the quadrupling of oil prices and the massive current account imbalances that ensued, had without doubt thrown the world economy into a state of turmoil greater than anything previously seen since the immediate post-war period. The intensity of the recession that followed is witness to that. The fact that the world economy was in a disturbed state does not, however, in itself imply that an agreed system was unnecessary or unattainable: indeed, the converse proposition is arguable — that it is precisely in a situation where drastic changes need to be accommodated without provoking international disharmony that the need for an agreed framework of rules is greatest. And even to the extent that it was true that the installation of a reformed system would have to await a calmer environment, that provides no reason for not agreeing on the basic shape of the system that it is desired to construct when circumstances permit. This was, after all, very much the procedure followed when the IMF was created: the Bretton Woods Agreement was negotiated and ratified over a decade before it really became operational. Accordingly, there is no ground for giving any credence to the view that the disturbed state of the world provides an explanation of, rather than an alibi for, the failure of the reform exercise.

To say this is not to deny that it would have been impossible to introduce a system based on such blueprint as the C-20 had constructed in the existing circumstances. This is, of course, because the early agreement to base the system on 'stable but adjustable par values' implied that introduction of the reform would have to await a markedly calmer environment — unless, at least, there were a revolution in the willingness of governments to subjugate their financial policies to the dictates of the balance of payments, of which there was no sign. The key question is, however, whether it made any sense to opt for a fair-weather system that was workable only under calm circumstances. I am no futurologist: I make no pretensions to knowing whether the future will bring the formation of new cartels, or the break-up of old ones; the near-exhaustion of key natural resources, or the development of synthetic substitutes; conflict between East and West, or North and South; harvest failures or climatic changes; further excesses in monetary expansion, or a dedicated attempt to eradicate inflation through monetary discipline; or a breakdown of the international capital market caused by widespread debt default. What is most unlikely is that the future will be characterized by the absence of any such shocks. These shocks will create a need for further payments adjustments and, so long as capital mobility persists, the attempt to secure such adjustments through the adjustable peg will provoke massive speculative capital flows that will overwhelm any system that is not consistent with the maintenance of asset-market equilibrium. What needs to be blamed for the failure to achieve reform is not, therefore, the ill grace of the world for declining to behave in a manner that would permit the negotiators' blueprint to work, but the misguided decision of the negotiators to opt for a fair-weather system in a world where the weather is notoriously variable.

Conflicts of national interests

When nations fail to agree, a frequent explanation is that there exist deep-seated conflicts of interest. Differences of interest are indeed always arising in international monetary relations and it is necessary to examine the possibility that it was these that prevented a successful outcome to the reform negotiations.

Until August 1971 it seemed to many Europeans that the United States had a strong national interest in the maintenance of a dollar standard. Gottfried Haberler and Thomas Willett[1] had been most explicit in arguing that this in no way precluded the United States achieving and maintaining full employment: if other countries chose to run current account surpluses and so impose a current account deficit on the United States, she could expand domestic demand to offset the effect of the deficit on employment. If other countries did not want surpluses, they could adjust, as they chose, through appreciation, expansionary demand-management policies or restrictions: it would be regrettable if they chose the latter, but it did not affect any vital US interest. Many Europeans regarded this analysis as correct, at least so far as US interests were concerned, although they also believed, for reasons described in Chapter 5, that the gain to the United States through 'benign neglect' was less than the losses that the policy imposed on them. It seemed doubtful, however, whether these losses were so great as to justify risking a major diplomatic rupture with the United States in order to correct them. This meant that, as long as the United States pursued her interest in the maintenance of a dollar standard in a non-provocative way, it would have been very difficult indeed to secure any change.

In August 1971, however, the Nixon Administration bowed to the mercantilist sentiment that pointed to the loss of jobs occasioned by a current account deficit, and jettisoned the formal gold exchange standard and with it the *de facto* dollar standard. From that point on the United States acted as though the great problem in establishing a reformed system was the conflict of interests occasioned by the desire of each country to have as large a surplus as possible. And the United States was not alone in seeing this as an important source of conflict: the Japanese certainly believed that export-led growth was the key to their success, and many Europeans felt to some extent the same way. Jeremy Morse endorsed the view that this was the key issue. In answer to the question '[do] you think that the other countries of the world are willing to give the United States the type of adjustment that it needs to make the dollar convertible?' he replied:[2]

> I don't know whether they are, but that's the essence of the reform. If they are, well then we shall have a nice reform; if they're not, then we shall have something else ...

In the end, of course, the United States got her surplus but the world

1. G. Haberler and T. D. Willett, *A Strategy for U.S. Balance of Payments Policy*, American Enterprise Institute, Washington DC, 1971.
2. *IMF Survey*, 12 February 1973, p.36.

did not get its reform, which might throw some doubt on the view that this was such a key issue. It is nevertheless of interest to examine how real the perceived conflict of interest over balance-of-payments objectives in fact was.

It is generally conceded that cyclical factors can result in competitive current account objectives. During a global recession, each country is able to improve its own employment position at the expense of its trading partners by increasing its current account surplus; conversely, during a boom, there is an incentive to compete for current account deficits to the extent that reserve ease permits, in order to relieve the burden on domestic stabilization policy. The founding fathers of Bretton Woods were well aware of this danger because of the competitive depreciations of the 1930s and they introduced the criterion of 'fundamental disequilibrium' precisely for the purpose of permitting the international community to restrain competitive exchange rate policies motivated by the conjunctural situation. The Bretton Woods system did not in fact witness any overt examples of competitive depreciation, and by the early 1970s the opinion was being expressed that competitive exchange rate policies need no longer be judged a serious danger. This confidence was perhaps premature. The 1973 boom brought several appreciations in which the desire to strengthen anti-inflationary policy was clearly the dominant factor, and in some of these cases, where there was an associated relaxation of domestic policy, it is at least arguable that the resultant export of inflation was anti-social. And exchange rate movements and import restrictions during the 1975 recession — which is, after all, the first recession since the war to have been sufficiently sharp to create any strong temptations — may yet provide more disquieting proof that international constraints remain necessary. Indeed, it is possible that this is where the inadequacies of the post-C-20 non-system may prove most acute.

These cyclical factors are familiar, but they were not what was in the minds of those who saw competitive payments objectives as a key problem. The cyclical explanation suggests that countries will sometimes be competing for surpluses and at other times for deficits, whereas what was envisaged as being the problem was a more or less permanent competition for surpluses. The problem of possible inconsistency in overall payments objectives had been recognized in the 1960s. It was to accommodate the desire of most countries to see their reserves increase over time that it had been judged necessary to create the SDR: an absolute dearth, or an inadequate growth, of liquidity was expected to result in inconsistent payments objectives that would have led to general deflation, the escalation of payments restrictions, interest rate 'wars', and competitive devaluation, in the course of which all countries would have stood to lose. The key question is why the United States eventually decided that this mechanism could not be relied on, and needed to be supplemented by a reserve indicator system. The answer may be that US officials came to the conclusion that the more conservative Europeans, notably the Germans, would never agree to SDR allocations on the scale that they judged to be necessary to avoid inconsistency in objectives, unless the objectives of some countries were forcibly modified by the adoption of the indicator system.

There remains the question whether the major surplus countries really did have a strong national interest in the preservation of their surplus position. It seems fairly clear that none of them felt that they had any such interest in the maintenance of massive reserve increases: not only did they deny any such ambitions unequivocally, but both Germany and Japan backed this up with vigorous steps to promote net capital exports. What is more plausible is the charge that they felt themselves to have an interest in the maintenance of substantial current account surpluses. Because of the structural dislocation that would result from rapid elimination of a current surplus, they had a real interest in avoiding being pressured into too hasty a change; but this does not imply that they had an interest in the permanent maintenance of a current account surplus. Orthodox neo-classical theory provides little basis for regarding a permanent current surplus as a rational objective. This theory views countries as sharing a common interest, qualified only by the divergence between marginal national social and marginal private products of investment mentioned in Chapter 4, in the achievement of whatever current account outcomes are necessary to effect a real transfer equal to the underlying capital flow. The qualification suggests that countries would generally find it advantageous to compete for current account deficits (so long as they can be financed) rather than surpluses: real resources generally yield a higher return than financial capital.

In so far as the view that countries' interests are in permanent conflict in the search for current account surpluses is not based on simple mercantilism or a failure to observe that the world has not suffered from a chronic deficiency of demand in the post-war period, it presumably stems from one or other of the theories of export-led growth. Now the theory of export-led growth does contain important insights: notably, that investment is stimulated by an assurance that a payments deficit will not compel the authorities to deflate output, and by the ability to supply profitably markets sufficiently large to permit the realization of economies of scale; the greater efficiency of investment designed to serve a market of adequate size; and perhaps also the greater ease of shifting resources from net exports to investment than from consumption to investment when an investment boom materializes. But none of these factors suggests that a continuing net transfer of real resources to the rest of the world is in itself a cause of growth — which is the proposition that has to be proved to establish that an export surplus will always lead to faster growth even for a country that has ample liquidity. To believe that, one has to believe that output is usually constrained by a Keynesian lack of demand rather than by supply constraints arising from limited capacity. There is a strong Marxist tradition that amounts to asserting that this is the case, but it is an unconvincing portrayal of the post-war world; moreover, it would suggest that the world has unlimited opportunities for accelerating its growth through shipping goods to mid-ocean and dumping them there.

Nevertheless, the theory of export-led growth does suggest that, while inconsistent current account objectives are by no means a certainty, they are a possibility that cannot be ruled out. The growth rate (of capacity) is dependent on the rate of investment, which may be limited either by available resources (a neo-classical constraint) or by the inducement to invest (a Keynesian constraint). A bigger current account surplus tends to increase the incentive to invest, thus relaxing the Keynesian constraint on growth, but simultaneously to reduce the resources available for (domestic) investment, thus intensifying the neo-classical constraint. Hence there will, *ceteris paribus*, be some particular current account surplus (when the investment and savings constraints are equal) that will maximize the growth rate. Unless one has a fairly extreme neo-classical faith in the role of the interest rate in equating savings and investment, one cannot rule out the possibility that over the world as a whole it is the investment — i.e., Keynesian —constraint that is binding, and hence that a concern for growth maximization might lead countries into inconsistent ambitions for current account surpluses.

The main reason for hesitating to give much credence to this possibility is that it depends critically on the *ceteris paribus*; if the incentive to invest is proving the limiting factor, countries can usually (unless they are suffering from a reserve shortage) stimulate investment through domestic policy instruments, rather than needing to rely on stimulation from the external sector. The basis for believing that in general important real conflicts of national interest arise in the pursuit of current account targets is therefore rather tenuous. Although one cannot deny that countries do have objectives that are inconsistent, the fact that their achievement is not a matter of vital national concern implies that there may still be scope for successful negotiation (which may in part have to be educational).[3] And it is far from clear that the degree of target inconsistency was in fact at all large (at least before the oil price increase): after all the Europeans welcomed, and the Japanese concurred in without great reluctance, the second dollar devaluation. The crucial difference between the first and second dollar devaluations was that the world was in a recession in 1971 and a boom in 1973. Hence one is led back to the view that the real problem of target inconsistency is the cyclical one. This is highly significant, because one of the major motivations for wanting an agreed system is the common interest that countries share in ensuring that problems of cyclical stabilization are not tackled by a self-defeating attempt on the part of each individual country to load its problems on to others.

One area in which interests do conflict in international monetary relations is — as in other parts of economics — in regard to distributional questions. In particular, the distribution of the seigniorage resulting from reserve creation creates a direct conflict of national interests on a whole series of questions : the rate at which monetary gold is released on to the market, the extent of a reserve currency system and the obligations of the reserve centre with regard to convertibility, the yield on the SDR, the terms on which assets acquired by a substitution facility are to be serviced by the debtor, the distribution of new SDR allocations, and so on.[4] To make matters more difficult, countries not only have easily identifiable short-run interests in these questions, but the nature of their interests tends to remain the same over time. (This is in contrast to the situation concerning payments objectives, where countries must anticipate the possibility that their payments position will be reversed on some future occasion, or that some other country might export inflation or unemployment to them next time round if there were no rules restraining such behaviour.) Nevertheless, there are only two issues where the sums at stake are sufficiently large to make it rational for countries to consider allowing their financial interests to rule out an agreement that was felt

3. I have argued elsewhere that in the particular context of distributing the current account deficits that are the counterpart to the OPEC surplus, a real problem has been created by the temporary excess of voluntary full employment savings over desired investment, which calls for international action to assign current account deficits — i.e., involuntary reductions in savings — in a fair way. See J. Williamson, Chapter 6 in E. R. Fried and C. L. Schultze, eds., *Higher Oil Prices and the World Economy*, Brookings Institution, Washington DC, 1975. Once savings and investment have adjusted, I would expect this conflict of national interests over current account objectives to disappear.
4. I examined the nature of countries' financial interests in these questions in 'The Financial Implications of Reserve Supply Arrangements', IMF *Staff Papers*, November 1974.

worthwhile on other grounds. The first relates to gold. The fact is, however, that, so long as gold was not being aggressively hounded out of the system, which might have thrust countries such as Germany (which probably has sufficiently large gold holdings to give her a marginal financial interest in gold remonetization) into the arms of the gold lobby, the latter did not have enough strength to exercise a veto. This was demonstrated in 1968 by the fact that the French ultimately joined the SDR scheme. The second relates to the financial advantage to the United States of an inconvertible dollar standard. In principle this was not an interest that the United States was claiming to defend, for throughout the reform negotiations she maintained her offer to restore dollar convertibility when her external position permitted, subject to the acceptance of a reserve indicator system. In practice there is room to doubt whether the United States had really reconciled herself to a circumscription of the role of the dollar, and it is possible that her interest in perpetuating the use of the dollar led to a certain ambivalence as regards her anxiety to see an agreed reform achieved: this possibility is discussed in the next section. This is, however, a different proposition from an assertion that reform was unattainable because of a tenacious US defence of a vested financial interest in the avoidance of an SDR standard.

So far as an economic interpretation of national interests is concerned, I conclude that there were no deep-seated conflicts of interest that compelled countries to adopt incompatible positions. It remains possible that I am guilty of professional narrow-mindedness in taking it as axiomatic that national interests should be more or less identified with the integral of the discounted utility of expected future consumption of the nations' citizens. Governments are, it is asserted, concerned with other objectives, such as power, influence, prestige and autonomy. Having lived most of my life under a series of governments that dedicated their foreign policy to such ends more than to economic ones, in the process not merely impoverishing their citizens but also generally making themselves look rather ridiculous, I would not care to deny that such factors can intrude into an economic negotiation. I do, however, find it difficult to see what issues of this character might have been supposed to be at stake in the reform negotiations. Military security was not an issue one way or the other. The battle of the 1960s about gold versus credit reserves, in which prestige had indeed become heavily involved, had been buried along with its inventor, de Gaulle. The question of the economic power that would accrue to the United States under a dollar standard had been largely defused by the resort to widespread floating in March 1973. By the time that the reform negotiations had got well under way, therefore, there were no noneconomic diversions preventing countries from acting on the basis of their economic interests.

Lack of political will

In the course of an address summarizing the work of the Committee delivered shortly before its final meeting, Jeremy Morse discussed his view on why the C-20 failed to negotiate a reform.[5] Although he made a decent obeisance to the official view that the failure was a consequence of the disturbed state of the world economy, he acknowledged that this in itself would not have precluded the C-20 completing its design of a reformed system, even if it would have prevented its immediate implementation. Neither did he suggest that the explanation lay in the existence of irreconcilable conflicts of national interests. He focused instead on the lack of sufficient political will:[6]

> ... there has been no lack of courtesy, or of the understanding of the interests of others ... What has been insufficient ... is the will to active cooperation ... By this I mean the will to agree and do things together in the common interest even though they may not be precisely what any of the parties would have chosen, and the will to help or accommodate others in the expectation of receiving similar help or accommodation in future.

This was perhaps somewhat unfair to the Europeans who, with the exception of the Germans, were willing to concede the link to the developing countries, and who made a series of efforts to accommodate the US desire for a greater certainty that adjustment pressures would apply to surplus as well as to deficit countries. First they suggested adopting a basic balance indicator; then they suggested using a reserve indicator as a trigger to a strengthened consultations procedure in the IMF; and finally they suggested penalties on countries with excess reserve holdings. These proposals do suggest a certain willingness to engage in serious negotiations, which it is not surprising to find since it was the Europeans who felt their interests to be most threatened by the absence of a formal system following the Smithsonian Conference. The United States, however, never displayed any similar willingness to concede to either of the other parties. She held out against asset settlement through thick

5. C. J. Morse, 'The Evolving Monetary System', an address delivered to the International Monetary Conference in Williamsburg, Va., on 7 June 1974, and partially reprinted in the IMF *Survey*, 17 June 1974.
6. *Ibid.*, p.137.

and thin, defending her position with arguments (about elasticity and the danger of her being subjected to financial losses due to reserve shifts through a Substitution Account) that were invalid if the comparison were with a system of on-demand convertibility, as it ostensibly was since this was the position that she was espousing. And she was equally uncompromising in her opposition to the link. The developing countries also defended marginal interests, such as freedom of reserve composition and virtual exemption from the operation of an indicator system, with a tenacity that hardly contributed to the chances of a successful outcome.

Fred Hirsch has argued that there is a general reason for expecting attempts to construct an SDR standard to be hampered by a lack of political will.[7] The reason is that the benefits of an SDR standard are diffused and at any time likely to appear abstract, while the costs are specific and easily identifiable. For example, a developing country being asked to agree to restraints on its own reserve-holding behaviour in the interest of establishing an SDR standard, had to weigh the immediate and apparent inconvenience and loss of interest income against the hopes that in due course it would benefit from larger SDR allocations and that world cyclical fluctuations might be mitigated. Since the developing countries were only too conscious that the feedbacks from their own individual actions to the behaviour of the system as a whole were negligible, it was no doubt difficult for them to realize that collectively this was not true, and that an agreed system required that they shoulder obligations as well as collect benefits. This failure to accept the need to undertake responsibilities all too often reduced the developing countries to a position that looked more like begging than bargaining, while some quite valuable bargaining counters (such as an offer to accept limitations on reserve placements in the Euro-markets) were never exploited to advance their particular demands (such as the link). This may have been explicable on the basis of divided interests within the group of developing countries — the richer Latin American countries, for example, might have expected to lose by the trade just described — but the fact remains that, while their attitude remained one of all asking and no bargaining, the strictures of Jeremy Morse seem understandable.

So far as the United States was concerned, the problem was perhaps less that the benefits of reform were intangible and the feedbacks small, than that she thought she had already achieved her main interest — the ability to change her exchange rate in order to correct her long-

7. F. Hirsch, *An SDR Standard: Impetus, Elements and Impediments*, Princeton Essays in International Finance No.99, Princeton, 1973.

standing deficit — before the reform negotiations even began. The question arises, therefore, of what the United States thought she stood to gain from a successful negotiation, especially after the advent of generalized floating in March 1973. I shall argue in the next chapter that present arrangements are not without their danger to the United States, but there is no reason to think that the particular disadvantage I diagnose in present exchange rate arrangements is one that was recognized in Washington. Probably her main motivation was less any hope of tangible economic benefits than a feeling that she had a moral obligation to try and help construct a system that was less offensive to the rest of the world.[8] This sort of motivation may not have counted for much with President Nixon, whose lack of passionate concern for the monetary problems of the United States' partners became public knowledge when the Watergate tapes were published,[9] but it was probably enough to give Paul Volcker (the principal US Deputy in the C-20 and the driving force behind US policy) a genuine enough desire to see agreement reached. But even those Americans who were most concerned to achieve an agreed reform cannot have seen much hope of getting domestic political support for changes that would have seriously circumscribed the role of the dollar or threatened to reimpose any onerous external constraints on US policy. The US position that 'the system should neither ban nor encourage official holdings of foreign exchange'[10] certainly suggested that, as in the SDR

8. At the beginning of the reform negotiations, the United States sought to link trade concessions by the rest of the world with monetary concessions on her part, but in the event the trade negotiations developed largely independently and any chance of swapping concessions in the two fields was lost.

9. An extract from the tape for 23 June 1972 read:

HALDEMAN (H): Did you get the report that the British floated the pound?
PRESIDENT (P): No, I don't think so.
H: They did.
P: That's devaluation?
H: Yeah. Flanigan's got a report on it here.
P: I don't care about it. Nothing we can do about it.
H: You want a run-down?
P: No, I don't.
H: He argues it shows the wisdom of our refusal to consider convertibility until we get a new monetary system.
P: Good. I think he's right. It's too complicated for me to get into. (unintelligible) I understand.
H: Burns expects a 5-day percent (*sic*) devaluation against the dollar.
P: Yeah. O.K. Fine.
H: Burns is concerned about speculation about the lira.
P: Well, I don't give a (expletive deleted) about the lira.

10. *The US Proposals*, para.28(g).

negotiations, the United States still thought of the SDR as providing a substitute for gold rather than for the dollar. The fact that the United States believed that she could live without discomfort without a reform implied that she could not be expected to make any costly concessions in the interest of reaching agreement.

As I have already indicated, the Europeans were more anxious to see an agreement achieved and more ready to modify their positions in the interest of finding a compromise. They can perhaps be charged with a certain lack of realism in expecting the United States to meet them more than half way, in so far as they expected to win asset settlement without conceding more than a nominal indicator system. The facts of life demanded that, unless the Europeans were prepared and able convincingly to threaten to organize the eastern hemisphere into a new monetary system that would exclude the United States, it should be they who made the major concessions. The continued clinging to gold by some of the Europeans also impeded their ability to offer a package that might have been acceptable to the United States.

My own judgement would therefore be that there was indeed truth in the charge that there was a certain lack of political will, even though it was more lacking in some quarters than others. On the other hand, a fair amount of political capital had been invested in launching the reform effort in the first place, and if there had been a technical consensus the politicians would no doubt have been delighted to take the credit for forging a new chapter in the history of international cooperation. It is true that in the past agreements on important subjects have come only under the spur of a crisis which created a sufficiently general feeling that an agreement was essential, but then in the past the system tended to create deep-seated conflicts of national interests. Where no such irremovable conflicts exist one might have hoped that the technicians could achieve agreements even if the gains they promise are only modest. The experience of the C-20 does nothing to confirm this hope, but in order to see whether it refutes the hope it is necessary to examine the performance of the technicians.

The conduct of the negotiations

The view has sometimes been expressed that the restoration of an international monetary system based on a consciously designed constitution such as that agreed at Bretton Woods is unlikely to materialize because of the sheer difficulties of negotiation in present circumstances.[11] The negotiations that culminated at Bretton Woods

11. See, for example, A. T. Hayes, *Emerging Arrangements in International Payments — Public and Private*, Per Jacobsson Foundation, Washington DC, 1975.

enjoyed advantages (which are unlikely to be repeated in the future) over those conducted in the C-20. First, they were dominated by two participants, the United States and the United Kingdom, whose power was sufficiently unequal to leave no doubt as to whose will must prevail in the last resort. Second, there was a high degree of political harmony fostered by the common war-time struggle and sacrifices. Third, White and Keynes provided outstanding leadership. It is concluded that, lacking these negotiating advantages, it was (and remains) unrealistic to seek a similar comprehensive agreement, and hence one would do better to seek more pragmatic and restricted agreements between a limited number of key countries. (The key currency approach has always had its adherents, especially in the United States: at the time of Bretton Woods they were represented by John H. Williams.[12])

It cannot be doubted that the Bretton Woods negotiations enjoyed these advantages. The world is a more complicated place than it was in 1944, in which power is more widely dispersed, political solidarity is less close than it was among the western Allies (though it should not be forgotten that the Soviet Union participated in the Bretton Woods conference and agreed to the IMF Articles, in spite of which she never joined the Fund), and the skewness of the analytical abilities of the population of negotiators is smaller. But it is also true that a whole tradition and technique of economic negotiation has been built up in the post-war period that was largely lacking in 1944. This tradition functioned with tolerable success — at least by the standards of international relations — in permitting realization of the benefits of cooperative international management of the system over a quarter of a century. And, although it is true that the SDR negotiations fudged some vital issues, the tradition did allow an agreed solution to be reached despite the fact that those negotiations also involved a large number of participants discussing complex issues on which national interests diverged in circumstances where political harmony was not pronounced and the negotiators were not intellectual giants. It is, therefore, worth examining this tradition in order to see whether one can isolate factors that may have contributed to the failure of the C-20 to achieve a success at least comparable to that of the SDR negotiations.

It seems to me that the post-war tradition of economic diplomacy was able to succeed as well as it did because of the widespread observance of two unarticulated rules of the game, in conjunction with a general presumption that achieving agreement is desirable and the assignment of an active innovative role to whatever international

---

12. J. H. Williams, *Post-War Monetary Plans and Other Essays*, Blackwell, Oxford, 1949.

secretariat is responsible for servicing the negotiations. The first rule is that one seeks to avoid positive harm to the interests of others: that one takes the *status quo* as a base point for negotiations, with not too many questions asked about how the world got to that point in the first place.[13] The second says that argument is centred around technical questions. In a sense this is a subterfuge, because countries select technical arguments in order to suit the case they want to make to promote their own interests or prejudices, and naturally the attention paid to an argument depends more on the power position of who says it than on its intellectual merit. Nevertheless, the rule is vital in allowing negotiations to proceed on the basis of analysis rather than just horse-trading, and hence in opening the door for an active role for the international secretariat, which can seek to refine analysis in ways that provide opportunities for countries to modify their attachment to lost causes, to reformulate proposals in ways that meet the essential interests of one party without prejudicing those of the other, to amend the language used to avoid terms that have acquired objectionable connotations to one party, to add elements to a package to provide something for everyone, or — when all else fails — to scale down the objective so as to reach limited agreement on those issues where agreement is possible and postpone those issues on which no consensus can be established. This second rule is of course violated at times and negotiations become politicized. Once that happens there is not much chance of securing an agreement unless a bargain with high-level political appeal can be devised. This may be feasible if the need to reach an agreement is generally felt to be acute, but that which is merely desirable does not stand much of a chance.

This interpretation suggests several factors that may have contributed to the failure of the C-20. In the first place, the circumstances were such as to make interpretation of the first rule ambiguous. The first rule is most useful when the *status quo* is clear and unambiguous. For example, in tariff negotiations the *status quo* is defined by the level of tariffs at the start of a GATT bargaining round: countries' obligations under GATT prevent them arbitrarily raising their tariff rates in order to strengthen their bargaining position. Tariffs are bargained down from their pre-existing level by countries striking bilateral bargains, which are then generalized to all other participants through the most favoured nation provision: since no country is obliged to strike any particular bargain, this procedure ensures that all

13. In terms of game-theoretic concepts, I am suggesting that in economic diplomacy the origin for negotiations is typically provided by the *status quo*, rather than by a threat point or by the independently attainable welfare level.

countries gain from the negotiation. In the C-20 negotiations, in contrast, there was no clear definition of the *status quo* similar to the initial tariff level: the existing system was felt by the Europeans to have resulted from an illicit unilateral renunciation of her responsibilities by the United States, and to take that as the base point seemed a bit like allowing one country to double all its tariffs just before a GATT round started. As described in Chapter 2, the United States took a different view of the matter. The result was that the United States regarded it as perfectly reasonable to demand an indicator system tailor made to protect her particular interests in return for the restoration of convertibility, while the Europeans could never quite bring themselves to feel that they had any obligation to take the idea seriously, despite the fact that, if one considers how little the United States stood to gain from the achievement of agreement, it would seem that the European position was unwise. Hence this unsettled argument about the apportionment of the blame for the breakdown of the Bretton Woods system was a factor complicating the task of negotiating a new system in the C-20. Another, though less central, area of ambiguity about the nature of the *status quo* concerned gold; as argued in the previous chapter, the major gold holders tended to define their base point on the assumption that their gold stock should be valued on the basis of its current market price.

A second possible element lay in an unwillingness to negotiate, as opposed to discuss, at the technical level. The Bureau appeared to view the essence of the negotiation as a horse trade in which, at some point, the three principal parties would get together and agree to concede the essential demands of the two other parties in return for their own principal demand: thus the United States would get a reserve indicator system, the Europeans would get asset settlement, and the developing countries would get the link. I would not dispute the view that in the absence of a political willingness to make these concessions the process of negotiation was a waste of time. That does not, however, imply that the real negotiation has to take place at ministerial level, as seemed to be inferred. Finance Ministers are busy people with a vast range of responsibilities and they cannot be expected to establish a technical mastery of the international monetary system sufficient to enable them to judge sensibly between alternative options, to engage in intelligent discussion of whether a proposal has been reformulated in a way that meets their vital concerns, or to accept a technical argument as dictating the necessity for as graceful a withdrawal as possible. Officials are supposed to be experts capable of undertaking these tasks, but if they abdicate their responsibilities by insisting on 'keeping the options open for their Ministers to decide' the chances are that the result will either be that the Ministers decide something silly or that they are unable to decide on anything at all. The task of the Ministers meeting collectively is in a sense largely the ceremonial one of announcing what has been agreed. This is not an unimportant task, because it is the necessity to have something for the Ministers to announce that provides the necessary pressure for the officials to hammer out an agreement.

A third possible contributory factor was the somewhat passive conception of its role on the part of the Bureau, which provided the international secretariat for the C-20. This may have stemmed from the view, which I have just argued to be mistaken, that once national proposals had been clarified and explored there was a need for an explicit ministerial decision on the general shape of the system, which the technicians would then complete by filling in the detail. This suggests that the role of the secretariat was essentially that of clarifying and presenting a full menu from which the Ministers could choose: hence, perhaps, the willingness to devote much time to the task of drafting reports that expressed dissenting positions. But if, as I have argued, it is unreasonable to expect Ministers themselves to master the technical material needed to reformulate proposals in a manner that can command general consent, this approach is doomed to failure. Someone has to undertake the crucial tasks of judging what may prove acceptable, of pushing forward analysis designed to muster support for a position that may provide the basis for a consensus, of assembling packages that provide something for everyone, and of synthesizing and modifying proposals so as to satisfy the essential interests of the several parties. National delegates can and do contribute to this process, but the fact remains that their first duty is, and must be, to ensure that their particular national interests are adequately defended in the process of reaching a compromise. Too much willingness to seek compromise solutions may merely succeed in surrendering a valuable bargaining counter with nothing to show in return. It follows that the prime responsibility for selecting proposals for discussion, analysing their implications and reformulating them with a view to reaching agreement, must rest with those charged with providing the international secretariat. There are undoubtedly dangers in international civil servants assuming such exposed positions: Schweitzer's fate is proof enough of that. The fact remains that agreement was reached at the Smithsonian — as indeed it was reached on the Guidelines for Floating and the valuation of the SDR (despite the fact that all five of the major powers opposed adoption of the standard basket through the greater part of the discussions), where the IMF staff, with their more active conception of the role of the secretariat, were charged with prime responsibility.

No one could claim that this more activist approach has always achieved complete success. During the SDR negotiations, for example, it was not merely such semantic issues as whether the SDR was a 'reserve asset' or a 'credit instrument' that were sidestepped in the interests of achieving an agreement, but also the quite fundamental question of whether the SDR was to be a substitute for gold or the dollar (or both). It was described merely as a 'supplement to existing reserve assets', and the agreement contained no provision for limiting the volume of other forms of liquidity or for substituting SDRs for outstanding reserve currency balances. Matters were even worse with the IMF's exchange rate report, where the failure to recognize consistency with asset market equilibrium as a basic condition for the viability of an exchange rate regime was inexcusable. What this demonstrates is not, however, that the international secretariat should restrict itself to secretarial functions, but that an excessive concern for achieving agreement even at the cost of ignoring viability, or an analytical failure to identify what is necessary for viability, may deprive any agreement that is achieved of value. In the age of negotiations involving 126 or more nations, an active and analytically-able secretariat with an institutional commitment to the achievement of agreement is almost certainly a necessary condition for a successful negotiation. By comparison with this factor, the number of people in the room (which attracted considerable press comment) is inconsequential.

Intellectual failings

I have already argued at length that the principal and crucial intellectual error of the C-20 lay in the decision to opt for restoration of the adjustable peg at a time when this system had ceased to be viable because of the development of capital mobility. In my view this error not only meant that any agreed system would have been unlikely to be implemented and, if implemented, would not have operated successfully, but it also bears much of the onus for the failure to secure agreement on other issues. This is primarily because of the incompatibility of indicators and the adjustable peg.

There were, as indicated in Chapter 5, several reasons why the reserve indicator system as proposed by the United States was likely to remain unacceptable to the rest of the world, but only one of these objections was of the basic irremovable variety, rather than the sort of difference that international secretariats are employed to find mutually satisfactory solutions to.[14] This basic difficulty stemmed from the fact that there were already far too many indications of when countries were likely to change their par values to allow the adjustable peg to operate smoothly with the existing degree of capital mobility, and it therefore seemed unwise to confer an official status on one particular indicator. This was a difficulty that stemmed directly and inescapably from the attempt to associate an indicator system with the adjustable peg. And, without some form of effective indicator system, the United States was unambiguously unprepared to concede asset settlement, which was the essence of the reform in European eyes. Moreover, asset settlement was a risky commitment for the United States to undertake, after she had become accustomed to the luxury of living without convertibility, with an exchange rate regime that was guaranteed to beget irregular but ever-more-massive speculative flows.

Why, then, did the C-20 decide to condemn itself to futility within 6 months of its creation? It was not a decision that was made after a close and dispassionate study of the alternatives, but more in the nature of a reflex action. Inevitably, therefore, any explanation offered must be speculative. Perhaps part of the explanation is to be found in the innate conservatism of the international financial establishment and the feeling that, despite its ultimate breakdown, the Bretton Woods system had served the world well. Part goes back to the failure of the 1970 IMF report on exchange rates to identify the ability of the system to accommodate changes without violating the conditions for asset market equilibrium as a prerequisite for a viable exchange rate regime. Perhaps a part can be explained by a rational appraisal of self-interest on the part of the developing countries, which saw advantages in the industrial countries having substantial reserve needs (thus promising them potential SDR allocations), and which may also have welcomed the possibility of themselves making occasional speculative profits through judicious reserve switching before par value changes.

But perhaps the prime element was the lack of a widely acceptable alternative. It is often said that a theory is never displaced by the uncovering of facts that are inconsistent with it, but only by the development of a better theory. This is as it should be, since the intellectual framework provided by a deficient theory is preferable to the absence of any intellectual framework at all. Similarly, a recognition

14. One of the technical failings in the C-20 was, however, the failure of either the Bureau or the IMF staff to make much of a contribution to refashioning the indicator proposal in a manner that satisfied the essential interests of the several parties.

of the deficiencies of the adjustable peg was not in itself enough to cause its abandonment; it was first necessary to identify a superior alternative. Completely fixed and freely floating rates were both ruled out, for reasons discussed in Chapter 5. The crawling peg was disliked, not because it was too flexible, but because governments could not bring themselves to contemplate the degree of discipline involved in admitting that their par value was wrong but nonetheless making the necessary correction gradually rather than in one fell swoop. Managed floating seemed to be ruled out because the lack of the framework provided by a par value system apparently precluded the type of international management that was aspired to. One cannot, for example, introduce multicurrency intervention without a rule for determining the choice of intervention currency, such as is provided in a par value system by the rule that one intervenes in the currency against which one is at the margin. And one cannot expect the issuer of an intervention currency to agree to asset settlement unless the balances of its currency acquired in intervention were obtained in the course of intervention of which it approves; it would, for example, be unthinkable for the United States to be expected to convert dollars acquired in intervention undertaken to keep the dollar overvalued. Once again, a par value system provides the necessary framework, since intervention undertaken in defence of an agreed set of par values cannot be considered detrimental to the interests of the intervention currency country so long as it maintains that its par value is correct. On this interpretation, therefore, the adjustable peg was chosen, notwithstanding its deficiencies, because it was felt that a par value system was needed to provide a framework for the desired degree of international management, and the only alternative form of the par value system — the crawling peg — implied an unacceptable degree of discipline. Unfortunately the deficiencies of the adjustable peg were altogether more serious and more irremovable than was acknowledged.

I therefore conclude that the reform negotiations failed through a combination of weak political will and technical inadequacy. Political will was most lacking in the United States, which was not surprising since she had the least to gain through a replacement of the present arrangements. More generally, however, once the world had taken the plunge into generalized floating and discovered that, while not quite the utopia depicted in part of the academic literature, the system was better than the one that had been propped up with such difficulty for so long, the incentives to reach agreement were not overwhelming.

Since there were no acute conflicts of national interest, a sufficiently bold and resourceful set of technicians might have nonetheless achieved a worthwhile measure of agreement. But the Bureau failed to fill the active innovatory role that is a necessary condition for fostering a consensus in a multicountry negotiation. And the technicians irresponsibly chose to push back far too much of the burden of decision making to their Ministers, who are in no position to engage in the sort of technical dialogue out of which agreements can be forged. The combination of technical weakness and the absence of a compelling need to reach agreement was fatal.

8

The future

It was argued in the previous chapter that a sufficient condition for the failure of the reform exercise was the lack of any proposal for an exchange rate regime consistent both with the current facts of life and such collective aspirations as the C-20 had. However, ideas on this front developed rapidly after the move to generalized floating, and the lacuna that existed when the C-20 was discussing the exchange rate regime has now been filled. The first section of this chapter, therefore, is devoted to an exposition of a form of managed floating, based on the 'reference rate proposal', which would be capable of providing the basis for a reformed system. The second section sketches the reasons for believing that a system of this character would both be technically consistent and respect the vital interests of all parties. The final section of the chapter examines the reasons for supposing that such a system would be preferable to the non-system that presently exists.

The reference rate proposal

The basic idea of the reference rate proposal [1] is that an agreed structure of exchange rates, regularly revised at pre-specified intervals, would provide the basis for intervention *rights* but would not impose intervention *obligations*. The agreed structure of rates would be known

---

1. Both the term and the idea were introduced by W. Ethier and A. I. Bloomfield in a paper entitled 'The Management of Floating Exchange Rates' which was presented to the Conference on World Monetary Disorder sponsored by the Center for International Business and Management of Pepperdine University held in May 1974. A revised version of their paper entitled *Managing the Managed Float* appeared as Princeton Essays in International Finance No.112, Princeton, 1975. I discussed this proposal and its potentiality for application to a reformed system, on the general lines followed in the text, in 'The Future Exchange Rate Regime', Banca Nazionale del Lavoro *Quarterly Review*, June 1975.

as the set of reference rates, and would be similar in general concept to a set of par values; that is, it would be a set of rates that represented an official and agreed view as to what rates ought to be. Countries would be entitled to intervene if, and only if, intervention served either to push the exchange rate toward the reference rate or left the rate within a specified band around the reference rate. Countries would never, however, be obliged to intervene; and it is the obligation to intervene to defend a specified margin that creates the one-way options that are the fatal weakness of the adjustable peg.

A similar idea to the reference rate proposal emerged simultaneously in the IMF, in the course of the construction of the Fund's Guidelines for Floating, and is incorporated in Guideline 3. As outlined in Chapter 5, Guideline 3 employs the concept of ' .... some target zone of rates ... within the range of reasonable estimates of the medium-term norm'. Guideline 3 (a) provides that any country wishing to intervene other than defensively must secure the Fund's agreement to such a target zone and that aggressive intervention must be confined to that which will push the rate toward the target zone, while 3 (b) allows the Fund to encourage the member to act to promote the return of its rate towards such a norm if it has deviated so far as to threaten the interests of other countries. Guideline 3, therefore, goes a considerable part of the way towards the reference rate proposal, for both embody the principle of seeking international agreement on what the official world conceives to be an appropriate structure of rates without accompanying such agreement by a commitment to override the market if the market disagrees with that judgement.

At the time that the C-20 was debating the exchange rate regime, this idea was not on the table. The Guidelines had not been thought of, let alone agreed, and Ethier and Bloomfield had not conceived, let alone published, their proposal. Discussion at that time took it as axiomatic that a floating rate regime involved the authorities abstaining from any kind of commitment to a particular exchange rate: about the only existing proposal for the management of floating rates was Paul Wonnacott's suggestion, which is embodied in Guideline 2, for 'leaning against the wind' to slow down any movement in the rate.[2] The C-20 therefore had no opportunity of considering whether the reference rate proposal might have provided the basis for a reformed system.

There are three differences between the Guidelines and the Ethier-Bloomfield proposal that are non-fundamental, in the sense that either approach could easily be amended to embrace the procedure adopted in the alternative approach. The first concerns whether the rules are to

2. See references in Chapter 5, n.24 (p.123).

be restricted to intervention policies or are to be used to judge all policies that may be used for purposes of exchange rate management — notably official foreign borrowing and lending, intervention in the forward market, capital restrictions and monetary policies adopted for reasons other than domestic stabilization purposes. Ethier and Bloomfield advanced their proposal for the limited purpose of providing a technique to restrain possible aggressive central bank policies in an environment that lacked any such defences, and therefore confined their proposal to intervention policy, while the Guidelines emphasize that they are intended to apply to all policies of exchange rate management. It seems clear that the wider interpretation is the appropriate one when considering the reference rate proposal for the more ambitious role of providing the foundation of an agreed system. The second inessential difference concerns whether short-run smoothing intervention of the type encouraged by Guideline 1 should be encouraged at all times, as it is by the Guidelines, or whether smoothing should be prohibited in one direction (except in a zone around the reference rate), as it is by the original reference rate proposal. The latter clearly could be, and perhaps should be, amended to permit such short-run smoothing at all times. The third inessential difference concerns a topic that is of vital importance: whether the structure of reference rates should be published (as Ethier and Bloomfield assume) or maintained secret (as has so far occurred with any understandings that the Fund may have reached as to what constitute acceptable target exchange-rate zones). Since the only times when governments have an interest in concealing their views about what they believe an appropriate exchange rate to be are when they are trying to defend some other, unrealistic, rate, and the overwhelming advantage of managed floating is that it avoids the need for governments to engage in such antics, I shall assume that an integral part of the reference rate proposal is that the set of reference rates be published.

At a mechanistic level, the difference between the intervention rights and obligations entailed by a par value system, the existing Guidelines, and the reference rate proposal can be studied by considering Figure 8.1. The curve shows the exchange rate that would prevail in the absence of any intervention (and is drawn smoothly, thus ignoring the day-to-day movements that Guideline 1 is intended to suppress). It may be assumed for the sake of expositional clarity, although it is not an assumption whose plausibility I would defend for a moment, that this rate is independent of the exchange rate regime and of the history of previous intervention. It is also assumed that in each case the normal exchange rate — the par value, the centre of the target zone of rates within the range of reasonable estimates of the medium-term norm and the reference rate — is the same, x_n; and that the high and low rates surrounding the normal rate — respectively the margins, the boundaries of the target zone of rates within the range of reasonable estimates of the medium-term norm, and the boundaries of the specified band around the reference rate within which intervention is unrestricted — are similarly the same, at x_h and x_l.

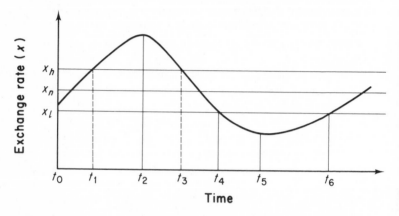

Figure 8·1 x = foreign exchange per unit of domestic currency.

Between t_0 and t_1 both the par value system and the reference rate proposal would permit intervention in either (or no) direction, while the Guidelines would permit intervention to slow down the appreciation of the rate by the central bank purchasing foreign exchange. Between t_1 and t_2 the Guidelines would still permit intervention to limit the appreciation, and so would the reference rate proposal, while the par value system would require the central bank to intervene to hold the rate at x_h. Between t_2 and t_3 there would still be an obligation to intervene to hold the rate at x_h under a par value system, and the right, but not the obligation, to buy foreign exchange so as to depreciate the rate under the reference rate proposal. The Guidelines, however, provide contradictory rights in this case: Guideline 2 permits intervention to limit the depreciation, while Guideline 3 (a) permits intervention to accelerate it, so that a country would be free to do anything short of intervening so strongly by selling foreign exchange as to turn the depreciation into an appreciation. Between t_3 and t_4 both the par value system and the reference rate proposal would permit intervention in either direction provided that it were not so strong as to push the rate above x_h or below x_l, while the Guidelines would only allow a country to sell foreign exchange so as to limit the depreciation.

Between t_4 and t_5 the par value system would obligate the central bank to sell foreign exchange to the extent necessary to hold the rate at x_l, while both the reference rate proposal and the Guidelines would permit but not compel the sale of foreign exchange so as to limit the depreciation. And so on.

There are, therefore, formal differences between the intervention rights and obligations entailed under the three approaches. One way of appraising the approaches would be to endeavour to assess which set of rights and obligations would best suppress short-run swings in exchange rates while allowing orderly evolution to changes in underlying conditions. Provided that the par value is correct, the par value system is admirable from the first standpoint, but its fatal weakness lies in its inability to satisfy the second criterion. So far as the choice between the Guidelines and the reference rate proposal is concerned, the difference lies in the fact that the Guidelines define intervention rights with respect to both the change in the rate and x_n, while the reference rate proposal assigns no role to changes in the rate and therefore implies a correspondingly greater role for x_n. One may therefore expect[3] the reference rate proposal to perform better if, and only if, the authorities are generally able to form a reasonable estimate of the equilibrium rate x_n and to adjust x_n promptly to reflect changes in underlying conditions.

Whether Guideline 2 should be suppressed, thus implicitly increasing the role of Guideline 3, is, however, of less consequence than whether agreement on a reference rate should be required as a condition of being allowed to intervene at all (except perhaps for short-term smoothing of the character sanctioned by Guideline 1). It is the requirement for regular negotiation of a comprehensive structure of reference rates that would permit the construction of a symmetrical and internationally managed system of the character that was being sought by the C-20. The obvious occasions for these regular negotiations would be the thrice-yearly meetings of the IMF Council, if that body is ever created, which would therefore exercise its proposed responsibilities for supervision of the adjustment process primarily by approving the set of reference rates. Modification of the previous set of reference rates would no doubt be guided by the sort of 'indicators' that used to be discussed as offering automatic or presumptive rules for parity adjustment in a crawling-peg system: notably, how market

---

3. I base this conclusion on the analysis in my paper 'Exchange Rate Flexibility and Reserve Use', *Scandinavian Journal of Economics*, 1976(2). The conclusion is, however, tentative, mainly because the model presented in that paper was solved only to a very limited extent (even with the valuable extension of my discussant, Stanley Black).

rates had been behaving, and how reserves had been moving relative to a desirable norm. One would expect actual movements in market rates to be validated by changes in reference rates in many cases, although not automatically, for that would defeat the object of having reference rates at all; rather, the authorities would be required to judge whether a particular rate movement represented a short-term 'blip' or a basic adjustment to changes in underlying conditions, and reference rates will no doubt not be taken seriously by the market unless and until the authorities demonstrate their ability to avoid being stampeded into following the market on errant paths. It would also be both easy and appropriate to give a role to reserves in guiding the choice of reference rates, in other words to have some form of reserve indicator system. This would be easy because the knowledge that reference rates might be revised because of reserve changes would not create the danger of disequilibrating capital movements in the way that comparable knowledge does under a par value system, for the simple reason that central banks would not be required to step in and defend a particular reference rate pending its revision. And it would be appropriate because, as argued in Chapter 5, the stock of reserves does provide a logical basis with respect to which to define a country's adjustment obligations.

It would, naturally, be desirable to minimize the number of occasions when reference rates become inappropriate. One way of doing this would be to allow reference rates to crawl in order to accommodate secular differences in inflation rates. The regular international negotiations would therefore need to determine both a set of current reference rates, and also a set of planned future reference rates as of the date planned for the next IMF Council. The actual reference rate would then crawl from the one rate to the other over the intervening period. A country with an atypically low inflation rate would generally select a planned future reference rate modestly above its current reference rate, and its actual reference rate would then appreciate continuously, until the next date for revising reference rates arrived. Naturally no well-run country would choose a planned future reference rate so different from its current reference rate as to imply a rate of appreciation or depreciation greater than could be neutralized by an acceptable interest rate differential, for reasons familiar from the theory of the crawling peg. But well-run countries would not be characterized by a refusal to plan a future rate different from the current rate: on the contrary, financial officials would take a certain pride in their planned future rate turning out to be an accurate forecast of the actual future reference rate, and — so long as the need for exchange rate changes persists — this will not in general be possible with planned future rates set equal to current rates.

One strand of academic writing of which insufficient note has up to now been taken in official circles concerns *ex ante* coordination of monetary policies. The ideas have been most fully developed by Ronald McKinnon,[4] who has elaborated the conditions regarding domestic credit expansion (DCE) and sterilization needed to enforce fixed exchange rates between countries. The essence of the matter is that planned rates of DCE should diverge only to the extent needed to accommodate differences in the increase in the demand for money caused by divergences in trend rates of real growth, while the unplanned element of DCE caused by the sterilization of reserve inflows and outflows should be limited to ensure that sterilization is only partial, thus providing a monetary adjustment mechanism of the character embodied in the gold standard. The framework being suggested here is a much looser one, in which reference rates would be allowed to crawl against one another as a result of deliberate planning, and in which countries would, in any event, not be expected to enforce their plans if it appeared that such enforcement was going to be costly. There do, nevertheless, appear to be grounds for seeking consistency in planned monetary policies (which in this case would also allow for planned rates of DCE to differ to the extent needed to provide the monetary growth to feed the anticipated differential inflation rates that cause the crawls of the reference rates). First, this would tend to discipline individual countries into formulating an internally consistent set of policies, and, while changes in those policies would in no way be precluded, it would do something to ensure that changes in policy were made after due thought rather than in a fit of absent-mindedness. Second, it would help to ensure that the global implications of the sum of the monetary policies being pursued by individual countries were spotted relatively early, before inflation or deflation had got out of hand. Third, one of the classic advantages of a system of fixed rates is that it enables domestically induced changes in demand, including the effects of domestic monetary 'mistakes', to be dispersed rather than turned in on the country where they originate; to the extent that countries intervened as their rates departed from their reference rates, and avoided complete sterilization of the monetary effects of their intervention, one would introduce an element of this stabilizing feedback into the system. Even though such *ex ante* coordination of monetary policy may be desirable, however, it may also be true that it is politically unrealistic for the time being. What does seem clear is that

4. R. I. McKinnon, 'Sterilization in Three Dimensions ... ', in R. Z. Aliber, ed., *National Monetary Policies and the International Financial System*, University of Chicago Press, Chicago, 1974, and 'On Securing a Common Monetary Policy in Europe', Banca

any future move to try to stabilize exchange rates (beyond the reduction in volatility that might be achieved by adoption of the reference rate proposal) should start by seeking to achieve consistency in monetary policies, rather than by pegging exchange rates while allowing countries to pursue monetary policies that are ultimately inconsistent with the maintenance of fixed rates.

A reformed system

It has already been argued in the previous section that the reference rate proposal would assign a natural and legitimate place to one of the most contentious proposals advanced in the C-20 negotiations — the reserve indicator system — without raising the danger of provoking speculative capital movements, which constituted the fundamental objection to that proposal in the context in which it was advanced. It is also true that an agreed structure of reference rates would provide the necessary framework for introducing the two other elements that emerged in the C-20 discussions as essential to the achievement of symmetry in rights and obligations : multicurrency intervention and asset settlement.

MCI is impractical under managed floating as it presently operates because the avoidance of conflict in intervention policies demands the existence of rules governing which currency may be used in intervention, and this requires a criterion as to whether a currency should be regarded as weak or strong. The reference rate would provide such a criterion. It would be possible to stipulate that intervention should always take place in a currency that would be pushed towards its reference rate by the intervention being undertaken.

Similarly, asset settlement is precluded by floating as at present operated because a country can hardly be required to convert all balances of its currency that other countries acquire in intervention into reserve assets, irrespective of its view of the appropriateness of that intervention for its own exchange rate. The essential condition for asset settlement to be a proposal that an issuing country can take seriously is that it can be assured that the balances that it is required to convert should always be acquired in accordance with a set of rules that safeguard its interests. Balances acquired under MCI conducted according to the rule in the previous paragraph would certainly satisfy this criterion.

Suppose, therefore, that the reference rate proposal was accompanied by MCI and asset settlement. The operation of the system may be illustrated by the following examples. A country wishing to intervene to support its currency would be obliged to buy its own currency by selling a currency that was standing above its reference rate, which it could obtain by virtue of the obligation that each issuing country would have to sell its currency in exchange for reserves so long as its rate was above its reference rate.[5] Conversely, a country that wished to limit the appreciation of its currency would do so by using it to buy a currency that was standing below its reference rate; the currency balances so acquired would then be converted into reserves, which the country whose currency had been bought would be obliged to sell while its currency was below the reference rate. In order to ensure asset settlement, the rules would, of course, have to be written in such a way as to ensure that conversion actually occurred (in both directions) as assumed in the above examples.

No matter how much care was taken in determining planned future as well as current reference rates, occasions would no doubt periodically arise when it would become apparent that a particular reference rate was no longer appropriate. If this happened to a currency outside the MCI group, no problem would arise: the country would simply allow its rate to adjust and would seek an appropriate revision of its reference rate during the next international negotiation. If, however, it happened to a country inside the MCI group, there would be a danger that the right of other countries to limit the deviation of the market rate from the reference rate would reintroduce the rigidities of the par value system. For example, if it became clear that the lira was undervalued, deficit countries that wished to support their rates would be entitled to sell lire for their currencies, thus preventing an appreciation of the lira which the Italian authorities might urgently desire in order to stem an unwanted capital inflow at bargain rates. No doubt most cases of this nature could be dealt with by informal inter-central bank cooperation: there would be no great cost to a country in acceding to another's request not to use its currency in intervention for the time being, since there would always be other currencies available for intervention (unlike the present situation). And the position of countries with intervention currencies could be further safeguarded by providing for the temporary suspension of convertibility obligations pending the settlement of a request for a changed reference rate. This would mean that, in the above example, the Italian authorities would be relieved of their obligation to buy reserves from other countries; in the converse case, the issuing country would be obliged to redeem its currency only when the new reference rate had gone into effect, which would be liable to

5. It is assumed that reserves would be exchanged for intervention currencies at current market exchange rates (and not at reference rates) so that central banks would not be offered the possibility of realizing profits through arbitrage. This is the practice already followed with regard to SDR transactions.

impose a capital loss on a country that insisted on intervening in the overvalued currency.

Just as an indicator system would avoid the dangers that the Europeans feared most, provided that it were embodied in a system based on reference rates rather than par values, so would asset settlement appear in a different and more attractive light to the United States in a system of MCI and reference rates. A run on the dollar would no longer threaten the United States with the need to revoke her newly accepted obligations before the ink on them was dry, but could be fended off, as it is now, by permitting a depreciation of the dollar. This would give her adequate protection, of the sort she tried so hard to establish through an indicator system and quaintly hoped to preserve through 'elasticity' in settlement arrangements, without requiring any revocation of her international obligations or involving disruption in the exchange rate relationships of the rest of the world.

Another of the attractive features of the reference rate proposal is that it permits a far more realistic approach to the troublesome question of sanctions. Instead of the Fund having to choose from a long list of pressures to be applied to a country that failed to fulfil its adjustment obligations, the international community would simply decline to sanction a reference rate that did not reflect a willingness to adjust. The lack of a reference rate would automatically serve to prohibit intervention. This would penalize the recalcitrant country, since the ability to intervene is, in general, advantageous, but it would be the sort of penalty that countries might be induced to accept since free floating is an inconvenience rather than a disaster. And it would have the important incidental advantage of generally providing a remedy as well as a penalty. This is altogether more realistic than the opposite suggestion in para.13 of the *Outline* that the Fund might withdraw its authorization for a country to float as a penalty for failure to observe the Guidelines. The fact that countries that wish to maintain their par values do not always succeed would preclude any simple test of whether a country had tried to hold its par value when instructed to do so by the IMF, while the mere knowledge that a country did not want to observe its par value would make it impractical to hold that par value even if it tried. There is no similar ambiguity about whether a country has satisfied an obligation to abstain from intervention, so that defiance of the rules would be possible only by a country prepared to defy them outright. Defiance might also be impeded by other central banks declining to enter into transactions with the offending central bank. (If reference rates were determined partially in the light of reserve holdings relative to an internationally-agreed norm, it might be a case of overkill to introduce interest penalties for excess reserve holdings, on the lines mentioned in Chapter 5, as well, but there would be no technical inconsistency in so doing if it were considered desirable in the interests of symmetrical adjustment pressures.)

The remaining elements of the reform programme discussed in the C-20 all involve the arrangements governing the supply of reserve assets. They can be dealt with far more briefly, since they do not raise unresolved interlocking technical issues in the way that the questions of adjustment, exchange rates, intervention and settlement do. The key element in establishing an SDR standard is, in any event, the introduction of asset settlement. The interdependencies that do exist are perhaps more political than technical. For example, it would seem improbable that the developing countries could be induced to agree to controls on reserve placements in the Euro-markets unless asset settlement were guaranteed, since in the absence of asset settlement the likely consequence of such controls would be increased holdings of dollars in New York and therefore increased seigniorage for the United States rather than increased SDR allocations. Even then, one might expect the developing countries to demand the link in return. It was argued in Chapter 6 that the link does not in itself raise any significant dangers provided that it does not impede the adoption of a competitive interest rate on the SDR, so that a formula-determined competitive rate of interest on the SDR might become the condition for concession of the link. And if the SDR interest rate were being settled once and for all, it would be natural to endorse the standard basket as the permanent method of SDR valuation as well (and preferably to accompany this endorsement by the adoption of rules that would govern periodic revisions in the composition of the basket while guaranteeing that revisions would not lead to sudden changes in the value of the SDR). This set of measures could be expected to lead to an SDR standard quite rapidly, provided that continual further growth in the value of gold reserves is avoided. A safeguard against this danger could be provided by varying the rate at which monetary gold is released on the market with a view to limiting fluctuations in the price of gold.

This system even offers the opportunity of an elegant solution to the unimportant little problem of inconsistency between par values — or, in this case, reference rates — and transactions values of the SDR. Presumably reference rates would in general be expressed in terms of the SDR (which would have the incidental effect of leading those countries that continued pegging — a practice in no way precluded by the reference rate proposal — to peg to the SDR rather than to an individual currency). But general and cumulative deviations of reference rates from transactions values could be avoided as a result of the fact that the complete set of reference rates would be systematically revised at regular intervals. Those currencies included in the basket could first have their reference rates negotiated simultaneously in terms of one another (thus recognizing the economic fact that there are a limited number of currencies whose importance is sufficient to require simultaneous determination), and then have their absolute reference rates in terms of the SDR calculated mechanically by the requirement that the reference rates be consistent with the transactions value of the SDR as determined by the basket on a pre-specified date. Meanwhile all other countries would negotiate directly about their absolute reference rates in terms of the SDR, thus recognizing that, while it is important that the reference rates of even the smaller countries be chosen appropriately, the rate chosen for any individual currency would not have a sufficient feedback to justify changing the rates of other currencies.

Is reform still desirable?

Although I am not enough of an expert on international relations to discuss the subject at length, I suspect that the strongest argument for desiring to see an agreed international monetary system installed may well be political. In the absence of an agreed framework of rules governing countries' rights and obligations in the economic and monetary fields, there is clearly potential scope for the inevitable differences in national interests to foment political disharmony. The trans-Atlantic differences of view about the role of the dollar that developed during the 1960s provide a leading example of how international relations can be poisoned by an inadequate framework of rules. Not only does one need rules, but they need to be essentially symmetrical among countries; even if differences imply both advantages and disadvantages that may seem reasonably balanced to an impartial observer, it is only too likely that countries will focus attention on the disadvantages to themselves and the advantages to others, so that differences *per se* can foster grievances. This does not mean that the international community cannot grant specially favourable treatment to those of its members suffering from severe handicaps without threatening to arouse resentment; developing countries receive aid, special treatment under GATT, access to the Extended Fund Facility and so on. But where there is no compelling rationale for preferential treatment, it would seem prudent to build in as much symmetry as technically feasible. Not only does this avoid the invitation to manufacture grievances, but it also minimizes the extent to which one country will find its interests are contrary to those of others when decisions on new policies need to be made. The asymmetry of the Bretton Woods system surely fostered the highly unfortunate situation of the early 1970s, when, because her interests were in fact so different from those of other countries, the United States repeatedly found herself in a tiny minority in international monetary debates and consequently seemed to come to regard herself as constituting a permanent opposition. The IMF cannot, of course, hope to function effectively without the cooperation of its largest member.

In addition to this general political reason for desiring that whatever system exists receive an explicit endorsement which the present non-system lacks, five features of the existing arrangements give cause for concern on economic grounds. The first relates to the degree of volatility that exchange rates have exhibited during the floating period. It is an established historical fact that exchange rate variations were pronounced during the first $2^1/_2$ years of generalized floating,[6] despite the occurrence of substantial central bank intervention designed to smooth rate fluctuations. Day-to-day changes in exchange rates of up to 4 per cent have been recorded, week-to-week movements have approached 10 per cent, and short-term swings lasting a quarter or two have exceeded 20 per cent on occasion.[7] Such movements have often been reversed, rather than always being explicable as prompt adaptations of rates to changes in underlying conditions as and when these were perceived by the market. Over the longer term, variations in effective exchange rates have indeed tended to be such as to offset differential inflation rates, but the fact remains that this has occurred against a background of considerable short-term volatility.

It does, of course, need to be asked whether this short-term volatility matters very much. It has resulted in a substantial widening in bid-ask spreads in foreign exchange markets, to compensate dealers for the additional risk that they have to bear in maintaining the open positions necessary to permit the markets to work efficiently, but even the approximate doubling in the spread that seems to have occurred[8] leaves the cost of foreign exchange transactions as a trivial element of the cost of engaging in foreign trade. Forward markets remain available to enable traders to protect themselves against the exchange risk involved in any particular transaction: while the evidence as to whether the use of forward markets has expanded or contracted since the advent of floating is contradictory, the most systematic evidence indicates that, in the Swedish case, the use of the forward market has

---

6. See IMF, *Annual Report*, 1975, chapter 2A; F. Hirsch and D. Higham, 'Floating Rates — Expectations and Experience', *Three Banks Review*, June 1974; and S. Katz, *'Managed Floating' As An Interim International Exchange Rate Regime, 1973-75*, Bulletin of the Graduate School of Business Administration of New York University, 1975-3.
7. IMF, *loc.cit.*
8. *Ibid.*, p.26.

roughly doubled.[9] It is, however, mistaken to suppose that use of the forward market enables a trader to gain complete protection against the risk caused by large random variations in exchange rates. Since forward rates are subject to much the same volatility as spot rates, a firm involved in a continuing series of external transactions, all of which it covers forward, is subject to much the same increase in the variation of receipts as if it settles in the spot market. All that use of the forward market does is to ensure that it will not find itself completing particular transactions that it would rather not have undertaken. It seems inevitable, therefore, that erratic variations in exchange rates will have some protective or 'anti-trade' effect, although this may operate largely in the long run as investment plans are modified to reflect a greater or lesser commitment to serve foreign markets. The absence of evidence to date that exchange rate variability has hampered trade is therefore not conclusive.

The next question is whether one can reasonably expect that agreement on, and publication of, an agreed set of reference rates will help to reduce the volatility of exchange rates. My own view is that such an expectation is reasonable. In the short run the level of a freely floating exchange rate is not determined by the intersection of current account (or basic balance) demand and supply schedules for foreign exchange, but by the conditions of asset market equilibrium — which depend on the average view of market operators as to what the equilibrium rate is. There is no particular reason for expecting market operators to be more skilled in this task than national authorities, while there is a compelling reason for expecting the authorities to have an advantage: namely, that the equilibrium rate depends *inter alia* on the future policies to be pursued by the authorities themselves. Moreover, it is not simply a case of the authorities being better able to predict their own future actions than market operators: a commitment to relate policies of exchange rate management to a particular rate will in and of itself introduce feedbacks into the actions of the authorities that will tend to validate the agreed rate. In particular, if reserves are bought (sold), and the monetary effect of this reserve acquisition (loss) is not completely sterilized, when the exchange rate is above (below) the reference rate, this will introduce an element of the gold standard adjustment mechanism tending to reinforce the reference rate. In the absence of knowledge of the future intentions of the authorities, including any intention they may have to direct their exchange rate management policies to the reinforcement of a particular rate, market

9. S. Grassman, 'Currency Distribution and Forward Cover in Foreign Trade: Sweden Revisited 1973', mimeo, 1975.

operators must be expected to have only hazy — and also volatile — notions on what the equilibrium rate is (which is not at all inconsistent with their sometimes developing very strong views on what the equilibrium rate is *not*, thus giving rise to the billion-dollar-per-hour flow sometimes observed under pegged rates). They cannot, therefore, be expected to step in with a considerable volume of stabilizing speculation until the rate has departed convincingly from its equilibrium level; thus one should expect the wide swings in rates that have in fact occurred. A strength of this explanation is that it also explains convincingly the relative stability of the Canadian dollar, where the 1:1 relationship with the US dollar serves as a psychological parity to focus the views of the market. And a corollary of the explanation is that an announced reference rate, which informs the market as to what the authorities believe to be a realistic estimate of the equilibrium rate which their actions will to some extent reinforce and which will provide a basis for informed public debate, can hope to provide a similar focus for stabilizing speculation.

The second economic inadequacy of present arrangements is the total lack of control over the volume of international liquidity. As analysed in Chapter 6, this lack of control arises from the absence of asset settlement, the unconstrained freedom to place reserves in the Euro-markets and the fluctuations in the gold price. Once again there is room for debate about how much weight should be attached to this factor. So far as variations in foreign exchange reserves are concerned, it can be argued that floating gives countries individually far more power to avoid major unintended reserve accumulations or losses than the par value system did, and therefore that the danger of a major general surfeit or shortage of reserves emerging and provoking global inflation or deflation is substantially reduced. On the other hand, this elasticity in the supply of reserves means that one cannot expect any positive contribution from a tautness in the reserve supply to a global anti-inflationary policy. What seems potentially more disruptive than variations in foreign exchange reserves is, however, variations in the value of gold reserves. If gold reserves are effectively remonetized by the agreement of August 1975, countries in general could find their reserves carried far above their optimal level by some new speculative bubble in the gold market. Each country acting rationally would then tend to seek to dispose of its excess reserves, but the fact that they were all floating would not help the system as a whole to dispose of the excess reserves. Two outcomes would be possible: the United States might react passively and allow other currencies to appreciate against the dollar, thus providing the rest of the world with real resources corresponding to the writing up in the value of reserves, or else the United States might join in the attempt to dispose of its excess reserves by an expansionary monetary policy, export restrictions, or even by attempting to intervene at cross purposes with other countries. Even if the ultimate disaster of inconsistent intervention were avoided, the other possible forms of US reaction would produce precisely those results that have always been feared would result from a surfeit of reserves. The former outcome demands of the United States a rather substantial willingness to make sacrifices for the sake of other countries, and is the type of asymmetry that has in the past created endless tensions and disagreements.

The third unsatisfactory economic aspect of the present situation, at least in the eyes of many, is the maldistribution of seigniorage. With an elastic supply of reserves such as is provided by present arrangements, it seems unlikely that sufficient reserve stringency could develop to convince the necessary 85 per cent of the IMF membership that new SDR allocations are called for. Seigniorage will therefore continue to be distributed arbitrarily to reserve centres and possibly to gold holders, rather than on the agreed basis reflected in the distribution of SDR allocations.

The fourth economic disadvantage of existing arrangements relates to the continued asymmetry in the position of the US dollar. There seems to be a tendency in some quarters, especially in the United States, to imagine that the problem posed by the asymmetrical position of the dollar has been relieved by the change from the par value system to one of managed floating. This presumably rests on the continuing tendency to treat managed floating as a mildly deviant form of free floating (in which the problem of asymmetry would indeed disappear), rather than as a distinct exchange rate regime. It is, however, more revealing to recall that under the Bretton Woods system the particular limitation on US freedom of action, as compared to that of other countries, lay in her inability to take an initiative designed to influence the dollar exchange rate within the margins; and what the advent of managed floating has done is to extend the margins from 2·25 per cent to infinity. Accordingly, the asymmetry in the opportunities for national exchange rate management has been intensified rather than relieved.

There is once again room for debate as to the significance of this factor. With high capital mobility and a firmly held view in the market as to what constitutes an equilibrium exchange rate, the asymmetry would be unimportant: if, for example, during a global recession the rest of the world attempted to export its unemployment to the United States by buying dollars and so appreciating the dollar, the major result would be to induce large capital outflows from the United States in the expectation of a rebound in the rate, and the countries seeking competitive depreciations would find it prohibitively expensive to buy up these dollars in order to maintain their depreciated rates. While capital mobility is indeed high, the observed volatility of exchange rates refutes the hypothesis that the market has firm views of equilibrium exchange rates. It follows that there is potential scope for countries other than the United States to obtain a useful contribution to their domestic stabilization objectives through exchange rate manipulation, if they so choose, and do not find themselves unduly constrained by the existing IMF Guidelines. Whether this will in fact lead to a major intensification of the problem of demand management in the United States, and therefore to political tension, remains to be seen.

The final cause for concern in present arrangements is the weakness of the defences against the pursuit of agressive exchange rate policies for anti-cyclical (or, for that matter, any other) purposes. It is true that the Guidelines provide some protection in this respect, but nevertheless a country that wished to secure a competitive depreciation could take advantage of, or perhaps, by suitable policy pronouncements, engineer, a temporary depreciation of its rate, and then resist a rebound by Guideline 2, and the only recourse of the international community would be to try to invoke Guideline 3 (b). In the absence of an agreed structure of reference rates, however, it seems only too likely that this would prove difficult. In contrast, the reference rate proposal would make any intervention at all contingent on the establishment of an agreed reference rate, so that a country bent on aggressive policies could easily be restrained by a refusal to sanction its proposed reference rate. Indeed, since anti-cyclical depreciations or appreciations would have to be explicitly agreed during the negotiations establishing reference rates — rather than permitting all anti-cyclical rate movements that can be accommodated within the band, as the par value system does — the reference rate proposal would create stronger defences against anti-social anti-cyclical exchange rate policies than those under the Bretton Woods system. A country with a stronger (weaker) pressure of demand than that in the world as a whole could still appropriately seek a higher (lower) reference rate than otherwise, but such variations would have to be negotiated and therefore accepted as justifiable by other countries.

There do seem to be reasons for judging this factor to be of some importance, despite the absence of overt evidence of aggressive exchange rate policies. The speed with which the industrialized countries passed the oil deficit on to the primary producers, the ability of many of which to finance substantial deficits for an extended period is open to question, is a ground for genuine concern. The most obvious possible cause of major economic crisis in the next few years is the danger of widespread debt default by developing countries as a consequence of the maldistribution of the oil deficit. The discipline of being forced to negotiate regularly a set of mutually consistent reference rates could provide an international mechanism to ensure a more equitable and sustainable distribution of the oil deficit.

None of these arguments for desiring to see the present set of *ad hoc* arrangements replaced by a more formal and agreed system can be considered individually overwhelming. They indicate that a preferable system to the one that currently exists is conceivable and they make one regret that the C-20 failed to conceive it. But they do not indicate that the failure of the C-20 to reach agreement was a disaster. There has been no monetary collapse despite the absence of reform and the turbulent circumstances of the times, and there is no strong reason for supposing that present arrangements are not viable indefinitely. Managed floating provides an effective and crisis-proof adjustment mechanism and it defuses the most potent sources of conflict in international monetary relations in the past, such as the question of distribution of the responsibility for initiating adjustment (not only because exchange rate adjustment no longer requires a formal initiative, but also because where exchange rate changes are used as a part of the adjustment process the real economic burden of undertaking adjustment is no longer associated with which country initiates adjustment). Indeed, since there is every reason for supposing that the adjustable peg would have performed markedly worse than managed floating has done, the failure of the C-20 to reach agreement along the lines that it was pursuing must be counted as a blessing in disguise, at least by those who believe that an attempt might have been made to translate any agreement into reality.

I have nevertheless argued that there remains scope for general gain through a C-20 type of reform, provided that it is based on the reference rate proposal rather than the adjustable peg. All countries could be expected to gain through the removal of potential sources of political tension and the reduction in exchange rate volatility: the Europeans would value the establishment of control over international liquidity; the developing countries would benefit through their share (especially if this were increased through the link) in the seigniorage from reserves being increased through SDR allocations rather than through the growth in reserve currencies or gold remonetization; and the United States might gain through a greater symmetry in exchange rate relationships. The unhappy fact is, however, that at least up to now it has proved difficult to secure significant reforms except under the stimulus of a crisis, and now that the momentum that created the C-20 has been dissipated and major crises appear less likely than in the past, it is perhaps unlikely that major changes will be attempted. It may be that some of the causes for dissatisfaction with the present system analysed above — or some other source of tension that I have overlooked — will prove sufficiently acute to provoke a resumption of the reform effort. It is even conceivable that discussion on reform will resume without the spur of a crisis, or that change will evolve along these lines by the evolutionary process envisaged by the C-20 when it finally conceded defeat. It is perhaps more likely that future writers will look back on the C-20 as a hopelessly over-optimistic exercise in constitution writing. It will be a pity for the world, but not a disaster, if that is the verdict of history.

BIBLIOGRAPHY

Aliber, R. Z., *Choices for the Dollar,* National Planning Association, Washington, D.C., 1969.

Aliber, R. Z., (ed.), *National Monetary Policies and the International Financial System,* University of Chicago Press, London, 1974.

Artus, J. R., and Rhomberg, R. R., 'A Multilateral Exchange Rate Model', IMF *Staff Papers,* November 1973.

Balogh, T., *The Dollar Crisis: Causes and Cure,* Blackwell, Oxford, 1950.

Bergsten, D. F., Halm, G. N., Machlup, F., and Roosa, R. V., (eds.), *Approaches to Greater Flexibility of Exchange Rates: The Bürgenstock Papers,* Princeton University Press, Princeton, 1970.

Britton, A. J. C., "The Dynamic Stability of the Foreign Exchange Market", *Economic Journal,* March 1970.

Cambridge Economic Policy Group, *Economic Policy Review,* No.1, 1975.

Cohen, S. D., *International Monetary Reform 1964-69,* Praeger, London, 1970.

Cooper, R. N., "Eurodollars, Reserve Dollars, and Asymmetries in the International Monetary System", *Journal of International Economics,* 1972.

Corden, W. M., *Monetary Integration,* Princeton Essays in International Finance, No.92, Princeton, 1972.

Corden, W. M., Little, I. M. D., and Scott, M. fg., *Import Controls versus Devaluation and Britain's Economic Prospects,* Trade Policy Research Centre, London, 1975.

Cmd. 6436, *Proposals for an International Clearing Union* (Keynes Plan), HMSO, London, 1943.

Diaz-Alejandro, C.F., *Less Developed Countries and the Post-1971 International Financial System,* Princeton Essays in International Finance, No.108, Princeton, April 1975.

Dunn, R. M., *Canada's Experience with Fixed and Flexible Exchange Rates in a North American Capital Market,* Canadian-American Committee, Washington, D.C., 1971.

Emminger, O., *Inflation and the International Monetary System,* Per Jacobsson Foundation, Washington, D.C., 1973.

Ethier, W., and Bloomfield, A. I., "The Management of Floating Exchange

Rates", paper presented to the Conference on World Monetary Disorder, Centre for International Business and Management, Pepperdine University, May 1974; subsequently revised as *Managing the Managed Float,* Princeton Essays in International Finance, No.112, Princeton, 1975.

Ezekiel, H., "The Present System of Reserve Creation in the Fund", IMF *Staff Papers,* November 1966.

Fleming, J. M., "International Liquidity: Ends and Means", IMF *Staff Papers,* December 1961.

— *Towards Assessing the Need for International Reserves,* Princeton Essays in International Finance, No.58, Princeton, 1967.

— "On Exchange Rate Unification", *Economic Journal,* September 1971.

Friedman, M., "Commodity Reserve Currency", *Journal of Political Economy,* June 1951, reprinted in his *Essays in Positive Economics,* University of Chicago Press, London, 1953.

— "The Case for Flexible Exchange Rates", in his *Essays in Positive Economics,* University of Chicago Press, London, 1953.

Gardner, R. N., *Sterling-Dollar Diplomacy,* McGraw Hill, London, new edition, 1969.

Gilbert, M., *The Gold Dollar System: Conditions of Equilibrium and the Price of Gold,* Princeton Essays in International Finance, No.70, Princeton, 1968.

Girton, L., "SDR Creation and the Real-Bills Doctrine", *Southern Economic Journal,* July 1974.

Grassman, S., "Currency Distribution and Forward Cover in Foreign Trade: Sweden Revisited 1973", mimeo, 1975.

Greene, M. L., "Reserve Asset Preferences Revisited", in Kenen, P. B., and Lawrence, R., (eds.) *The Open Economy,* Columbia University Press, London, 1968.

Group of Ten, *Report of the Study Group on the Creation of Reserve Assets,* (Ossola Report), 1965.

Grubel, H. G. (ed.), *World Monetary Reform,* Stanford University Press, Stanford, 1963.

Gutowski, A., "Flexible Exchange Rates Versus Controls", in Machlup, F., Gutowski, A., and Lutz, F. A., (eds.), *International Monetary Problems,* American Enterprise Institute, Washington, D.C., 1972.

Haan, R. L., *Special Drawing Rights and Development,* Stenfert Kroese, N. V., Leyden, 1971.

Haberler, G., "Prospects for the Dollar Standard", *Lloyds Bank Review,* July 1972.

Haberler, G., and Willet, T. D., *A Strategy for US Balance of Payments Policy,* American Enterprise Institute, Washington, D.C., 1971.

Halm, G. N., *The 'Band' Proposal: The Limits of Permissible Exchange Rate Fluctuations,* Princeton Special Papers in International Economics, No.6 Princeton, January 1965.

Harrod, R. F., *The Life of John Maynard Keynes,* Macmillan, London, 1951.

Haynes, A. T., *Emerging Arrangements in International Payments — Public and Private,* Per Jacobsson Foundation, Washington, D.C., 1975.

Hewson, J., and Sakakibara, E., "The Eurodollar Multiplier: A Portfolio Approach", IMF *Staff Papers,* July 1974.

Hicks, J., "An Inaugural Lecture", *Oxford Economic Papers,* June 1953.

Hirsch, F., *Money International,* Penguin, London, 1967.

— *An SDR Standard: Impetus, Elements and Impediments,* Princeton Essays in International Finance, No.99, Princeton, 1973.

Hirsch, F., and Higgins, I., "An Indicator of Effective Exchange Rates", IMF *Staff Papers,* October 1970.

Hirsch, F., and Higham, D., "Floating Rates — Expectations and Experience", *Three Banks Review,* June 1974.

Horsefield, J. K., *The International Monetary Fund 1945-1965,* IMF, Washington, D.C., 1969.

Høst-Madsen, P., "Gold Outflows from the US 1956-63", IMF *Staff Papers,* July 1964.

IMF, *Articles of Agreement,* adopted 1944, amended 1969.

— *International Reserves and Liquidity,* IMF, Washington, D.C., 1958.

— *International Reserves: Needs and Availability,* IMF, Washington, D.C., 1970.

— *The Role of Exchange Rates in the Adjustment of International Payments: A Report by the Executive Directors,* IMF, Washington, D.C., 1970.

— *Reforming the International Monetary System: A Report by the Executive Directors to the Board of Governors,* IMF, Washington, D.C., 1972.

— *International Monetary Reform: Documents of the Committee of Twenty (C-20 Documents),* IMF, Washington, D.C., 1974.

— *Survey,* 12 February 1973, 17 June 1974.

— *Annual Report: 1975,* IMF, Washington, D.C., 1975.

Johnson, H. G., "Theoretical Problems of the International Monetary System", *Pakistan Development Review,* Spring 1967.

— *Further Essays in Monetary Economics,* Allen and Unwin, London, 1972.

— "The Link that Chains", *Foreign Policy,* Fall 1972.

— *Inflation and the Monetarist Controversy,* North Holland, Amsterdam, 1972.

Johnson, H. G., and Frenkel, J. A., (eds.), *The Monetary Approach to the Balance of Payments,* Allen and Unwin, London, 1976.

Katz, S. I., '"Managed Floating" as an Interim International Exchange Rate Regime, 1973-75', *Bulletin* of the New York University Graduate School of Business Administration, 1975(3).

Kenen, P. B., *Reserve Asset Preferences of Central Banks and Stability of the Gold Exchange Standard,* Princeton Studies in International Finance, No.10, Princeton, 1963.

— "After Nairobi — Beware the Rhinopotamus", *Euromoney, November 1973.*

— "Floats, Glides and Indicators", *Journal of International Economics,* 1975.

Keynes, J. M., "The International Control of Raw Materials", *Journal of International Economics,* 1974.

Kindleberger, C. P., *Balance of Payments Deficits and the International Market for Liquidity*, Princeton Essays in International Finance, No.46, Princeton, 1965.
— *The Politics of International Money and World Language*, Princeton Essays in International Finance, No.61, Princeton, 1967.
MacDougall, G. D. A., *The World Dollar Problem*, Macmillan, London, 1957.
Machlup, F., *Plans for the Reform of the International Monetary System*, Princeton Special Papers in International Economics, No.3, Princeton, revised, 1964.
— *Remaking the International Monetary System: The Rio Agreement and Beyond*, Johns Hopkins, Baltimore, 1968.
Machlup, F., and Malkiel, B. G., (eds.), *International Monetary Arrangements: The Problem of Choice*, International Finance Section, Princeton University Press, Princeton, 1964.
Marris, S. N., "Decision Making on Exchange Rates", in Bergsten, D. F., Halm, G. N., Machlup, F., and Roosa, R. V., (eds.), *Approaches to Greater Flexibility of Exchange Rates*, Princeton University Press, Princeton, 1970.
McKinnon, R. I., "Optimum Currency Areas", *American Economic Review*, September 1963.
— "On Securing a Common Monetary Policy in Europe", Banca Nazionale del Lavoro *Quarterly Review*, March 1973.
— "Sterilization in Three Dimensions: Major Trading Countries, Euro-Currencies, and the US", in Aliber, R. Z. (ed.), *National Monetary Policies and the International Financial System*, University of Chicago Press, London, 1974.
Meade, J. E., *The Theory of International Economic Policy: Vol.I, The Balance of Payments*, Oxford University Press, London, 1951.
— "The International Monetary Mechanism", *Three Banks Review*, September 1964.
Modigliani, F., and Askari, H., "The International Transfer of Capital and the Propagation of Domestic Disturbances Under Alternative Payments Systems", Banca Nazionale del Lavoro *Quarterly Review*, December 1973.
Morse, C. J., "The Evolving Monetary System", paper delivered to the International Monetary Conference, Williamsburg, Va., 7 June 1974; partially reprinted in IMF *Survey*, 17 June 1974.
Mundell, R. A., "The Appropriate Use of Monetary and Fiscal Policy for Internal and External Stability", IMF *Staff Papers*, March 1962.
— *Monetary Theory*, Goodyear Publishing Company, Pacific Palisades, California, 1971.
— "The Optimum Balance of Payments Deficit", in Claassen, E., and Salin, P., (eds.), *Stabilization Policies in Interdependent Economies*, North Holland, London, 1972.
— "The Economic Consequences of Jacques Rueff", *Journal of Business*, July 1973.
Mundell, R. A., and Swoboda, A. K., (eds.), *Monetary Problems of the International Economy*, University of Chicago Press, London, 1969.

OECD, *The Balance of Payments Adjustment Process,* Paris, 1966.

Officer, L. H., "Reserve Asset Preferences in the Crisis Zone 1958-67", *Journal of Money, Credit, and Banking,* May 1974.

Oort, C. J., *Steps to International Monetary Order,* Per Jacobsson Foundation, Washington, D.C., 1974.

Oppenheimer, P. M., "World Monetary Developments and the Committee of Twenty", *Aussenwirtschaft,* September 1974.

Nybery, L., and Viotti, S., "Optimal Reserves and Adjustment Policies", *Swedish Journal of Economics,* December 1974.

Polak, J. J., "Monetary Analysis of Income Formation", IMF *Staff Papers,* November 1957.

— *Valuation and the Rate of Interest of the SDR,* IMF, Washington, D.C., 1974.

Posner, M. V., *The World Monetary System : A Minimal Reform Program,* Princeton Essays in International Finance, No.96, Princeton, 1972.

Roosa, R. V., *Monetary Reform for the World Economy,* Harper and Row, New York, 1965.

Roper, D. E., "On the Theory of the Devaluation Bias", *Kyklos,* 1972.

Rueff, J., "The West is Risking a Credit Collapse", *Fortune,* July 1961.

Russell, R. W., "Transgovernmental Interaction in the International Monetary System 1960-72", *International Organization,* Autumn 1973.

Salin, P., "The Problem of Symmetry in the Process of Adjustment and the Reform of the International Monetary System", mimeo, 1972.

Stamp, M., "The Reform of the International Monetary System", *Moorgate and Wall Street,* Summer 1965.

Symposium on "Flexible Exchange Rates and Stabilization Policy", *Scandinavian Journal of Economics,* 1976(2).

Triffin, R., *Gold and the Dollar Crisis,* Yale University Press, New Haven, 1960.

U.S. Treasury, *The U.S. Proposals for Using Reserves as an Indicator of the Need for Balance of Payments Adjustment,* (*The US Proposals*) published as Appendix A.5 to the 1973 Report of the Council of Economic Advisors, *Economic Report of the President,* US Government Printing Office, Washington, D.C., 1973.

Whitman, M. v. N., "The Current and Future Role of the Dollar : How Much Symmetry ?", *Brookings Papers on Economic Activity,* 1974.

— "The Payments Adjustment Process and the Exchange Rate Regime : What Have We Learned ?", *American Economic Review,* May 1975.

Williams, J. H., *Post-War Monetary Plans and Other Essays,* Blackwell, Oxford, 1949.

Williamson, J., *The Crawling Peg,* Princeton Essays in International Finance, No.50, Princeton, 1965.

— *The Choice of A Pivot for Parities,* Princeton Essays in International Finance, No.90, Princeton, 1971.

— "On the Normative Theory of Balance-of-Payments Adjustment", in Clayton, G., Gilbert, J. C., and Sedgwick, R., (eds.), *Monetary Theory and Monetary Policy in the 1970's,* Oxford University Press, Oxford, 1971.

— "International Liquidity — A Survey", *Economic Journal*, September 1973.

— "Payments Adjustment and Economic Welfare", IMF *Staff Papers*, November 1973.

— "The Financial Implications of Reserve Supply Arrangements", IMF *Staff Papers*, November 1974.

— "The Future Exchange Rate Regime", Banca Nazionale del Lavoro *Quarterly Review*, June 1975.

— "The Impact of European Monetary Integration on the Peripheral Areas", in Vaizey, J., (ed.), *Economic Sovereignty and Regional Policy*, Gill and Macmillan, Dublin, 1975.

— "The International Financial System", in Fried, E. R., and Schultze, C. L., (eds.), *Higher Oil Prices and the World Economy*, Brookings Institution, Washington, D.C., 1975.

— "Generalized Floating and the Reserve Needs of Developing Countries", in D. M. Leipziger, ed., *The International Monetary System and Developing Nations*, Agency for International Development, Washington, D.C., 1976.

— "Exchange Rate Flexibility and Reserve Use", *Scandinavian Journal of Economics*, 1976(2).

Witte, W. E., "Dynamic Adjustment in the Foreign Exchange Market", Ph.D. thesis, University of Wisconsin, Madison, 1975.

Wonnacott, P., "Exchange Stabilization in Canada 1950-54: A Comment", *Canadian Journal of Economics and Political Science*, May 1958.

— *The Canadian Dollar 1948-62*, University of Toronto Press, Toronto, 1965.

— *The Floating Canadian Dollar*, American Enterprise Institute, Washington, D.C., 1972.

Yeager, L. B., *International Monetary Relations*, Harper and Row, New York, 1966.

Index